The Strawberry Beds

Na Ceapóga Sú Talún

Patrick Troy

ORIGINAL WRITING

© 2013 & 2020 Patrick Troy

The cover photograph shows a typical cottage that lined the Lower Road along the Strawberry Beds in the past. This cottage belonged to Mary Byrne and lies at the bottom of the Rugged lane. The wonderful colours of aubrietia and wisteria, as seen here, would have been commonly grown to adorn the dwellings. Families would also grow climbing roses outside the front door of the cottages. Many of the cottages had a porch for shelter outside the front door and the roses would cover this shelter completely. These roses, which would give off a wonderful smell in the summertime, were a treasure for the bees and other insects.

The photograph on the back cover is The Wren's Nest weir. The weir was built in the late 1600s or the early 1700s. The original form was probably much more rudimentary than the present day structure.

Disclaimer: The author acknowledges that there may be errors in this publication. Every effort has been made to verify all contents within the book and the author accepts no responsibility for inaccuracies that have gone unnoticed. The author apologises for any errors that may have slipped through. The author has made every effort to identify the original owners of photographs and documents reproduced in this book. The author apologises if contact was not made with the individuals concerned.

All rights reserved. No part of this publication may be reproduced in any form or by any means—graphic, electronic or mechanical, including photocopying, recording, taping or information storage and retrieval systems—without the prior written permission of the author.

ISBNS
PARENT: 978-1-78237-124-3
EPUB: 978-1-78237-125-0
MOBI: 978-1-78237-126-7
PDF: 978-1-78237-127-4

A CIP catalogue for this book is available from the National Library.

Published by ORIGINAL WRITING LTD., Dublin, 2013.
Printed by ESSENTRA Glasnevin, Dublin 11

Dedication

This book is dedicated to my father, who had a wish to write about the Strawberry Beds from the day he moved on to the Lower Road in 1947. He always appreciated the uniqueness of the area with its agricultural tradition, market gardening, its richness of beauty, its cultural heritage and, of course, its people. Unfortunately he died in 1971 without having commenced the task.

I decided to undertake the task and fulfil his wish and, while I may not be as eloquent as he might have been, nonetheless I hope I have gone some way in describing the life and times of the Strawberry Beds.

While my father was the inspiration for the book, my mother, who, despite only coming to live on the Strawberry Beds in 1950, developed a great knowledge of the area and its people. She corrected a great many of my mistakes and I frequently sought her help.

James Patrick Troy BA.
1916 - 1971

Eileen Troy
1922 - 2013

Acknowledgements

In 1973 my sister Helen and I interviewed some of the oldest residents on the road. Ms. Mary Byrne was a wonderful source of local information with an amazing memory. Mrs. Carney, Mrs. Doyle, Jack Lovely, Mrs. Nash, Gertie Murray and May Tobin on Somerton Lane were a joy to gather history and stories from. Later on Ms. Shelia Doyle was of great assistance; she demonstrated great clarity of memory. Later still information was gathered from Ger Lanigan, Patrick Tobin, Maureen O'Rourke, Michael Harford, James Lynam and many others who filled in the details. Much of this information was gathered informally.

Photographs were kindly given by the following and are greatly appreciated:

Mary Eustace
Mary Shackleton
The Wren's Nest
The Strawberry Hall
The Anglers Rest
Gretta Higgins
John Higgins
Robert Fry
Shelia Kavanagh
Hugh O'Connor
Mick Harford
Caroline Corballis
Michael Daly
Gerard O'Byrne
Rose Blackburn.
Eileen Troy
Ordinance Survery of Ireland/Government of Ireland
Copyright Permit No. MP0003512.

Ordnance Survey Ireland
National Mapping Agency

The assistance of the Royal Society of Antiquities in providing stored photographs was invaluable. Permission granted by the National Library to use photographs from the Laurence Collection is acknowledged. Permission was granted by the National Archives to source information and reproduce it in this book. This permission is acknowledged and appreciated. The Ordinance Survey of Ireland granted permission for the maps contained within this publication to be reproduced.

Contents

Introduction	ix
Foreword	xiii
Chapter 1 Geology of the Strawberry Beds	1
Chapter 2 Early Inhabitants	3
Chapter 3 Maps of the Strawberry Beds	7
Chapter 4 The River	17
Chapter 5 The Mills	26
Chapter 6 The Main Houses	34
Chapter 7 Griffiths Valuation	41
Chapter 8 Census 1901 and 1911	52
Chapter 9 Employment	66
Chapter 10 Market Gardening	74
Chapter 11 Transport	78
Chapter 12 Strawberry Beds Improvement Association	82
Chapter 13 The Schools	92
Chapter 14 Irish Educational Act 1892	95
Chapter 15 Lower Road School	99

Chapter 16 The Teachers	*101*
Chapter 17 The School Registers	*106*
Chapter 18 Attendance	*134*
Chapter 19 The Lower Road School Closes	*137*
Chapter 20 The Community Centre	*143*
Chapter 21 The Sports Field	*157*
Chapter 22 All Things Change	*164*
Chapter 23 Reflections	*172*
Chapter 24 Appendix	*191*
References:	*224*

Introduction

The Strawberry Beds are to be found if one travels west of Dublin city for six miles. They lie on the banks of the River Liffey, the northern bank facing the sun, and are without doubt the best known feature of the Liffey Valley. One travels through Chapelizod, up Glenmaroon Hill, down Knockmaroon Hill and onto the Lower Road. From here, with the steep hills on your right hand, the river on your left, a pleasant journey awaits you, whether on foot, bicycle, car, or horse and trap as would have been the main mode of transport years ago. The Strawberry Beds are of course an agricultural feature where the local people have grown strawberries for nearly two hundred and fifty years. The strawberries, grown as a commercial crop, were transported to the city's fruit and vegetable markets for sale to the hotels, restaurants and homes. However, it was for the sale of the strawberries with fresh cream on cabbage leaves from the cottages to travellers, daytrippers or locals that the Strawberry Beds was renowned. It was a delight that hundreds of Dubliners would enjoy for years and years as they jaunted along the Strawberry Beds.

Strawberries date back to the late 1700s and it is mentioned in Cnuacha by O'Driscoll that Lord Annaly grew the fruit in his estate at Luttrellstown. The fruit grown at this period in time was a wild european variety and in 1780 a hybrid was developed in the USA. A series of new hybrid varieties were being grown in Europe by 1817. They were genetically modified to have a more succulent taste, a larger berry, and a more commercial viability. The name strawberry may have derived its name from the runners the plant puts out or 'stray berries'. The southern border of the Luttrellstown Estate and further hills along the Lower Road descend steeply to the river and it is on these slopes that the strawberry, exposed to the warmth of the sun would ripen into a tasty succulent fruit.

Cottages, a distinctive feature of the Strawberry Beds, were always placed at the bottom of the slopes along the roadside. These cottages lined the roadside from the bridge at Lucan to Knockmaroon Hill. The hills that were cultivated rose up behind the houses and every square foot would be brought into production. Up until the early 1900s land was held by lease, so it was important that produce was maximised.

Cottages on the Strawberry Beds.
(Courtesy National Library)

The photograph above, which is part of the Laurence Collection, features typical cottages on the Strawberry Beds. They are on the road edge, which is a dusty track, they have thatched roofs, are whitewashed in colour and single storey in elevation. They probably had no more than two to three rooms for the family. The actual position of the houses in the photograph above is difficult to pinpoint because they lie on both sides of the road. Currently, there are only three houses on the riverbank between Shackletons Mill and the bottom of Knockmaroon Hill. Building so close to the river carries obvious flooding risks. The photograph here may have been taken at Knockmaroon Hill because the road rises at this point and the view is looking towards the Anglers Rest public house. It is from cottages such as these that the strawberries and cream would be sold.

The concept of this book, while accounting for the evolution, history, and culture of the area, is ultimately to remember the names and peoples of the Strawberry Beds that have gone before and to describe the evolution of this rural community. Information was sourced from elderly residents as far back as 1973. Many of the stories are descriptive, sometimes recollections, or anecdotal. More formal information was gathered later on from archives, schools, various documents and written correspondence. Informal public house chats also filled in gaps in the tales and stories.

Photograph of the most elderly residents taken in 1968 in the Old School House. James White, Bridie Fagan, Mary Byrne are in the back row while Mrs. White, Mrs. Carney and Mrs. Plunkett are seated in front.

Mary Byrne had a wonderful memory and her recollections went back to end of the 1800s. She could relate the visit of Queen Victoria to Ireland in 1900. Queen Victoria's entourage travelled along the Strawberry Beds on its way to Lutttrellstown Castle where she was hosted. Mary described the Queen as 'a small frail woman' sitting in her horse-drawn carriage as she passed by. This was Queen Victoria's fourth visit to Ireland, a country she was very fond of. Her first visit to the country was in 1849 when she was named 'The Famine Queen'. She was in her eightieth year in 1900 so the description of being frail and small was probably very accurate.

Mrs. Byrne reared Peter Melia and his brother Patrick Melia. The two boys went to the Lower Road National School in the year of 1924. The cottage in which she lived (see cover) is one of the few remaining classical cottages that were characteristic of the Strawberry Beds. From the seventies onwards more and more similar cottages were demolished by families moving onto the Beds with a desire to live at the top of the hills. Mrs. Byrne died at home and she passed the cottage on to Peter Melia who in turn died in 1997. Mary Byrne's cottage was probably built in the early 1800s or perhaps even earlier. Thankfully the cottage is well preserved and being cared for most ably by Ms. Marie Therese Eustace.

Mrs. Carney also contributed to this book with her stories of market gardening and of life on the road at the turn of twentieth century. She described the peelers, as they would ride by on horseback along the road doing their patrols. They were stationed in Chapelizod and would continue on to Lucan and back by the Galway road. Her husband Peadar Carney, who was deceased at the time of the above photograph, used to work for Maxi Arnott in his riding stables in Clonsilla. Peadar Carney rode many races in the Phoenix Park for Maxi Arnott. In his later years he had the 'bowed legs' characteristic of retired jockeys.

Mrs. Doyle provided much information on the growing of the strawberries, how they were grown, picked and transported to the city's market. The Doyle's always had a pony and trap to ferry their fruit. Not all growers were as well off in this regard, many had to make the trip on foot.

This rural community of the Strawberry Beds, while not unique, was still special and of significance because of the agricultural, industrial, and social contribution it made to the fabric of Dublin's history. Many who travelled there on day trips or ultimately to live were always aware of the unique beauty of the Liffey Valley. The Strawberry Beds, home to the market gardeners, the 'pinks', and the strawberries and cream on cabbage leaves, coupled with a pleasant meander along the riverbank will always be remembered fondly.

The 'Tea house' or 'Coffee house' on Lucan Bridge at the start of the twentieth century. This house served the workers of Hills mills. Note the boy on the right is in bare feet.
(Courtesy Mrs. Mary Shackleton).

Foreword

In past times place names, townlands, and local names were used extensively to describe or localise an area. A crossroads would have a name to identify it, a field might be known by a family name, a road or lane might be known by its descriptive condition. Farmers would name their fields to identify them when discussing some relevant matter. Today all areas are mapped on Google earth, so one can view the Strawberry Beds from the other side of the world. Indeed, so accurate is the mapping that a car in a driveway can be visualised. Nowadays one has postcodes, extensive mapping, GPS locating and road numbering. People are more mobile now, few walk the roads, so historical place names are becoming redundant. When I asked my brother Denis to carry out the initial proof reading of this book, he confessed that he didn't know the location of some of the place names and he had grown up in the Strawberry Beds. Because this local knowledge can disappear so rapidly, I have introduced a glossary at the start of the book so readers can become aware of the area, cottage, lane, that they read about.

Airfield: the original name for Summerton / Somerton, home of the Brooke and Laidlaw families.

Anna Liffey (mill): also previously known as 'Devil's Mill', lying at the bottom of Tinkers Hill opposite the Luttrellstown Estate.

Astagob (or Castagob): a townland covering the Strawberry Beds divided into two electoral divisions - Clonsilla and Castleknock.

Broomfield: a townland and walled residence bordering the River Liffey lying just east of Anna Liffey mill.

Cannons Lane: a lane joining Porterstown Road with Carpenterstown Road. This may have been known originally as Keenans Lane.

Castleknock: a barony, townland and electoral division, originally belonging to the Tyrell family with a castle therein.

Diswellstown: a townland and (house) residence, the original home of the Ducswell family, a Norman family.

Farmleigh (Farmley): a residence of the Guinness family on the Tower Road bordering the Phoenix Park.

Ferry: a boat crossing the river with a boom linking the Strawberry Beds to Mill Lane, Palmerstown.

Glen: footpath joining the Lower Road to Sandpits. Forms the western boundary of Knockmaroon Estate. Runs alongside a stream, a townland boundary.

Glenmaroon: residence for The Sisters of Charity at the entrance to the Phoenix Park at Knockmaroon Gate. (Hill) road running down into Chapelizod.

Grand Lodge: gate lodge and main entrance to Luttrellstown Castle from the Lower Road.

Knockmaroon: residence of the Guinness family. (Hill) at the end of the Lower Road up to the Phoenix Park gate.

Lower Road: roadway from Lucan to Knockmaroon Hill along the riverbank. Given name to distinguish it from the Dublin to Galway road.

Mardyke: residence and site of an old mill at Palmerstown Weir. Start of towpath running from Palmerstown Weir to Chapelizod along the riverbank.

Oatlands: large residence opposite Diswellstown House.

Pickering Forest: large house and farm in Celbridge, once owned by the Brooke family.

Porterstown: townland, named after the Porter family, a Norman family.

Rag Well: site of an old pump serving cottages at the Sandpits. Overlooks the Glen. Originally the site of a holy well with a whitethorn bush. Locals would tie small rags to the bush and pray.

Rugged Lane: a lane running up from the Lower Road to Porterstown Road. Also forms the eastern boundary of Luttrellstown Estate.

Sandpits: row of cottages belonging to Knockmaroon Estate at the junction of College Road, Capenterstown Road and Porterstown Road. Also known as Sand Holes where sand was extracted.

Somerton: (lane, house): a roadway running from the Strawberry Beds to Porterstown road. Residence of the Laidlaw family.

Tinker's Hill: a roadway opposite Shackleton's Mill (Anna Liffey) going from the Lower Road to Porterstown Road on the western edge of Luttrelstown Estate. Also known as St Josephs Hill.

Woolly Corner: crossroad at Somerton Lane and Porterstown Road, site of sheep dealing or sheep stealing in past times. (folklore)

Woodlands: first cottage after the Grand Lodge travelling from Lucan. It lies east of Luttrelstown Estate. A Mass path runs from this cottage up onto the Rugged Lane.

Woodland cottage as it is today.
This cottage is the starting point of the Strawberry Beds.

The Strawberry Beds

Na Ceapóga Sú Talún

Chapter 1
GEOLOGY OF THE STRAWBERRY BEDS

The Liffey Valley was formed following the last ice age in a process known as 'River Rejuvenation'. The last Ice Age occurred around 20,000 years ago. The process is as follows: the weight of the ice, which is present for thousands of years initially, depresses the landscape. As the earth's temperature increases and the glaciers retreat, the land rises up with the weight removed. This process is known as 'Isostasy'. Rivers form beneath the melting glaciers forcing a path to the sea. Later on, the River Liffey, which rises in the Dublin Mountains, would down-cut into the rising landscape forming a V shaped channel from Leixlip to Island Bridge on its way to the sea. Similar erosions occurred in the Dodder and Tolka regions. As the river travels to the sea it forms flood plains and it is here that rich fertile soil is deposited both from the receding glaciers and the active river. During periods of flood the river would simply flow out to cover tracts of land and recede when levels dropped, leaving small particles of soil in their wake. Deposits of stone and gravel were also made at deeper levels and were a source of building material when quarried at a later date. The soil along the River Liffey and valley is deep and tremendously fertile due to the many, many years of mineral deposits and decomposition of organic material, which makes it perfectly suitable for agriculture.

Starting in St. Catherine's, west of Lucan, the high banks on either side of the river are evidence of this 'Isostacy'. The steep bank on the northern side of the river continues to Woodlands Cottage - the eastern edge of Luttrellstown Estate - where the first flood plain starts. The Strawberry Beds is a descriptive local name, noted firstly on maps of 1836. The name predates this, however, and was probably used in the 1700s. The Strawberry Beds really starts at the first flood plain (Woodlands Cottage) and continues along the Lower Road to finish at Knockmaroon Hill. The total extent of the Strawberry Beds is about three miles.

The slopes, which were cultivated, are south facing, giving it a distinct ecology. Protected from severe climate changes due to their depth, closeness to the river, and the shading afforded by the large woodlands, the land enjoyed mild winters and warm temperatures in summer. This lengthened the growing season on the Strawberry Beds compared to other competitive regions. The Liffey Valley is considered to be the second warmest in Ireland - the first being in Cork on the River Lee.

The River Liffey flows on a limestone bed, which underlies the soil of Kildare and Dublin. Because of this the river forms shallows and rapids along its way to the sea. Unfortunately this prohibits navigation along the river unlike the Barrow or Shannon. While the great benefits of the river are evident, it also posed a barrier, which had to be negotiated by anyone who wished to navigate in or out of the Strawberry Beds. This barrier would have a much greater influence in winter than in summer with the heavier water flow. While floods could be expected in wintertime, they often surprised the Strawberry Beds inhabitants in summer.

So in essence the Strawberry Beds is blessed with rich soil, ample water, south-facing orientation, good farmers and market gardeners. Above all it is its closeness to the city of Dublin with its vegetable and flower markets at six miles distance, that brought a source of income to build and support the community.

****

Chapter 2
EARLY INHABITANTS

Habitation of nomadic people always took place along a river or stream ways. This provided a food and water source, both being vital for survival. Ireland has been inhabited for nine thousand years or more, and for the first 2000 years the people were nomadic. During the last Ice Age, 20,000 years ago, the sea levels were much lower than they are today so land bridges existed between Ireland and England and the mainland of Europe. As the ice receded, Ireland became heavily forested, abundant in wildlife, with ample water in the rivers and streams, and so became attractive to migrating peoples from the mainland of Europe. This was the Mesolithic period of man where stone and flint – the best deposits were to be found in Antrim - were the working tools.

The benefit of rich alluvial soil for cultivation on the banks of rivers encouraged the people to move from a nomadic life to a settled agricultural lifestyle. Settlements grew along the rivers with concentrations at fording points. Dome-shaped huts were constructed, food grown, food gathered and animals kept. Rivers might also have religious or cultural significance for the people. The River Boyne, with the passage tombs of Newgrange, Dowth and Knowth, is one such river. The tombs were built by Stone Age people six thousand years ago and were constructed prior to the arrival of the Celts. The River Liffey did not have the same religious or cultural significance as that of the Boyne. However, it is a large river, was a rich source of food and bracketed by fertile lands, all that an evolving society would require for their growth and survival.

The inhabitants evolved through the centuries from nomadic hunter-gatherers to pastoralists and formed settlements with a social order. This settlement of the peoples would have cultural, social and organisational significance throughout the land. By the year 400 AD, seven thousand years after the first arrival of man on the island, Ireland became a land of learning and education with the Christian belief at its core. Abbeys were built along riverbanks, such as Clonmacnoise, and these abbeys became the literary centre for all of Europe. It was in these educational establishments that the Bible would be translated into the Gaelic language and the day-to-day living of the Irish people would be chronicled. Saints and scholars would leave the island to spread their teaching on the mainland of Europe. It is evident that contact between Ireland and the Continent was prolific throughout the ages. The monks that lived in the abbeys had a great awareness of life in Europe and elsewhere.

The year 841 AD saw the first Viking incursion into Ireland. These seafarers from the Norwegian lands sailed all along the coastline of Europe, from the Mediterranean regions to all the islands that lie to the west. In 964 AD they were established in 'Dubh Linn' or Dublin, having sailed up the river to initially plunder and later form a trading port. Dublin was to become the centre of trading for the Vikings by the year 1000 AD because of its central location with respect to their sailing routes. This would ensure that Dublin was exposed to many different cultures and peoples from distant places. Indeed Dublin was the capital slave-trading port at this time. Slaves would be sought locally, or acquired in other lands, and sold on the market in Dublin. As the Strawberry Beds is only six miles from the river mouth it is certain that the Viking people moved up along the river. The name Leixlip derives from the Viking words *Lax Haup*, which translates as salmon leap, or *Leim an Bhradain* in Irish. The Vikings fought the Battle of Confey, near Leixlip, against the native Irish in 917 AD. The Strawberry Beds did suffer Viking influence whatever its nature.

The earliest documented signs of inhabitants in the Strawberry Beds come from bones unearthed in Somerton in the early 1970s. Fields were being tilled in the moat field above the Huntsman House (Scully's), when the plough unearthed bones of women and children who had suffered a violent death. There were many skull fractures amongst the slain and over a hundred bodies were excavated. There were no bones of men in the remains. Investigation of the discovery by the National Museum suggested that the find might have been an encampment or village settlement that would have overlooked the river from the high ground. Whether this was a temporary settlement for a nomadic tribe or a settled people is not known. The National Museum dated the bodies to the year 1000 AD or perhaps the Battle of Clontarf (1014). The women and children could have been massacred while the men were away fighting but that they died a violent death is certain. The camp might also have been raided to procure slaves with the men being taken and the women and children slaughtered. Their remains were subsequently interred in Mulhuddart Cemetery following the archeological investigation.

The Normans invaded Ireland soon after, in 1100 AD, and took lands beside the main cities and ports of the time. Cities such as Waterford, Cork, Dublin and Limerick were the first areas to be invaded and the Norman power would spread out into the hinterland from these bases. King John, who came to Ireland in 1204, granted the lands at Luttrellstown to the Lutteral family. The Porter and Dueswell families are Norman in origin, and so the further evolution of the Strawberry Beds with these new settlers continued. These new conquerors would introduce a feudal system of government with land acquisition and ownership at the heart of its power. These landlords would endure for the next 800 years with their control of the land and hence the people.

The oldest accurate records of the number of inhabitants living in the area, and in Ireland generally arrive with the recording of Griffith Valuation in 1843 by Richard Griffith. This recording is followed by the census of 1901 and 1911. Previous censuses, of 1821, 1841 and 1851, carried out all over Ireland have only partial records surviving or have been destroyed in their entirety. Unfortunately none of the surviving records relate to the townlands that encompass the Strawberry Beds. The numbers of people living in the locality, as recorded in Griffiths Valuation and the Census of 1901 and 1911 are approximately similar. A figure of 350 to 400 persons would represent the stable population of the area with fluctuations on occasions.

The Strawberry Beds and surrounding areas would always have had a changing population. The presence of the military in the Phoenix Park, the Viceregal Lodge, the Ordinance Survey, and the Military Hospitals would have had a changing staff all the time. These newcomers might lodge in the local houses as boarders. Houses might be leased for a number of domestics, gardeners or horsemen to live in. Professionals or skilled persons might be commissioned for short periods of time for a specific task and so live in the area before returning home. A typical example would be the hiring of skilled persons during the all-Ireland survey of 1841 to 1843.

Suppliers of produce or services to the military and all its constituents would wax and wane due to the prevailing political circumstances of the time. Farriers would be needed when there was an increase in cavalry activity, food consumption would increase and hence more suppliers would be needed. Hospital care would require nurses and doctors. General domestic staff for the houses, hospitals or barracks would be in demand. All manner of needs had to be catered for and manpower was necessary to fulfill most roles. It is noticeable on examining the census details, that the part of the townland of Castleknock that covers the Strawberry Beds had large numbers of boarders and lodgers. Their names, such as Bale, Higginbotham, Herrevin, Dumbrell or Willoughby are not of local origin and their place of birth is England, Scotland or Dublin city. Many of the migrants would subsequently integrate with the local community, marry and settle down as residents of the Strawberry Beds. Conversely, the local population might decline with the closure of a mill or the changing ownership of an estate that incorporated the loss of jobs.

There is no doubt that the Strawberry Beds and surrounding townlands were populated from the earliest times. Successful conquest and unsuccessful defence shaped the lives and livelihoods of the people. However, despite the ever-changing political situation, it is evident that the overall number of inhabitants remained stable during the seventeen, eighteen and nineteen hundreds.

*Crossing the river by boat to meet the tram on the Galway road.
(Courtesy Mrs. Blackburn)*

Chapter 3
MAPS OF THE STRAWBERRY BEDS

All areas of dense population such as cities were mapped from the earliest times. The hinterland would also have been well known to the local people. However, the countryside, far from the cities, would be less well known the land was still in the hands of the native Irish. Dublin and its hinterland was no exception in this regard, its surrounds would have been well known from the outset. Dublin was the gateway to Ireland used by traders, merchants and, of course, invading forces. The Viking forces landed in Howth around 850AD and were using the city as a strategic trading port by the year 964AD. Missionaries sailed from Dublin to the Continent (via the River Liffey.) St Columbanus is thought to have sailed from Dublin or Dubh Linn, as it was known then, on his way to establish a monastery in Italy in the year 641AD. Rivers form a pathway to the interior of a country. Knowledge of the land and its river routes was always present, but the lands needed to be charted for exploration, exploitation, and control.

Dublin was to become the second city of the British Empire. The Normans having conquered England landed in Ireland in 1100 AD and set about annexing the island to their domain. This domination was accomplished through military might, strategic alliances or, as happened with Strongbow, a suitable marriage. The Norman influence was evident in the large fortified castles that can be found at strategic points in the cities and on the rivers of Ireland. King John visited Ireland in the 1200s and had a castle built in Carlow on the River Barrow. A further castle was built on the River Boyne at Trim, County Meath, by Hugh de Lacey. King John ordered a bridge to be built in Lucan to cross the Liffey. This was the early Anglo-Norman influence in Ireland. The Anglo-Normans were in full control of Dublin and an area of hinterland known as the Pale. The Pale would expand or shrink in size according to the strengths of the Royal forces or the native Irish forces outside the Pale. Trim Castle lay on the boundary of the Pale; hence the Strawberry Beds always lay within its influence.

The philosophy of the Norman feudal system was based on the acquisition of land and the introduction of a peasantry to toil on their behalf. Lands that were confiscated would be granted to Royal supporters or those who had earned gratuities through service. Furthermore, lands belonging to local Irish families or Clans were seized and granted to soldiers within the English forces or to the native Irish forces that might fight alongside the English. The inability of the Irish Clans to form a unified force and repel the foreign forces was always present. This pattern of disorganisation would continue up until the Irish Lords, O'Neill and O'Donnell, would almost defeat the English in 1601 at the Battle of Kinsale. With the final defeat of the Irish Clan system all of Ireland would fall under the control of the Monarchy. Mapping of the conquered lands was now necessary for acquisition, control and land grants for the supporters of the Royal forces.

The earliest map discovered in my research of the area west of Dublin is the Down Survey of 1659. This is a rudimentary map with few features; the barony of Castleknock is marked with no boundaries as it extends westward to the County of Meath. A castle belonging to the Tyrell's of Castleknock is marked, as is a reference to Luttrellstown. There had been eight Barons of Tyrell who owned or controlled all of the lands around Castleknock in the sixteenth and seventeenth centuries. The Tyrell family would have their lands confiscated in time.

Taylor and Skinner were cartographers who, in 1778, produced maps for traveling out from Dublin to the rest of the country. One such map included here, outlines the passage to be taken from Dublin to Sligo via Longford. The road west has milestones and it can be seen that the Strawberry Beds lies between the fourth and sixth milestone. At the fifth milestone a mill is marked as Black Mill. This is the site of the New Holland Mill on the Lower Road and, further on, Broomfield is marked. The houses of Knockmaroon and Diswellstown are marked. Diswellstown was the seat of Thomas Keenan Esq. On the Palmerstown side of the river the name Brooke Esq. is noted. This was the first home of the Brooke family and was purchased by Major Francis Brooke. The house was named Brooklawn and Major Brooke lived there with his wife and twelve children. George Fredrick Brooke, the sixth child, was born there in 1779 and would eventually come to live in Summerton and end his life there in 1865. He would die in full view of his birth home, Brooklawn. An iron mill is marked at Lucan Bridge. Luttrellstown, which was heavily wooded at the time, belonging to Lord Carhampton, is also charted.

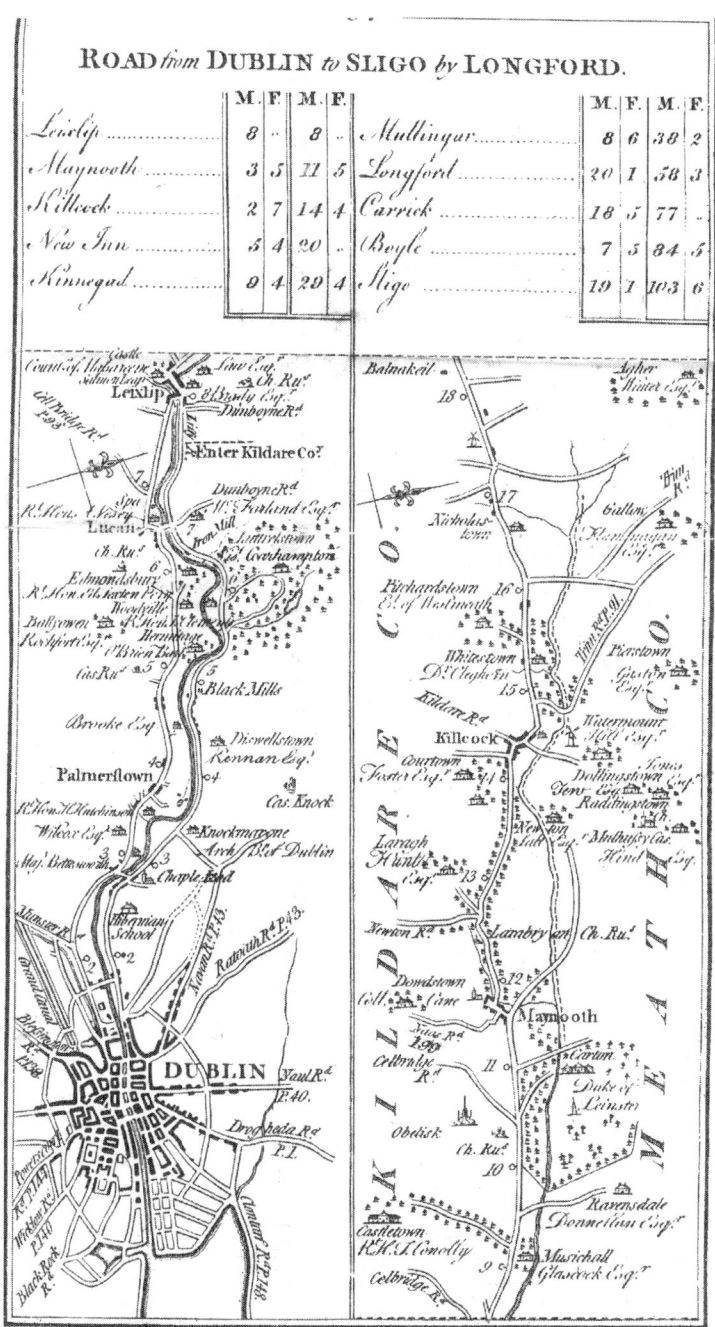

Map of the road from Dublin to Sligo via Longford in the year 1778.
(Taylor and Skinner, 1778)

Maps with the following dates, 1836–1843, 1870, 1907–1911 and 1936–1937 exist for Ireland and offer a great deal of information. Initially the British army, through the Ordinance Survey, which was within its command, carried out these surveys. Post independence the Ordinance Survey of Ireland continued its surveying tasks without military influence. The time taken to complete the all-Ireland surveys lay between four and seven years, an impressive accomplishment. In the nineteenth century Ireland was the most extensively mapped country in Europe. This was partly due to the training of military surveyors for the Empire, but also for the landlords to determine the extent of their ownership of lands granted to them, lands they might never see, as they were often absentee landlords.

These maps show the passage of time and features or remnants on these maps are still evident today. In 1836, starting at Lucan Bridge, a site of an old iron mill existed. Millers and Mills, 1850, make reference to this mill as existing in the 1300s. As we move along the road we note the weir and flourmill at the Devils Mill. Broomfield is noted, as is Woodlands (Luttrellstown). Woodlands is the townland name. The start of the Strawberry Beds is marked, the New Holland Mill for iron and starch works and the Wren's Nest public house. Diswellstown House is marked, whereas Somerton is known as Airfield at this time (1836).

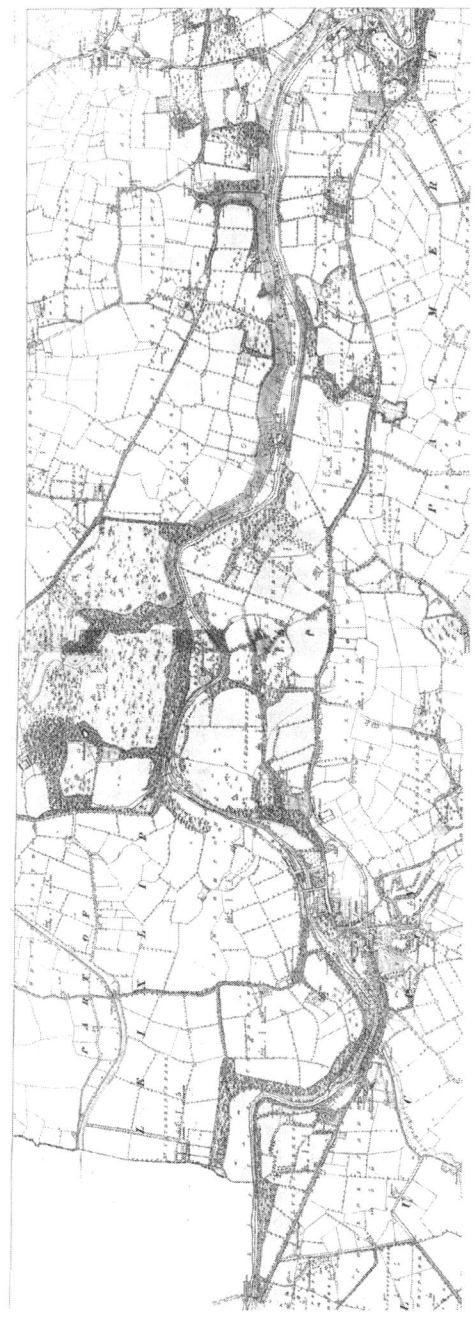

Map of 1836

In 1836 a National School for primary education existed adjacent to where the Strawberry Hall public house now stands. The public house was not built until later. The river could be forded at this point and the cobbled flagstones on the riverbed to assist the horses and carts are present to this day. From this ford a small bridge crossed the millrace on the opposite bank of the river. The millrace, which starts at the New Holland Mill or Wren's Nest weir, flows east, parallel to the river, to Palmerstown where the water rejoins the river having fulfilled its tasks. The next notable markings on the map of 1836 are the two ferries that crossed the river. One is situated at the bottom of Knockmaroon Hill.

Ferryman 'Grandfather' Michael Treacy Senior c. 1930

The second ferry was about a half-mile upstream where the iron bridge now stands. It is suspected that this second ferry was a private affair for use by the Guinness family, as they owned land on the south bank of the river. The iron bridge would eventually replace the ferry. Mapping of marked crossing points on the river were essential to travellers as they journeyed around the country be it on horseback or on foot.

Several mills and supporting weirs are marked on the 1836 map lying on both banks of the river. On the Palmerstown side there was an iron mill, a cotton mill and a lead and copper works. A flourmill, on the north bank at the site of Mardyke House, is also marked on this map.

There is little change of note in the map of 1870 (see appendix). Woodlands Cottage is marked, the recognised start of the Strawberry Beds, Airfield has now become known as Summerton, as the Brookes are now in residence, and there are distinct markings of the division of property and dwellings. Only one ferry now exists, the one closest to Palmerstown weir. A towpath for horses under load is marked along the riverbank from Mardyke to Chapelizod. This towpath enabled the horses to avoid Knockmaroon and Glenmaroon hills. The dray would drop down from the Lower Road at the start of Knockmaroon Hill and follow the riverbank to exit at the bottom of Glenmaroon Hill. This pathway is now in private ownership.

The 1907 (see appendix) mapping shows the woollen mill at Lucan Bridge, Hills Mill, and the 'Devils Mill', now called the Anna Liffey Mill for corn processing. The Strawberry Hall public house and the Anglers Hotel are also recorded. The Guinness metal bridge is present. This was a private bridge for the family and never fell into the public domain. The corn mill at Mardyke on the Palmerstown Weir is no longer marked.

Photograph of the Guinness metal bridge built, between 1870 and 1907. It also shows the heavily wooded slopes that now exist on the Strawberry Beds.

Finally, the map of 1936 shows significant change from its predecessor. Ireland is now self-governed and is struggling to develop its services. Electrification lines are present; sewerage systems are marked, as are accurate boundary markings of property and dwellings. The National School has been relocated to the bottom of Somerton Hill. This school was built in 1909. Property had been in the private ownership of the estates prior to the late 1800s, but with the change in the land commission legislation that followed, a proliferation of individual holdings in full private ownership are now evident along the road.

The main road from Dublin to the west ran through Palmerstown and reaching this road was essential for transporting goods and services. The river could only be crossed safely at the bridges in Lucan or Chapelizod. The ford at the Strawberry Hall public house was dependent on river conditions. Flooding was always a frequent feature of the river as there was no control of floodwaters. Even the summer season could not guarantee a safe crossing at the ford. Despite the construction of the dams at Ballymore Eustace and Leixlip in the nineteen thirties and forties, flooding, while more controlled, still persists to this day.

Flooding at Iron Bank near Lucan in late 1898.
The chimney at Hills mills is in the background.
(Courtesy Mrs. Mary Shackleton)

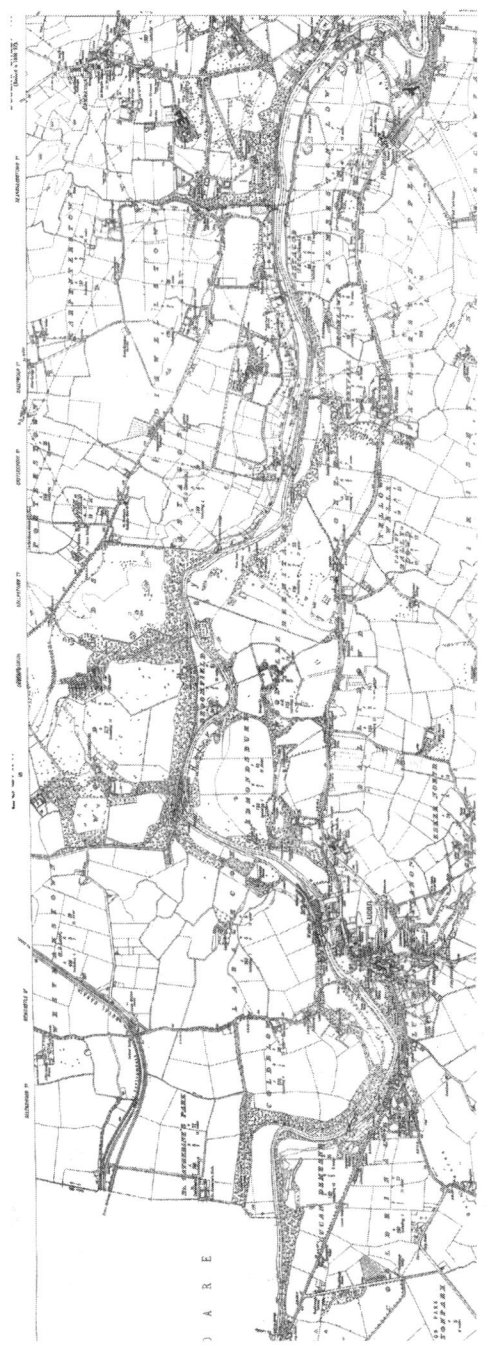

Map of 1936

Ferries continued to assist those on foot to cross the river. Many families also had their own boats to cross to the south bank. These boats were used in all seasons, even in flood times, because the boatmen and women understood the river flow. The Lower Road, up to the introduction of tar macadam in the 1930s, was just a mud track in winter, with persistent dust in summer. Prior to the covering of the road, men were employed by the local councils to scrape the mud off the roadway and form the banks we see today along the road. Drainage was also an important feature of road maintenance and ditches were kept viable to collect the run off water from the hills. Drainage in recent times has been neglected, contributing to flooding of the road.

*This photograph dates from 1889 and shows the school children standing outside their school in Lucan Village. The road is muddied and full of potholes. The Lower Road would have been in a similar condition.
(Courtesy Mrs. Mary Shackleton)*

Chapter 4
THE RIVER

The Liffey rises in the Dublin Mountains and it drains a large catchment area. The fields, mountains, lakes, hills, drains, small rivers and streams of Wicklow, Kildare and Dublin all feed the river. Flooding was a frequent occurrence all through the ages prior to its flow being controlled by the building of the dams in the twentieth century. The river is fifty miles in length as it meanders on its journey to the sea through the city of Dublin. Towns, villages and estates sprung up along its passage. The availability of the water was vital for communities who lived off the land for irrigation of crops and for farming animals. All households needed water for day-to-day living. It was also a source of fish, so it was vital for survival of the people.

The river could be harnessed to supply power, which could be extracted for energy purposes. This power was used for the manufacturing of necessary items and implements. So along the river weirs were constructed at selected points to power water wheels for the various mills that were built. The earliest record of a water-powered mill on the River Liffey is in the 1200s. This was by way of a horizontal water wheel. These wheels were the first design type and the power was generated using the natural direction of flow of the stream or river. However, the construction of millraces introduced the vertical wheel. This engineering advance was more appropriate for larger manufacturing projects. A constant flow of water could now be delivered to the wheel unlike the high and low flow rates of a natural stream. The vertical wheel was more efficient in energy production, it produced greater power and torque and, using belts and gears, the direction of the power generated could be changed when necessary. Larger wheels, and sometimes multiple wheels, could now be employed to generate greater torque as water could now be directed to any part of the circumference of the wheel by a series of strategically placed aqua ducts. Hence many processes could now take place within a mill using the sole power source.

Because the bed of the River Liffey consists of limestone it could not be navigated. Too many shallows and rapids prevented the transport of goods and people up and down the river, unlike (for example) the River Barrow. The river is tidal at its mouth, the first shallows as one sails upstream are at Chapelizod, so produce produced upstream of Chapelizod, was transported by dray to the boats moored at the quays.

The river divided the countryside, north from south. Lucan and Chapelizod bridges were considered vital from early times. They controlled the development of the Strawberry Beds. As mentioned before, King John had directed that a stone bridge be constructed over the Liffey at Lucan village. Prior to this the river was forded at Lucan. The ford, owned by Michael Lutteral was part of the Lutteral estate. This well-built stone bridge is thought to have lasted until 1768 whereupon it was washed away by floodwaters. The fact that this bridge lasted 500 years may be speculative because a bridge built by the Hon. Vesey in 1771 only lasted until 1786. A further bridge didn't last more than thirty years. Remnants of the buttress of one of these bridges can still be seen on the southern bank just above the Lucan weir. This bridge would have had three arches to cross the river and hence been more vulnerable to heavy flood destruction.

Lucan Weir with the stone buttress of a previous bridge still evident on left.

The present Lucan bridge was constructed or finished in 1814. This bridge is a single arch bridge and a masterpiece in design and construction. It is the longest single-span masonry arch bridge in Ireland. It has a span of 110 feet with a rise of 22 feet. The Royal Phoenix Ironworks in Parkgate Street made the iron balustrade. From Leixlip onwards the River Liffey is joined by the River Rye, channeling greater amounts of water downstream placing further strain on the multi-arched bridges. This would have led to the failure of the earlier bridges in Lucan.

Lucan Bridge built in 1814.

Chapelizod Bridge was built in 1660. A long millrace upstream divides the river flowing beneath this bridge. This millrace is more than fifty feet wide and has twelve-foot high stonewalls on either side. Two large vertical mill wheels powered the Phoenix Park Distillery in Chapelizod village. The mill wheels were considerable in size as can be seen in the drawing below.

The mill wheel measured 50 feet in breath and 18 feet in diameter. It was the said to be the largest in the United Kingdom at the time. (Sketch)

The Phoenix Park Distillery was owned by a Scottish Distillery Company and was an impressive five storey stone building in the heart of the village. The distillery ceased production in 1922 following the political changes in Ireland. The company also built a small Kirk in the village in which its staff could worship. The Port and Docks Company then acquired the building for storage use. Unfortunately, in 1979, the building was burnt down in a large fire. Chapelizod Bridge itself is unusual as it has four arches with the two central supports much larger than the side supports. The millrace, which must be one of the largest on the River Liffey protected the bridge with flow diversion. It is known as Anna Liffey Bridge.

*The main street of Chapelizod in 1904.
The Phoenix Distillery is the large stone building in the background.
(Courtesy of Gerard O'Byrne)*

The bridge at Islandbridge was built in 1577 and lasted until the flood in 1768. The current bridge was constructed in 1793 and is a single span masonry arch design similar to Lucan Bridge. The name given to the bridge was Sarah Bridge after Sarah Countess of Westmorland but was renamed Island Bridge after Independence in 1922. Despite its impressive span of 106 feet, it is still surpassed by the bridge at Lucan.

There are many recorded episodes of severe flooding from the Liffey and the damage inflicted on the communities, houses, farmland, factories and the city itself. In 1657 a great flood put low parts of Dublin city under water for up to six feet. In 1768 the bridge at Islandbridge was washed away in a flood, as was the iron mill at Lucan. The iron mill lay on the north bank where the Hill family would construct their woollen mill in 1863. A beautiful wooden bridge constructed by Lord Carhampton of Luttrellstown directly opposite the Grand Lodge suffered the same destruction in the flood of 1768.

Flooding at Clonboy House at the same time as the flooding of Iron Bank. (Courtesy Mrs. Mary Shackleton).

Flooding again occurred in 1898. In recent times, in 1954 for example, river waters burst their banks, entered people's homes to force evacuations of the houses, damage to property and the livelihoods of the farmers and market gardeners. There would have been a multitude of other floods, but the ones mentioned were recorded due to the significant damage caused.

Extreme climate changes did occur from time to time. Severe frosts froze the river solid in December of 1357 and the great freeze lasted for two months. People danced, travelled and even cooked on the river during this period. Another severe frost hit the country in the year 1759 and after initial fanfare and fun it became evident that crops could not be planted. Hunger fell over the country, which lasted for two years. Seed potatoes and livestock were consumed and after the freezing period ended there was

THE STRAWBERRY BEDS

little to plant or harvest. Statistically, more people died in these two years than in the great famine of the 1840s. A tidal wave struck in September 1767 and the level of the river is reported to have dropped two feet to rise four feet moments later before settling again.

Skating on the lake in Luttrellstown in 1897.
(Courtesy Mrs. Mary Shackleton)

Despite these calamities the river has provided well for the people of the Strawberry Beds. It provided energy for the eleven mills on its banks, four on the north bank and seven on the south bank at Palmerstown. The river gave employment to the people in the mills on both banks with some workers being ferried over and back from the Strawberry Beds. Four weirs were constructed to provide the required power: Lucan Weir, Anna Liffey Weir, Wren's Nest Weir and Palmerstown Weir.

The rich alluvial soil was suitable for agriculture and hence the market gardening culture. A source of water for household and farming needs was always at hand. Drawing water from the river must have been a laborious chore, as it required carrying to the top of the hills for irrigation of the crops. Domestic duties such as washing of clothes were carried out on the riverbank with the notorious 'washing boards'.

Fishing was possible; it was an excellent salmon and trout river, and perch, roach, eels and pike are all to be found. Prior to the early fifties the number of salmon passing up the Liffey was considerable. It was said that a poacher could shoot the salmon with a gun as they jumped high in the air to pass a weir. The course fish, such as perch, rudd, roach, and pike, were introduced to Ireland and are not native. However, they have thrived in our waters and were a good food source.

Although fish might have been abundant in the river they were not always available to the people. The landlords, who employed bailiffs to dissuade and deter those wishing to poach, owned the fishing rights. Even after the sale of a property by a landlord, the fishing or hunting rights might not be included in the agreement. Records of the fishing rights to the River Liffey dating from the 1200s, coinciding with the arrival of the Normans, still exist and are archived by the Irish Fisheries Board. It appears that many of the rights are no longer exercised and now fishing takes place under license for salmon and trout. For the past forty years fewer and fewer salmon have been recorded running upstream to spawn. The recording of the salmon is carried out at the Leixlip dam at the electrical power station. The reason for the depletion of the stocks is not fully understood and both salmon and trout are currently a protected species. Currently there is a complete ban on salmon and trout fishing on the river until stocks return to acceptable levels.

The eel numbers have also declined all over Ireland. Where once elvers were easy to pick on the weirs, they are now a vanishing species. The cause for this is unknown. The condition of the river is probably not solely responsible for their demise, as the rapid decline in eel numbers is noted worldwide.

Otters are still to be found on the riverbanks but they are scarce. However, few European countries can boast of having otters in their rivers that ultimately flow through their capital cities. Indeed in many European countries the otter is now extinct. Other wildlife, such as herons, waterfowl, swans, water rats, frogs, and ducks, are all to be found along the river. Plant life along the riverbank is abundant and thrives, especially in the wooded areas bordering the river.

The river also provided pleasure and pastimes. Boating took place, sometimes as a need to cross the river, sometimes for the pleasure of day-trippers to travel upstream and feast on strawberries and cream at the Strawberry

THE STRAWBERRY BEDS

Hall. The boats were rowed from Palmerstown upriver to moor at the Strawberry Hall, the site of the old ford crossing. Swimming was another past time and although there have been drowning fatalities no local person is known to have drowned in the river, but this may not be entirely true. Favourite sites to swim were at the Lucan, Wren's Nest and Palmerstown weirs. For those who chose not to swim then a restful day could be spent on the riverbank if the weather was fine. Boyfriend and girlfriend could spend happy times together by the riverside.

Boating on the river on their trip up stream, possibly to get strawberries and cream. The girls in the boat are Eva Kemp, Ester Dobbin and Mary Maguire, while John Murray and Hugh O Connor are two of the three men. (Courtesy Hugh O'Connor)

In many ways the river has become wild again. The water is no longer used for mill power. The two dams at Ballymore Eustace and Leixlip generate electricity, which powers the factories. Water for factories is drawn from the mains water supply or possibly pumped from the river directly. There is little irrigation need for vegetables, flowers, or fruit as very little is grown locally now with so much being imported. The riverbanks are much overgrown with fallen trees, heavy bush growth and heavy weed growth, possibly assisted by the increased nitrogen flowing into the river from fertilising practices upstream of the Strawberry Beds.

The river in past times would have been kept to a high standard due to necessity. The riverbanks would provide firewood for heating and cooking in the homes so the banks would have been quite bare. But perhaps its return to a feral nature will help it maintain and enhance the wildlife that depends on the river. Apart from swimming and canoeing, there is now little human activity on the river between Lucan and Knockmaroon Hill.

One disturbing fact now is that, with the total consumption of water that is currently being drawn from the river in the city and suburbs, the city engineers could prevent all waters flowing to the sea and utilise it for industrial and household requirements. The reality is our consumption and waste is so great that the river could be drained dry. The flow of water that is allowed to continue is only that amount that is sufficient to maintain fish life. Such a thought is incomprehensible, but greater rivers than the Liffey no longer reach the sea.

****

Chapter 5

THE MILLS

From recorded times four mills existed between Lucan village and Knockmaroon Hill on the north bank of the River Liffey. The first one at Lucan Bridge was an iron mill. Records exist to show that in 1484 the title of the iron mill was passed to a Thomas Prior of Worchester in England. Some years later it passed to Sir Godfrey Lutteral of Luttrellstown who had been granted vast estates under the reign of King John. This mill appears to have been in existence in the 1300s and was a producer of small iron implements. The mill functioned without a weir in its early stages using a horizontal water wheel arrangement for power. Its site is marked in the map of 1778. (Taylor and Skinner). The weir at Lucan was built in the early 1700s with a small millrace to provide a water supply, which in turn rotated the now vertical water wheels of the iron mill. However, in 1768 the entire mill was washed away in a massive flood. It could be construed that the weir construction, the flooding of the mill (1768), and the stone bridge destruction (1771) were all connected. All three happenings appear to take place within a span of twenty years.

In 1863 Hills of Bluebell purchased the site of the old mill and constructed a woollen mill that lasted until 1988. In its 120 year existence it provided employment, workers houses, income and resources for the people of Lucan. The woollen mill was well known for its good quality blankets, rugs, tweeds and uniforms. It supplied uniforms to the allies in both wars. Fires broke out within the mill from time to time but, despite various setbacks in its 120 years, the woollen mill continued in business. The Hill family lived in Clanaboy House, home of the current Concrete Products Ireland site (CPI). Their home first appeared on the map of 1870.

The 'Devil's Mill' or Anna Liffey Mill as it is now known, also appeared on the earliest maps. It is noted on the map of 1778. Legend has it that the mill was constructed overnight in a pact between the Lutteral family and Satan. It appears that Henry Lutteral, the dealmaker, was able to extract himself from offering his soul to Satan, which had been his promise to the deal. Henry Lutteral was intensely disliked in Dublin and London and was assassinated in his sedan chair in Dublin in 1717. This date of the assassination means that the 'Devil's Mill' was built long before 1717. Henry Lutteral was in his eighties at his death.

*Hills mills in 1900. The chimney is the last remnant of the mill.
It still stands proud at Lucan Bridge.
(Courtesy Mrs. Mary Shackleton)*

*Anna Liffey mill 1800s.
(Courtesy Mrs. Mary Shackleton)*

Anna Liffey Mill had always been a corn/flour mill and Mr. Joseph Shackleton from Ballitore, County Kildare, purchased it in 1860. The previous miller was Richard Rainsfort, under lease, and the owner was William Delaney. Mr. Delaney was residing in the townland of Woodlands at the time and may have purchased or more likely leased the mill from the Lutteral family. The net annual valuation, according to Griffiths Valuation, was £146.00 per annum. The weir and millrace provided power for the milling process and Mr. Richard Shackleton in later years was proud to show that the mill now contributes electrical power to the national grid.

New Holland Mill was situated at the Wren's Nest weir. The Wren's Nest pub was once known as New Holland, so this gives certainty to the pub's and the mill's very early origin. It is unknown when it was build, but Millers and Mills of Ireland mention the mill in the townland of Astagob in 1723. The owner was Thomas Keenan Esq., the largest landowner in the Diswellstown area at this period. It is marked on the earliest maps and legend has it that a Dutch immigrant had constructed it. Samuel Price was the miller in production at New Holland mill in 1725. The weir, with aqua ducts and horizontal water wheels provided power for the mill. The weir itself is thought to have been constructed at some time in the 1600s. According to Millers and Mills of Ireland the mill itself produced iron and starch. The iron was in fact wire and there were four wire mill wheels to produce the wire. Later on the mill was used in the cotton printing process, using starch. The slave trade used for cotton harvesting was thriving at this period in time. Perhaps the raw material for the printing process in the Strawberry Beds came from those parts of the globe where the practice of slave labour was still in existence.

In Griffiths Valuation 1843, the leaseholder of New Holland Mill was Thomas Liddy Esq. and the owner is a Thomas Lee Esq. The mill in 1843, produced paper for Mr. Liddy, a paper merchant, who had offices in Upper Ormond Quay. Mr. Lee may have purchased the mill from Mr. Thomas Keenan, whose family still resided in Diswellstown, or may have held a simple sub-letting agreement. Titles to a 970 year lease made in November 1806 still exist. The lease was made between Alexander Maguire and Dr. Thomas Lee and Roger Hamill. Roger Hamill was married to a Margaret Troy, a distant family relative. Another lease of title for the mill, between Letitia Mossop and Benjamin Glorney for 800 years was made in 1852. The title exists in the Land Registry Office.

The Wrens Nest Weir was built in the late 1600s.

The ruins of New Holland mill in the early seventies. The entrance to the mill was through this archway. Unfortunately the mill was knocked down in the seventies as it became structurally unsound and was a hazard to the swimmers, day-trippers or lovers who used to visit the river either to swim or just relax on the banks in the sunshine.
(Courtesy Denis Troy)

New Holland Mill became known as Glorney's Mill in later years as Benjamin Glorney now controlled the lease. Leasing and sub-leasing of property was the method of property exchange at this time. No title was freehold in Ireland, so ground rent was always payable to the landlord. Land, mills, houses always stayed in the ownership of the estate. This practice of property transfer originated in England following the Norman invasion.

Large substantial stone buildings with powered machinery and manufacturing processes were put to a multitude of purposes. The end products of the New Holland Mill changed from iron to starch to cotton printing and finally paper production in 1843. This pattern of change of use was not unusual, because the mills, with the wherewithal to power machinery, access to a trained workforce, and a good transport structure, could store all produce effectively.

The water level of the millrace was controlled by the sluice gates at the Wrens Nest weir. The weir provided a head of water to power the New Holland Mill and also provide power to the mills at Palmerstown downstream.

The lease of New Holland Mill by Benjamin Glorney in 1852 would have been strategic and profitable. It is not known what he produced in the mill. However, he would now have influence and perhaps control of the millrace on the opposite bank of the river. The millrace, which starts at the Wren's Nest weir, runs for nearly two miles and supplies water to the mills at Palmerstown where Benjamin Glorney had further mills. The millrace bypassed the shallows that start immediately downstream of the weir. The water level was controlled by four sluice gates. The first was at the Wren's Nest weir; the second was opposite the Strawberry Hall, the third and fourth were at Palmerstown. There are four small bridges still in existence that cross the millrace. This millrace is the longest on the River Liffey.

It was always thought that the millrace was used for transporting goods from New Holland to Palmerstown lane and hence on to the Dublin - Galway road. While this may have happened, it is unlikely, as loading on the south bank would mean crossing the river upstream of the Wren's Nest weir with the cargo. The millrace is too narrow for a barge of any size and low draught would be required to pass under the small bridges. Furthermore, the river could be forded at the Strawberry Hall with a roadway up to the Dublin - Galway road, a more efficient route for moving cargo. There are, however, mooring rings to tether boats in the millrace at this point, so one cannot say for certainty the race was not used to transport goods.

Horses would ford the river in the late 1700s and would pass through this gate, cross the millrace via a small bridge and make their way to the Dublin - Galway road.

*Bridge over the millrace.
There were four such small bridges along its two-mile length.*

The main function of the millrace was to provide power to the many mills at Palmerstown. In 1721 Palmerstown was a thriving industrial region with mills for iron and lead works, which were followed by cotton mills, flourmills, printing works, linen and calico mills. Starch production was a vital ingredient for cloth and printing so this was also in produced in the mills. The water supply from the river could be used both in the manufacturing process and generating power for the actual process. Pollution may have been an issue, but was probably ignored to a great degree. Production was possible as long as the water flow was ample. Flooding was troublesome; however, low water conditions were a much greater annoyance to the millers.

Law and regulation restricted water supply. The use of water for manufacturing purposes was limited to eight hours per day in periods of drought. Farmers and households would also be drawing water from the river, all be it with horse and cart, so legislation was enacted to conserve and regulate this vital resource. The quantity used by the mills could be considerable, so the legislation passed was to curb their usage as opposed to domestic use.

The last mill on the northern bank was at Palmerstown weir and again the water supply and power was supplied via a small millrace. It was a flour and starch mill and in use prior to 1778. Mardyke Mill, as it was known, belonged to a Mr. John Macken in 1839. A towpath (still there) existed from the Mardyke Mill along the riverbank for horses and drays to carry their load to Chapelizod without having to climb Knockmaroon or Glenmaroon hills. Once in Chapelizod the horses would use the bridge to cross the river.

*Palmerstown Weir with the Mardyke mill on the right.
The hillside is cultivated for strawberry growing.
(Courtesy Laurence Collection)*

The weir, officially known as Palmerstown weir, became known as Glorney's Weir after Mr. Benjamin Glorney of Waterstown on the south bank. Mr. Glorney as mentioned before had many interests on Palmerstown Lane. At one stage he had four mills working for him.

The millrace rejoins the river just below Palmerstown weir through this aqueduct.

The mills slowly became obsolete as they could not compete with the production, efficiency and output of the larger English mills. In the early 1800s a mill would employ one hundred to two hundred men. In wintertime this number might fall to sixty. The mills on the Strawberry Beds and Palmerstown were once a thriving area of industry, enterprise and employment; however, they would not be able to adjust to the new demands of the industrial revolution. They would slowly disappear due to their limitations. An inability of the mills to use large substantial wheels similar to those in England was due to the topography of the area. The fall in elevation of the river from Lucan to Palmerstown is not steep enough. The weir at Lucan is only 67 feet above sea level, too little to give a substantial head of water. Furthermore, the riverbed was of limestone, and restricted excavation. The steam engine would soon make water-powered machinery obsolete in any case and hasten the demise of the Palmerstown Lane manufacturing industry.

Chapter 6

THE MAIN HOUSES

The houses that are included in the earliest map of 1778 (Taylor and Skinner) show Knockmaroon, Diswellstown and Luttrelstown. In residence in Diswellstown in 1778 were Thomas Keenan Esq. and family. Diswellstown was the original home of the Diswell family (Deuswell). The family gave their name to the townland. The Dueswell family purchased 598 acres from Tyrell, the eight baron of Castleknock in the fourteenth century. In 1357 John Owen Esq., who had wide-spreading lands in the neighboring townlands of Corduff and Carpenterstown, acquired Diswellstown from the Diswell's. In *The History of County Dublin* by Dr. Ball (Royal Society of Antiquities in Ireland) the next 300 years are turbulent with ravages on the Pale. The ownership of Diswellstown probably changed many times until the Keenan family acquired it. The native Irish clans, the O'Tooles and the O'Byrnes of Wicklow in particular, repeatedly attacked the lands within the Pale. The Pale itself varied in size according to the strength of the respective forces. Land seizures and cattle rustling were commonplace. On occasions whole armies would descend on the area. Owen Roe O'Neill, for example, visited Castleknock in 1647 and two years later in the summer of 1649 the Duke of Ormonde advanced with a force from Kilkenny to Castleknock. In 1672, all the lands of Diswellstown fell, for a period of time, into the ownership of the Luttrelstown Estate.

The English Monarch granted Woodlands to Sir Thomas Luttrell early in the thirteenth century, but no Luttrell resided there until 1500 when Sir Godfrey Luttrell took up residence. The castle was considered a small Pale Castle. An inquisition of 1435 finds Christopher Luttrell granted lands of Castleknock, Clonsillagh, and the towns of Timolin and Barberstown. In 1470 the lands of Mulhuddart and Lismullin were enjoined to the estate.

Simon Luttrell was a Member of Parliament for County Dublin in the reign of King James. He fought alongside King James at the Battle of the Boyne and with Patrick Sarsfield in Aughrim and Limerick in the year 1690. The Luttrell family also married into the Sarsfield family. On the defeated side Simon Luttrell fled to France. He was later pardoned and allowed to return to Ireland under the Williamites.

Prior to this the Luttrell's fought with the Royalists against Cromwell and were defeated. Colonel Hewson became Governor of Dublin on behalf of Cromwell. Colonel Hewson took up residence at Luttrellstown in 1654. On the death of Cromwell in 1658 the Royalists returned to power and the Luttrells reclaimed their property.

While the Williamites pardoned Simon Luttrell following the Battle of the Boyne, it was his brother Henry, through deception, who succeeded to the estate at Luttrellstown. Furthermore, Henry received titles to Diswellstown, Mulhuddart, Carpenterstown, Clonsilla as well as Luttrellstown. Henry was intensely disliked and was murdered after a long life in Dublin in 1717. He was eighty-seven years old at the time and is it reported that his passing was not mourned. Simon, the son of Henry, became the first Earl Carhampton and it was another Earl (the third) who developed the estate and gardens and unfortunately built the wooden bridge over the Liffey, subsequently washed away in 1768.

Luttrellstown was sold to Colonel Luke White, a self-made millionaire, around the start of the nineteenth century. Colonel White did not come from aristocracy and because of this the Luttrells attempted to re-purchase the estate or prevent its sale. However, the sale was necessary due to the debts incurred by the estate and went through. Colonel White changed the name of the estate from Luttrellstown to Woodlands (its townland name) such was the hatred for the Luttrell name. His son became first Lord Annaly and the third Lord Annaly restored the original name of Luttrellstown. For the next 100 years the White family resided on the estate. The ownership then passed to Major E. C. Hamilton in 1900 for a brief period before it was purchased for Mrs. Brinsley Plunkett, daughter of Hon. Ernest Guinness, as a birthday present. Prior to the final purchase in 1913 the castle was leased on many occasions.

Knockmaroon is also marked on the map of 1778. It was the family seat of Colonel Colby in 1837. The house in question is now the residence of the Sisters of St. Josephs (Holy Angels), home for children with special needs. The Guinness family would come, in due course, to own this residence, Farmleigh and the Knockmaroon estate. The Guinness family offered the local council of the time a roadway along the river bank from Chapelizod to the Strawberry Beds via the Mardyke towpath, which would dispense with the need to move goods up Glenmaroon and down Knockmaroon Hill. The hill divides the residence at Glenmaroon, which is linked by the footbridge. The council refused this proposal so the residence is as it is today. The title of Viscount was bestowed on Lord Iveagh in 1865. Knockmaroon became the family seat of Lord Moyne.

The avenue to Luttrellstown Castle from the Grand Lodge on the Lower Road. It had a beautiful archway and lodge midway along its path. (Courtesy Mrs. Mary Shackleton)

Airfield House was the family seat of R. Manders Esq. in 1827. This house would be renamed Summerton by the Brooke family in 1836 or so. The property consisted of ninety acres and a small eighteenth century house, which was substantial relative to the houses of the native Irish. Additional rooms were added over time. Thomas Keenan Esq. was the immediate lessor of the Brooke lease title according to Griffith Valuation (1843).

The Brooke family originally came from Northern Ireland. They were related to Viscount Brookeborough in the main family line and were substantial property owners in Belfast in 1765. Prior to purchasing Airfield, Major Francis Brooke purchased Brookelawn in 1765 on the south bank of the river. The family lived there in view of Airfield, which would be purchased by his son George Fredrick Brooke in 1830. George was known as 'The Governor' and along with Airfield he also owned Pickering Forest and lands in Celbridge, Kildare. The Governor and his family moved into Airfield in 1830 and stayed there until 1910. The Governor died in 1865 and his son Francis, born 1817, became head of the house. His eldest son George Fredrick, born 1849, would become Baronet in 1903 and lived until 1926. The name of the house was changed from Airfield to Summerton sometime between 1836 and 1870. The name Summerton comes from an English town with which the Brooke's were associated at the time. Superstition has it that it is unlucky to rename a house, but this myth does not appear to apply in this instance. It was finally sold in 1910 for financial reasons, as the farms in Kildare and Summerton were running at a loss. The Laidlaw family, who had initially purchased Diswellstown and Abbey Lodge with large land holdings, purchased Somerton. All three properties were now joined into one estate. Somerton would now have a strong influence in the area for the next eighty years.

Airfield house was renamed Summerton by the Brooke family when they came to live there and substantially expand the house. (Courtesy Mrs. T. K. Laidlaw)

As mentioned before, the titles to Somerton, Diswellstown, Luttrellstown and Knockmaroon changed frequently down the years. The Luttrells held their estate for five hundred years and Colonel White owned the castle for a further one hundred years. The Keenan family owned Diswellstown for over one hundred years. Somerton and Oatlands were initially part of Diswellstown and were subjected to lease to various families who came to live in the area.

The families that resided in many of the large houses came from the forces of the Crown. Thomas Keenan of Diswellstown was Captain of the 34th Regiment of Foot.

His lands are noted on the Taylor and Skinner map of 1778. It appears he was extremely wealthy with fortunes made from the ironmongery industry. He was the owner of Annfield and Ashtown Castle as well as the mill on the Lower Road. That such a wealthy landowner with substantial lands should appear on a map of the time is no surprise.

Colonel Sir Neville Chamberlain KCB was Inspector General of the Royal Irish Constabulary and lived in Diswellstown from 1900 to 1916. It appears he mistook the seriousness of the impending rebellion of 1916 and he retired from his post soon after. Colonel Colby resided in Glenmaroon and Oatlands at different times. He was a military surveyor and responsible for the excellent surveys of the country at the early part of the nineteenth century. He was a diligent perfectionist in his work and offered to carry out the survey for no pay to himself.

Anna Liffey House and Weir. This was the home for the Shackleton family. The river has a low flow as can be seen from the dry areas on the weir. Most of the water was directed beneath the house to the mill in the background to drive the mill wheels.
(Courtesy Mrs. Mary Shackleton)

The Brooke family also had military origins. Major Francis Brooke of the 18th Light Dragoons and father to George Fredrick Brooke, fought on behalf of the Crown in the American War of Independance. The Brooke ancestors were also in the 4th Kings Own Regiment, the 60th Rifles South Irish Horse, the 19th Lancers Indian Army and others. Captain Basil Brooke in 1633 had been granted most of the lands of the McMahon and Maguire clans in Fermanagh and hence was a vast landowner in that part of the country.

Some of the other large houses in the area that had significant influence in the Strawberry Beds were the residences of the Hill family and the Shackleton family.

Clanboy House was home to the Hill family. The Hill family provided employment for many workers throughout the years in their woollen mill. (Courtesy Mrs. Mary Shackleton)

The ownership of the land did not belong to the Irish. They had been displaced and the lands confiscated from the Irish Clans. Some of these confiscations and forfeiting of lands led to enormous estates of thirty to fifty thousand acre holdings in the ownership of landlords from England who had won favour with the Crown. The landlords may never have seen their estates in Ireland and allowed estate managers to handle their affairs. Corruption could prosper in these conditions. To maintain their position of power and wealth, families would form marriage alliances, change religion, change patronage, proffer loans to the Monarch, or even raise an army on behalf of the Crown.

Grants of land were often made where the Crown had no jurisdiction, as with Queen Elizabeth in 1561. These areas belonged to the native Irish and the clan system of rights; title and ownership of the land still prevailed. The native people, having lost their lands, simply laboured as a resource while paying rent to the estate owners. These sums, paid by way of rent, were often considerable. In 1830, for example, Colonel White rented out land in Clonsilla at £3 to £4 per acre. Considering he owned 357 acre in Clonsilla this represented a considerable income from one title alone. In 1650 one estate in Sligo was granted to a Captain from Cromwell's army on the defeat of the McMahons in battle. The grant comprised a large land holding which was expanded to 34,000 acres in the early 1800s. At one pound rent per acre, per annum, the income in today's terms would be more than 3 million pounds per year. About the same time (1830) wages for the native labourers was 7/- shillings a week. The right to land ownership was to change over the next fifty years to the benefit of the people.

****

Chapter 7
GRIFFITHS VALUATION

Richard Griffith, a Dublin geologist, carried out the Griffiths Valuation in 1843. Tithes and taxes needed to be raised on a consistent and reliable basis that could be used for social development purposes. The authorities commissioned Richard Griffith to preform the task. The valuations were intended to gather information for local taxation purposes by determining the productive capacity of properties and the potential rent from all buildings, businesses, land, or houses. The initial step taken by Richard Griffith was a comprehensive survey of the country. This survey covered all the counties, baronies, poor law union, civil parishes, and townlands of Ireland.

Townlands date from the earliest times in Ireland. They originate from the Gaelic system of geographical divisions of land. The Gaelic word in past times was 'baile', which translated as 'settlement' or 'homestead', and was the holding of an extended family. 'Baile' is incorrectly used now to denote a town. The Gaelic word of 'fearann' was also used. Examples of the use of Anglicised versions are 'Ballymena' or 'Farranfore'. The Irish had different names for the divisions of land as one moved about the country. The Irish words 'baile' and 'fearann' were translated to 'townland' in English and this was universally adopted to identify the land division.

Townlands were first recorded in church papers before the 12th century. There are 61,402 registered townlands in Ireland so the extent of the survey carried out by Richard Griffith is obvious. The size of the townlands relates to their fertility. The smallest townland in Ireland is one acre in size, a churchyard, and the largest is 7012 acres. Poor, underproductive land such as tracts of bog or mountains have larger townlands. The average size of townlands in Ireland is within the range of 200 to 400 acres. Gaelic townlands tended to be larger than the post Norman varieties. The names of the townlands have varied origins. 'Astagob' or 'Castagob' could have Gaelic or possibly Viking origin, whereas Diswellstown is named after Dueswell, a Norman family. Porterstown is another such example of a townland being named after the prominent family in the area, in this case the Norman Porter family. The division between the Gaelic townlands is often a stream, a river or a ditch. The Norman version could be enclosed by man-made boundaries such as a wall, as in the case of Woodlands or Broomfield. While the English adopted the townland divisions of land they altered many with the Plantations that took place down through the ages.

The Strawberry Beds

In the past, and even to this day, especially in rural areas, the townland name would be included in the address of a person. Where family names would be similar, it could be that only the townland would identify the correct individual. This requires a local knowledge that thankfully still persists in Ireland. In 1972 the Royal Mail tried to abolish the use of townland names in Northern Ireland and introduce postal codes instead. This issue actually brought the communities in Northern Ireland together, republican and unionist, to resist the change as they each felt their sense of belonging and identity was being attacked.

The townlands that are relevant to the Strawberry Beds are Annfield, Astagob (Clonsilla), Astagob North (Castleknock), Broomfield, Clonsilla, Diswellstown, Kellystown, Porterstown, and Woodlands. The following map shows the townland markings and divisions.

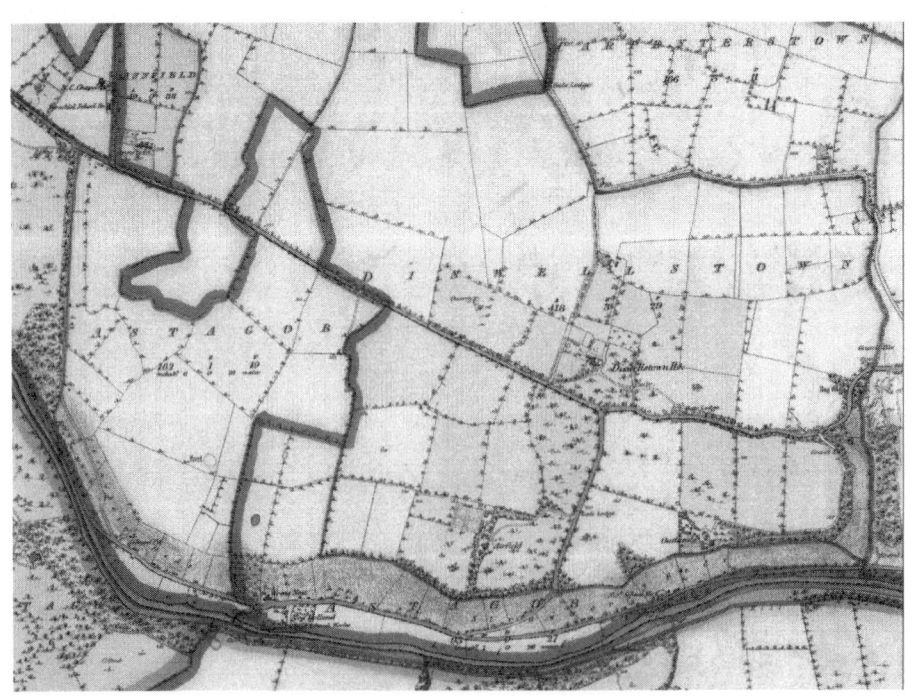

Townland map showing the divisions between Astagob, Diswellstown and Annfield. Porterstown lies next to Annfield while Woodlands has its boundary along the Rugged Lane. The Strawberry Beds continues into the townland of Castleknock, which starts at the Glen. Broomfield lies outside the extent of this map, as does Kellystown.
(Courtesy Ordinance Survey).

Griffiths Valuation lists every landowner and every household in Ireland. The survey summed the total acreage of each individual townland. Every rood, perch and acre was recorded. The occupier of the holding is named as the immediate lessor (owner or possibly a sub-letting), the content of land in size, the net annual valuation of the land, the net annual valuations of buildings, and finally the total net annual valuation of the property was calculated. A gravel yard of 2 perches 6 roods, for example, was valued at 10 shillings, whereas a garden of 20 roods was valued at 8 shillings.

These townlands give an idea of the extent of land ownership at the time. Some landowners could own many townlands. The valuation is not a census, however, and only those paying fees are recorded. However, for the first time names and families can be identified as living or farming in the area along the river from Lucan to Knockmaroon. It is not until the Census of 1901 and 1911 that all those living in the Strawberry Beds can be identified. The census of 1851 has been destroyed, which is unfortunate, as it was carried out just eight years after Griffiths Valuation.

The Lovely family, Simon and Edward, leased land from Col. Thomas White, as did the Halpin family. The Halpin family is thought to have come from St. Catherine's Estate in Lucan. The West family became the most prominent family in market gardening on the Strawberry Beds in the eighteen and nineteen hundreds. The brothers George and William leased land from Col. Thomas White in Astagob (Clonsilla) and Astagob North (Castleknock). Other names of note are Laurence Weldon, Carty, Kane, and Tuite, leasing in Woodlands from Col. Thomas White, while John McNeill in 1822 leased the land for the first national school, beside the Strawberry Hall, from Col. Thomas White.

The relevant extracts form Griffiths Valuation can be seen in the following pages. For complete details reference should be made to the National Archives for the comprehensive manuscript of Griffiths Valuation.

Griffiths Valuation 1843.

Name of Townland and Occupier	Name of Immediate Leaseholder.	Description of Tenement
Annfield		
Lawrence Reynolds	Thomas Keenan Esq	House Office Land
		Total 19 acres
Astagob (Castleknock) (North)		
Matthew Rice	Thomas Keenan Esq.	
Patrick Tuite	"	House, Office, Land
Thomas Maguire	"	House, Iron foundry Office.
Lucinda Wilson	"	House, Office, Land
Christopher Roe	"	House, Office, Land
Michael Burke	"	House, Land
Matthew Purcell	"	House, Land
James Durneen Cuffe	Col Thos. White	House, Office, Land
Thomas Liddy	Thomas Lee Esq.	House, Office, Land, Paper Mill.
Owen Scully	Col Thos. White	House, Office, Land
John Hughes	"	House, Land, Office
James Farrell	"	House, Land
James Keogh	"	House, Land
William Hughes	James Keogh	House
Bridget Keogh	"	House
Michael Carroll	Col Thos. White	House, Land
Patrick McDonnell	"	House, Land, Office
Catherine Carroll	Patrick McDonnell	House
Elizabeth Moore	Col Thos. White	House, Land
Michael Martin	"	House, Land, Office
Denis Sheerin	Michael Martin	House
Daniel Connelly	Col Thos. White	House, Land
John Hughes	Thomas Liddy	Land
Ellen Gibney	Col Thos. White	House, Land
Theresa Doyle	"	House, Land, Office
Owen Scully	"	House, Land
James Nevin	Owen Scully	House

James Brennan	"	House
William Bennett	Col Thos. White	House, Land
George West	"	House, Land
John McNeill	"	House, Land, Office
National School	John McNeill	School House
Edward O Neill	Col Thos. White	House, Land
Margaret Kelly	"	House, Land
Patrick Farrell	Margaret Kelly	House
Patrick Hickey	Col Thos. White	House, Land
Edward Lovely	"	House, Land, Office
John McNeill	"	Land
James Cuffe	Simon Lovely	Land
Simon Lovely	Col Thos. White	House, Land
William Reed	Simon Lovely	House
Jane Kane	Col Thos. White	House, Land
Edward Lovely	"	Land
William Panton	"	House, Land
Anne Halpin	"	House, Land, Office
William Ryan	Anne Halpin	House
Nicholas Delaney	Anne Halpin	House
Edward O Neill	Col Thos. White	Land

Total 93 acres.

The two main landowners in 1843 were Thomas Keenan Esq., who lived in Diswellstown, and Col. Thomas White of Luttrellstown. Lands, houses, mills, offices, and kilns, owned by the two families above, were leased to various people. Some of the families, or their descendants, named in Griffith Valuation are still living in the locality. The Balfe family, the Scully family, the Lovely Family, still have descendants on the Strawberry Beds.

Name of Townland and Occupier	Name of Immediate Leasehold	Description of Tenement
Astagob (Clonsilla)		
James Balfe	Thomas Keenan Esq.	House, Land, Office
Thomas Smith	"	Land
William Mahon	"	House, Land, Office
Matthew Rice	John Galloway Esq.	Land, Office
Richard Kennedy	Matthew Rice	House
Archibald Robinson	John Galloway Esq.	House, Land, Office
William West	Col Thos. White	House, Land, Office
William Furlong	"	House, Land
Denis Kane	"	House, Land, Office
Sarah Healy	"	House, Office
Mary Molloy and Mary Carty	"	House, Office
Alice Tuite	Thomas Keenan Esq.	House, Land, Office
John Curtis	Thomas Keenan Esq.	House, Land, Office
John Wm. Beech Esq.	John Curtis	House, Office
Patrick Heavy	John Curtis	House
Alice Tuite	Thomas Keenan Esq.	Land
John Doonigan	"	House, Land
Laurence Carty	"	House, Land
James Kane	"	House, Land, Office
Thomas Maguire	"	Land
Thomas Halpin	Thomas Maguire	House
Patrick Flood	Thomas Keenan Esq.	House, Land Office
Patrick Tuite	"	Land
John Heavy	"	Land
Sarah Martin	"	House, Land
Catherine Meleady	"	House, Land
John Hood	Catherine Meleady	House
William Tuite	Thomas Keenan Esq.	Land, Office, Water River Liffey

Total 162 acres

Name of Townland and Occupier	Name of Immediate Leasehold	Description of Tenement
Broomfield		
Rev Sheffing Thompson	Col Thos. White	House, Land, Office
Vacant	Rev S Thompson	Gate Lodge
		Water River Liffey
		Total 24 acres.

Name of Townland and Occupier	Name of Immediate Leasehold	Description of Tenement
Castleknock (Strawberry Beds area)		
George West	John Croker Esq.	Land
William Bennet	John Croker Esq.	Land
Benjamin Glorney Esq.	Thomas Pim Esq.	Flour, Mustard
Patrick Dillon	Sir Henry Marsh Bart.	Land
Joseph Coady	Patrick Dillon	House
Thos. Cavanaugh	Sir Henry Marsh Bart.	House, Office, Land
Rose, Daniel Crean	Sir Henry Marsh Bart	Land
James Coady	John Hawkins Esq.	House, Office, Land
Patrick Duffy	John Hawkins Esq.	House, Office, Land
William Cannon	Sir Henry Marsh Bart.	House, Office, Land
		Water of half the River Liffey
John West	Sir Henry Marsh Bart.	House, Land.
Andrew Clarke	Phillip Fea	House
William Clarke	Phillip Fea	House
James Kelly	Phillip Fea	House
		Total 13 acres.

Name of Townland and Occupier	Name of Immediate Leasehold	Description of Tenement
Diswellstown		
Patrick Balfe	Thomas Keenan Esq.	House, Land, Office
John Newport	"	House
Thomas Healy	Mid. G. Railway / Royal Canal Company	Bank of Canal
Mid. G Railway / Royal Canal Company	In fee	Railway
John Kelly	"	Bank of Canal.
James Balfe	Thomas Keenan Esq.	Meadow Land
Thomas Smith Esq.	"	House, Land, Office
George Bentley	"	Land
William Miller	"	House, Land, Office
Fitzmaurice Power	"	House, Land, Office
James Ledwich	"	Land
Thomas Keenan Esq.	In fee	House, Land, Office
John Donohue	Thomas Keenan Esq.	Gate Lodge
John Tiernan	"	Office, Land
John Seery	John Tiernan	House
George Brooke Esq.	Thomas Keenan Esq.	House, Land, Office
George Brooke Esq.	George Brooke Esq.	Gate Lodge
Patrick Flood	Thomas Keenan Esq.	Land
Colonel Hill	John Godley Esq.	House, Land, Office
Michael Martin	Colonel Hill	Gate Lodge
James Halpin	"	Land

Total 259 acres.

Name of Townland and Occupier	Name of Immediate Leasehold	Description of Tenement
Kellystown		
Peter Burill	Col Thos. White	House, Office, Land
George Aungier	Col Thos. White	House, Land
Peter Butterly	Col Thos. White	Land
Mid R.G. Railway and Royal Canal Co.	In fee	Land
Timothy Green	Col Thos. White	House, Office, Land
Michael Keogh	--- Kennedy Esq.	House, Office, Land
Gate Keeper	Michael Keogh	Gate Lodge
Anthony Smith	Col Thos. White	House, Office, Land.
Peter McDermott	Anthony Smith	House.
Peter Geraghty	Col Thos. White	House, Office, Land
R Catholic Church	Col Thos. White	Church, Lands.
------- Callaghan	Col Thos. White	School, Office.

Total 173 acres

Name of Townland and Occupier	Name of Immediate Leasehold	Description of Tenement
Porterstown		
John Dobbs	Col Samuel White	House, Land
Laurence Leonard	Col Samuel White	House, Office, Land
Thomas Keating	Col Samuel White	House, Office, Land
Thomas Fox	Thomas Keating	House
Owen Fox	Col Samuel White	House, Land
Roger Fox	Col Samuel White	House, Land
Henry Maguire	Col Samuel White	House, Land
James Smith	Henry Maguire	House
John Thompson	Henry Maguire	House
James Sheridan	Henry Maguire	House
George Aungier	Col Samuel White	Land
Patrick Gernon	Col Samuel White	House, Land
Joseph Kane	Col Samuel White	House, Land
Peter Butterley	Col Samuel White	House, Land
John Hogan	Col Samuel White	House, Office, Land
Patrick Kane	Col Samuel White	House, Office, Land

Peter Winters	Patrick Kane	House
Elizabeth Dardis	Col Samuel White	House, Land
Catherine Boylan	Elizabeth Dardis	House
Patrick Smith	Elizabeth Dardis	House
Mid G. W. Railway and Royal Canal Co.	In fee	Land
Thomas Healy	Mid G. W. Railway	Banks of canal
Catherine Shannon	William Coote	House
James Carlisle	William Coote	House
William Coote	Mid G. W. Railway	House, Land
Patrick Kane	Mid G. W. Railway	Smithy
Catherine Branagan	Patrick Kane	House
Andrew Gannon	Col Samuel White	Land
Vacant	Andrew Gannon	House
James Balfe	Col Samuel White	House, Land
James Balfe	Thomas Bannoe	Land

Total 219 acres

Name of Townland and Occupier	Name of Immediate Leasehold	Description of Tenement

Woodlands

Col Thos. White (Heirs)	In fee	House, Land, Office
James Curran	Col Thos. White	Gardeners House
Laurence Weldon	"	Gate Lodge
Fanny McMahon	"	Gate Lodge
James Doohan	"	Gate Lodge
Walter Teeling	"	House Free
James Fannin	"	Gate Lodge
Patrick Dunne	"	Gate Lodge
Richard Rainsford	William Delaney	Flour Mill, Office Kiln, and Water

Total 571 acres.

The valuations give some idea of the distribution of property in the early 1800s. The total acreage of the townlands selected is approximately 1600 acres, of which Col. Thomas White of Luttrellstown owned 1,114 acres. Thomas Keenan Esq. of Diswellstown owned over 400 acres. Col. Thomas White owned lands in Clonsilla, Barnhill, and Barberstown as well as lands in Westmeath.

Charles Trench Esq. lived in Farmley as it was then spelt; John Hawkins Esq. lived in Mountsacville, while Sir Henry Marsh Bart. lived in Haymount. In the townland of Diswellstown, Oatlands was now the seat of John Godley Esq. and family. Apart from Col Thomas White and Thomas Keenan Esq., who owned their lands, the other families' titles were sub-letting agreements.

A photograph of Veronica Ennis, Margaret Ennis and Hugh Ennis taken outside The Wrens Nest public house in 1920. Margaret Ennis has a small dog on her lap. (Courtesy Michael Daly)

Chapter 8
CENSUS 1901 AND 1911

The National Archives of Ireland have placed census details on their website. The census is based on the townlands of Ireland, as are the electoral divisions. The details from the two censuses, 1901 and 1911, that relate to the Strawberry Beds have been extracted and are included here, so comparison can be made over the ten year period. It is unfortunate that previous censuses (1821, 1841, 1851, 1861) for this area have been destroyed.

The details given here are the family name, the head of the house, his/her age and occupation. For each household there is separate recording, which gives more comprehensive family details: the names of the wife, husband, children, their ages, their occupations, the educational standards of family members, the children born and those still living. It also records ailments that family members may have. This information, while not included here, is available by a link to the website of the National Archives.

The census details of 1901 and 1911 relate to the townlands of Annfield, Astagob (Clonsilla), Astagob North (Castleknock), Porterstown, Diswellstown, Woodlands, Broomfield and part of Castleknock. (Ref. townland map). Walls surround the townlands of Annfield, Broomfield and Woodlands. These boundaries are man made and extend from the Norman influence on land division.

Astagob townland has two electoral divisions. The first is in the Clonsilla electoral division and the boundary line passes down the Rugged lane hugging Luttrellstown Castle wall, turning eastwards at Woodlands Cottage, along the Strawberry Beds and travels along before turning uphill at the Silver Hill next to the Wren's Nest public house. Here a stream marks the east boundary as it rises to meet the Porterstown townland in the 'moat' field. The second part of Astagob townland (Astagob North) starts again at the stream beside the Wren's Nest, along the southern boundary, the river, travels eastwards along the Lower Road to the stream at the 'Glen'. This strip is merely the hillside in depth as the Diswellstown townland commands all the area above the Beds stretching from Porterstown, Astagob (North) to Castleknock. The last townland of the Strawberry Beds runs from the stream at the Glen along the Lower Road, up Knockmaroon Hill to the Phoenix Park gate. This section falls into the Castleknock electoral division – hence only part of this census is included. The census returns for Castleknock are quite large.

By referring to the census, the number of households and persons living in the Strawberry Beds and surrounds can be counted. Hence, in 1911 there were in total 376 people living in the townlands of Annfield, Astagob (Clonsilla), Astagob (Castleknock), Broomfield, Diswellstown and Woodlands. Ten years earlier the same townlands had 434 people. This number included men, women and children. Assuming that more than sixty percent could not, would not, or did not have to work, then the eligible workforce would be approximately 200. This is too small a number of workers to meet the needs of the local farms, mills, the Ordinance Survey and other industries.

From these figures there is a drop of fifty-eight persons living in townlands between 1901 and 1911. This drop is also noted in the school attendance. Whether this is due to social upheaval, reduced birth rate, emigration or migration is open to speculation.

Ireland was heavily populated in the early 1800s prior to the famine and depleted thereafter. The population rose from 4.5 million in 1750 to 8 million by the famine time. This depletion was not universal across Ireland. In Clonsilla, for example, the population dropped only by seventy persons post famine, whereas in other parts of poorer Ireland, the townland population could drop by eighty percent. The population of Lucan actually increased during the famine by sixty-three persons. This reflects the reduced dependency on the potato crop that people had in this area and also the availability of work. Migration is also not dramatic, so the numbers extracted from the two censuses is an accurate account of the numbers available to work at this time.

The census details for Astagob in the electoral division of Clonsilla for the years 1901 and 1911 follows:

Astagob 1901

Surname	Forename	Townland	DED	Age	Sex	Birthplace	Occupation
Byrne	Teresa	Astagob	Clonsilla	24	F	Co Dublin	Labourer
Byrne	Christina	Astagob	Clonsilla	20	F	Co Dublin	Domestic Servant
Byrne	Bridget	Astagob	Clonsilla	55	F	Co Dublin	Labourer
Byrne	Bartle	Astagob	Clonsilla	31	M	Co Dublin	Labourer

Byrne	John	Astagob	Clonsilla	33	M	Co Dublin	Labourer
Byrne	Mary Jane	Astagob	Clonsilla	13	F	Co Dublin	Scholar
Clinton	Patrick	Astagob	Clonsilla	30	M	Co Dublin	Painter
Clinton	Catherine	Astagob	Clonsilla	50	F	Longford	
Clinton	John	Astagob	Clonsilla	60	M	Westmeath	Agricultural Labourer
Coates	Ellen	Astagob	Clonsilla	49	F	Dublin City	
Coates	William	Astagob	Clonsilla	68	M	Dublin City	House Builder
Curtis	Mary	Astagob	Clonsilla	31	F	Co Dublin	General Servant
Doyle	Amelia	Astagob	Clonsilla	28	F	Dublin	Servant
Doyle	John	Astagob	Clonsilla	70	M	Co Mayo	Farm Servant
Fagan	Simon	Astagob	Clonsilla	15	M	Co Dublin	Scholar
Fagan	John	Astagob	Clonsilla	24	M	Co Dublin	Farmer's Son
Fagan	Kathleen	Astagob	Clonsilla	17	F	Co Dublin	Farmer's Daughter
Fagan	James	Astagob	Clonsilla	22	M	Co Dublin	Farmer's Son
Fagan	James	Astagob	Clonsilla	53	M	Co Dublin	Farmer
Fagan	Eliza	Astagob	Clonsilla	18	F	Co Dublin	Farmer's Daughter
Flanigan	Mary	Astagob	Clonsilla	40	F	Co Dublin	Worker
Fullerton	Martha J	Astagob	Clonsilla	13	F	Co Dublin	Scholar
Fullerton	John A	Astagob	Clonsilla	51	M	Co Armagh	Gardener
Fullerton	John A	Astagob	Clonsilla	19	M	Co Armagh	Civil Assistant O.S.
Fullerton	Louise	Astagob	Clonsilla	21	F	Co Armagh	Teacher
Fullerton	Samuel J	Astagob	Clonsilla	9	M	Co Dublin	Scholar
Fullerton	Mary	Astagob	Clonsilla	11	F	Co Dublin	Scholar
Fullerton	Annie E	Astagob	Clonsilla	16	F	Co Dublin	House keeper
Fullerton	Jane	Astagob	Clonsilla	45	F	Co Armagh	Ladies Nurse
Fullerton	Eileen L	Astagob	Clonsilla	6	F	Co Dublin	Scholar
Fullerton	Herbert G	Astagob	Clonsilla	2	M	Dublin	
Gauntlet	Madaline	Astagob	Clonsilla	17	F	Dublin City	Scholar
Geraghty	James	Astagob	Clonsilla	49	M	Co Dublin	R.I.C. Pensioner
Geraghty	William	Astagob	Clonsilla	12	M	Co Dublin	Scholar
Geraghty	Patrick	Astagob	Clonsilla	1	M	Co Dublin	
Geraghty	Rosanna	Astagob	Clonsilla	6	F	Co Dublin	Scholar
Geraghty	Rosanna	Astagob	Clonsilla	30	F	Co Dublin	
Geraghty	Christina	Astagob	Clonsilla	2	F	Co Dublin	
Geraghty	John	Astagob	Clonsilla	11	M	Co Dublin	Scholar
Green	William	Astagob	Clonsilla	63	M	Co Dublin	Market Gardner
Green	Fredrick	Astagob	Clonsilla	24	M	Co Dublin	Farm Labourer
Green	Henry	Astagob	Clonsilla	28	M	Co Dublin	Farm Labourer
Green	George	Astagob	Clonsilla	33	M	Co Dublin	Farm Labourer
Hollywood	Olive	Astagob	Clonsilla	12	F	Co Down	Servant Domestic
Kearney	Eliza	Astagob	Clonsilla	60	F	Co Meath	Worker

Kellaghan	Mary	Astagob	Clonsilla	40	F	Co Dublin	House Keeper
Kellaghan	James	Astagob	Clonsilla	38	M	Co Dublin	Flour Mill Labourer
Kellaghan	Catherine	Astagob	Clonsilla	36	F	Co Dublin	House Keeper
Kellaghan	Mary	Astagob	Clonsilla	73	F	Wicklow	
Kellaghan	John	Astagob	Clonsilla	46	M	Co Dublin	Flour Mill Labourer
Madden	Peter	Astagob	Clonsilla	40	M	Co Kildare	Ag Labourer
Malone	James	Astagob	Clonsilla	11	M	Co Dublin	Scholar
Malone	Matthew	Astagob	Clonsilla	13	M	Co Kildare	Scholar
Malone	Annie	Astagob	Clonsilla	34	F	Co Kildare	
Neill	Mary	Astagob	Clonsilla	30	F	England	
Neill	James	Astagob	Clonsilla	36	M	Fermanagh	Farm Servant
Raby	John	Astagob	Clonsilla	43	M	England	Huntsman
Raby	Sarah	Astagob	Clonsilla	46	F	England	
Warren	Laurence	Astagob	Clonsilla	59	M	Co Dublin	Farmer
Warren	Margaret	Astagob	Clonsilla	45	F	Co Dublin	House Keeper
Warren	Margaret	Astagob	Clonsilla	61	F	Co Dublin	Assistant
West	Eliza	Astagob	Clonsilla	22	F	Co Dublin	
West	Esther	Astagob	Clonsilla	25	F	Co Dublin	
West	Nar?ian	Astagob	Clonsilla	66	F	Co Dublin	
West	Richard	Astagob	Clonsilla	76	M	Dublin	Market Gardener

Astagob 1911

Surname	Forename	Townland	DED	Age	Sex	Birthplace	Occupation
Armstrong	Nora	Astagob	Clonsilla	10	F	England	
Balfe	Peter	Astagob	Clonsilla	18	M	Dublin	Farmer
Balfe	William	Astagob	Clonsilla	15	M	Dublin	
Balfe	John	Astagob	Clonsilla	14	M	Dublin	Scholar
Balfe	James	Astagob	Clonsilla	24	M	Dublin	Farmer
Balfe	Mary Teresa	Astagob	Clonsilla	16	F	Dublin	
Balfe	Patrick	Astagob	Clonsilla	26	M	Dublin	Farmer
Byrne	Teresa	Astagob	Clonsilla	35	F	Co Dublin	
Byrne	Mary	Astagob	Clonsilla	23	F	Co Dublin	
Byrne	Bridget	Astagob	Clonsilla	70	F	Co Dublin	
Byrne	Maggie	Astagob	Clonsilla	33	F	Co Dublin	Cook House Keeper
Clinton	James	Astagob	Clonsilla	35	M	Co Dublin	General Labourer
Clinton	Catherine	Astagob	Clonsilla	68	F	Co Longford	
Clinton	Patrick	Astagob	Clonsilla	47	M	Co Dublin	General Labourer
Curtis	Isabella	Astagob	Clonsilla	38	F	Co Dublin	
Dunne	Fannie	Astagob	Clonsilla	29	F	Co Dublin	
Fagan	John	Astagob	Clonsilla	35	M	Co Dublin	Farmer

Fagan	Margaret	Astagob	Clonsilla	34	F	Co Dublin	
Fagan	Mary	Astagob	Clonsilla	0	F	Co Dublin	
Geraghty	Criss	Astagob	Clonsilla	10	F	Co Dublin	Scholars
Geraghty	Josephine	Astagob	Clonsilla	9	F	Co Dublin	Scholars
Geraghty	Peter	Astagob	Clonsilla	6	M	Co Dublin	Scholars
Geraghty	James	Astagob	Clonsilla	61	M	Co Dublin	Market Gardener
Geraghty	Mathew	Astagob	Clonsilla	4	M	Co Dublin	Scholar
Geraghty	Joseph	Astagob	Clonsilla	1	M	Co Dublin	
Geraghty	Roseanne	Astagob	Clonsilla	42	F	Co Dublin	
Geraghty	Christy	Astagob	Clonsilla	7	M	Co Dublin	Scholars
Geraghty	William	Astagob	Clonsilla	20	M	Co Dublin	Gardener
Geraghty	John	Astagob	Clonsilla	19	M	Co Dublin	Gardener
Geraghty	Rosanne	Astagob	Clonsilla	16	F	Co Dublin	
Geraghty	Bridget	Astagob	Clonsilla	3	F	Co Dublin	
Gill	Mary	Astagob	Clonsilla	21	F	Co Leitrim	General Servant
Greene	George	Astagob	Clonsilla	43	M	Co Dublin	Farm Servant
Greene	Mary	Astagob	Clonsilla	5	F	Co Dublin	
Greene	Bridget	Astagob	Clonsilla	2	F	Co Kildare	
Greene	Fredrick	Astagob	Clonsilla	0	M	Co Kildare	
Greene	Fredrick	Astagob	Clonsilla	33	M	Co Dublin	Garden Servant
Greene	Anne	Astagob	Clonsilla	26	F	Co Kildare	
Kelahan	James	Astagob	Clonsilla	51	M	Co Dublin	Flour Mill Labourer
Kelahan	Mary	Astagob	Clonsilla	53	F	Co Dublin	
Kelahan	Catherine	Astagob	Clonsilla	49	F	Co Dublin	
Long	Annie	Astagob	Clonsilla	39	F	Co Tyrone	
Long	Frederick C	Astagob	Clonsilla	34	M	England	Sapper Royal Engineers
McDermot	Patrick	Astagob	Clonsilla	52	M	Longford	Agricultural Labourer
McDermot	Kate	Astagob	Clonsilla	52	F	Longford	
McGovern	Daniel	Astagob	Clonsilla	27	M	Co Meath	Farm Servant
McKeon	Michael	Astagob	Clonsilla	62	M	Roscommon	Groom Servant
McKeon	Anne	Astagob	Clonsilla	60	F	Co Dublin	
McKeon	John	Astagob	Clonsilla	19	M	Co Kildare	Gardener Servant
Callaghan	Mary	Astagob	Clonsilla	47	F	Dublin	Farming
Callaghan	William	Astagob	Clonsilla	39	M	Meath	Farmer
Shea	Thomas	Astagob	Clonsilla	40	M	King's Co	Gardener
Shea	William	Astagob	Clonsilla	51	M	King's Co	Herd
Walsh	Brigid	Astagob	Clonsilla	44	F	Co Dublin	
Walsh	William	Astagob	Clonsilla	22	M	Co Dublin	Farm Labourer
Warren	Laurence	Astagob	Clonsilla	72	M	Co Dublin	Farmer
West	Esther	Astagob	Clonsilla	33	F	Co Dublin	
West	Mary Anne	Astagob	Clonsilla	75	F	Co Dublin	Farmer

PATRICK TROY

The census of Astagob in the electoral division of Castleknock for the years 1901 and 1911 follows.

Astagob 1901

Surname	Forename	Townland	DED	Age	Sex	Birthplace	Occupation
Brogan	Elizabeth	Astagob	Castleknock	60	F	Dublin	
Brogan	John	Astagob	Castleknock	73	M	Meath	Labourer
Butler	Patrick	Astagob	Castleknock	56	M	Westmeath	Labourer
Byrne	Bridget	Astagob	Castleknock	50	F	Carlow	Out Door Work
Byrne	Mary	Astagob	Castleknock	12	F	Co Dublin	Scholar
Byrne	Catherine	Astagob	Castleknock	46	F	Co Dublin	Farm Worker
Carroll	Kathleen	Astagob	Castleknock	3	F	Co Dublin	
Carroll	James	Astagob	Castleknock	73	M	Co Dublin	Gardener
Carroll	William	Astagob	Castleknock	34	M	Co Dublin	Shepherd
Carroll	Margaret	Astagob	Castleknock	6	F	Co Dublin	Scholar
Carroll	Margaret	Astagob	Castleknock	56	F	Co Dublin	
Carroll	Jane	Astagob	Castleknock	5	F	Co Dublin	
Carroll	Mary	Astagob	Castleknock	7	F	Co Dublin	Scholar
Carroll	Michael	Astagob	Castleknock	45	M	Co Dublin	Iron Moulder
Carroll	Mary	Astagob	Castleknock	33	F	Dublin City	
Clarke	Rose	Astagob	Castleknock	40	F	Co Dublin	
Clarke	Teresa	Astagob	Castleknock	2	F	Co Dublin	
Clarke	Winnefrid	Astagob	Castleknock	4	F	Co Dublin	Scholar
Clarke	James	Astagob	Castleknock	48	M	Co Dublin	Printer
Clarke	William	Astagob	Castleknock	16	M	Co Dublin	Farms Servant
Clarke	Mary	Astagob	Castleknock	20	F	Co Dublin	Bar Maid
Clarke	Anne	Astagob	Castleknock	6	F	Co Dublin	School Scholar
Clarke	John	Astagob	Castleknock	14	M	Co Dublin	Scholar
Clarke	Margaret	Astagob	Castleknock	11	F	Co Dublin	School Scholar
Clarke	Thomas	Astagob	Castleknock	9	M	Co Dublin	School Scholar
Costello	James	Astagob	Castleknock	20	M	Co Dublin	Farm Servant
Costello	Annie	Astagob	Castleknock	23	F	Co Dublin	General Servant
Cranny	Sarah	Astagob	Castleknock	23	F	Dublin	House Maid
Cunningham	Thomas	Astagob	Castleknock	12	M	Mansfield	Scholar
Cunningham	Ellen M	Astagob	Castleknock	8	F	Mansfield	Scholar
Cunningham	Patrick	Astagob	Castleknock	53	M	Co Meath	Labourer
Cunningham	Rose F	Astagob	Castleknock	6	F	Dublin	Scholar
Cunningham	Agnes	Astagob	Castleknock	10	F	Mansfield	Scholar
Curran	James	Astagob	Castleknock	56	M	Dublin City	Army Pensioner
Day	John	Astagob	Castleknock	45	M	Co Meath	Groom
Donnelly	Ellen	Astagob	Castleknock	49	F	Co Dublin	House Keeper

Donnelly	Kathleen	Astagob	Castleknock 15	F	Co Dublin	Scholar
Donnelly	Mary	Astagob	Castleknock 37	F	Co Wexford	
Donnelly	Thomas	Astagob	Castleknock 39	M	Co Dublin	General Labourer
Donnelly	John	Astagob	Castleknock 13	M	Co Dublin	Scholar
Donnelly	Catherine	Astagob	Castleknock 2	F	Co Dublin	
Donnelly	Mary Ellen	Astagob	Castleknock 10	F	Co Dublin	Scholar
Donnelly	John	Astagob	Castleknock 50	M	Co Dublin	Market Gardener
Donnelly	Annie	Astagob	Castleknock 0	F	Co Dublin	
Donnelly	Joseph	Astagob	Castleknock 7	M	Co Dublin	Scholar
Donnelly	Mary	Astagob	Castleknock 9	F	Co Dublin	Scholar
Donnelly	Joseph	Astagob	Castleknock 20	M	Co Dublin	Gardener
Donnelly	Thomas	Astagob	Castleknock 11	M	Co Dublin	Scholar
Downey	Thomas	Astagob	Castleknock 40	M	Kildare	Labourer
Downey	Catherine	Astagob	Castleknock 39	F	Dublin	
Downey	James P	Astagob	Castleknock 2	M	Dublin	
Downey	John J	Astagob	Castleknock 0	M	Dublin	
Doyle	Eliza	Astagob	Castleknock 9	F	Co Dublin	Going to school
Doyle	James	Astagob	Castleknock 16	M	Co Dublin	Domestic Servant
Doyle	Edward	Astagob	Castleknock 13	M	Co Dublin	Going to school
Doyle	Ellen	Astagob	Castleknock 21	F	Dublin Co	Domestic Servant
Doyle	Margret	Astagob	Castleknock	F	Queens Co	Housekeeping
Doyle	Joseph	Astagob	Castleknock 11	M	Co Dublin	Scholar
Doyle	Edward	Astagob	Castleknock 57	M	Co Wicklow	Domestic Servant
Doyle	Mary	Astagob	Castleknock 18	F	Co Dublin	Domestic Servant
Ennis	Hugh	Astagob	Castleknock 11	M	Co Dublin	Scholar
Ennis	Mary	Astagob	Castleknock 46	F	Co Dublin	House Keeper
Ennis	Luke	Astagob	Castleknock 54	M	Co Dublin	Vintner
Ennis	Thomas	Astagob	Castleknock 17	M	Co Dublin	Scholar
Ennis	Margaret	Astagob	Castleknock 19	F	Co Dublin	Mothers Help
Ennis	Veronica	Astagob	Castleknock 7	F	Co Dublin	Scholar
Ennis	James	Astagob	Castleknock 14	M	Co Dublin	Scholar
Feehan	Anne	Astagob	Castleknock 37	F	Blchdstown	Market Gardener
Feehan	Michael B	Astagob	Castleknock 56	M	Birr, K Co	Market Gardener
Flynn	Marcella	Astagob	Castleknock 21	F	Co Dublin	Servant
Galligan	William	Astagob	Castleknock 28	M	Queens Co	Labourer
Galligan	Mary	Astagob	Castleknock 26	F	Dublin	
Garaghty	Margaret	Astagob	Castleknock 45	F	Co Louth	Labourer
Garaghty	Patrick	Astagob	Castleknock 27	M	Dublin	Laborer
Glover	Eva	Astagob	Castleknock 31	F	Co Dublin	Shop Assistant
Glover	Agnes	Astagob	Castleknock 57	F	Co Dublin	Shop Assistant
Guidon	Ellen	Astagob	Castleknock 12	F	Co Dublin	Scholar

Guidon	Thomas	Astagob	Castleknock	18	M	Co Dublin	Labourer
Guidon	Alice	Astagob	Castleknock	45	F	Co Dublin	
Guidon	Thomas	Astagob	Castleknock	50	M	Co Dublin	Labourer
Guidon	Esther	Astagob	Castleknock	20	F	Co Dublin	
Guidon	Alice	Astagob	Castleknock	16	F	Co Dublin	
Guidon	Anne	Astagob	Castleknock	14	F	Co Dublin	
Halpin	Bridget	Astagob	Castleknock	23	F	Co Dublin	
Halpin	Edward	Astagob	Castleknock	2	M	Co Dublin	
Halpin	Kate	Astagob	Castleknock	24	F	Dublin City	Bar Maid
Halpin	Thomas	Astagob	Castleknock	27	M	Dublin	Gardner
Hegarty	Frank	Astagob	Castleknock	22	M	Co Dublin	Train Driver
Hetherington	Elizabeth	Astagob	Castleknock	2	F	Co Cork	Nothing
Hetherington	Lucy	Astagob	Castleknock	5	F	Co Kildare	Nothing
Hetherington	Joseph	Astagob	Castleknock	0	M	Co Dublin	Nothing
Hetherington	Maryanne	Astagob	Castleknock	27	F	Co Dublin	Nothing
Hetherington	Joseph	Astagob	Castleknock	29	M	England	Groom
Hetherington	Thomas	Astagob	Castleknock	1	M	Chapelizod	Nothing
Higgins	Mary	Astagob	Castleknock	26	F	City Dublin	Domestic Servant
Jones	Mary	Astagob	Castleknock	81	F	Co Dublin	Receiving Out Door Relief
Judge	Kathleen	Astagob	Castleknock	17	F	City Dublin	House Keeper
Lovely	Christopher	Astagob	Castleknock	16	M	Co Dublin	Farm Servant
Lynam	Kate	Astagob	Castleknock	58	F	Co Dublin	No Occupation
McKay	Robert	Astagob	Castleknock	75	M	Co Meath	Hesmegesty 2nd Foot
McNeill	John	Astagob	Castleknock	71	M	Co Dublin	
Mooney	John	Astagob	Castleknock	6	M	Co Dublin	Scholar
Mooney	Joanna	Astagob	Castleknock	49	F	Dublin	House Keeper
Mooney	Catherine	Astagob	Castleknock	14	F	Co Dublin	Scholar
Mooney	Serah	Astagob	Castleknock	16	F	Co Dublin	Outdoor Work
Mooney	Patrick	Astagob	Castleknock	50	M	Dublin	Engine Driver
Mooney	Patrick	Astagob	Castleknock	9	M	Co Dublin	Scholar
Moore	William	Astagob	Castleknock	23	M	England	Gardener Journey Man
Moore	William	Astagob	Castleknock	52	M	Dublin Co	Smith
Moore	Elizabeth	Astagob	Castleknock	38	F	Dublin Co	
Moore	Rose	Astagob	Castleknock	6	F	Dublin Co	Scholar
Moore	Rose	Astagob	Castleknock	80	F	King's Co	
Murray	Denis	Astagob	Castleknock	21	M	Co Dublin	Labourer
Murray	James	Astagob	Castleknock	12	M	Co Dublin	Scholar
Murray	Patrick	Astagob	Castleknock	54	M	Co Dublin	Gardener
Murray	Elizabeth	Astagob	Castleknock	19	F	Co Dublin	Servant Domestic
Murray	John	Astagob	Castleknock	16	M	Co Dublin	Labourer
Murray	Mary	Astagob	Castleknock	54	F	Co Dublin	

Murray	Joseph	Astagob	Castleknock	10	M	Co Dublin	Scholar
Murray	Bridget	Astagob	Castleknock	17	F	Co Dublin	Servant Domestic
Neill	Lawrence	Astagob	Castleknock	8	M	Co Dublin	Scholar
Neill	Peter	Astagob	Castleknock	43	M	Co Dublin	Farmer Servant
Neill	Mary	Astagob	Castleknock	48	F	Co Dublin	
Neill	James	Astagob	Castleknock	7	M	Co Dublin	Scholar
Neill	John	Astagob	Castleknock	44	M	Co Dublin	General Labourer
Niel	Joseph	Astagob	Castleknock	4	M	Co Dublin	Scholar
Niel	James	Astagob	Castleknock	38	M	Co Dublin	Builder
Niel	John	Astagob	Castleknock	15	M	Co Dublin	Labourer
Niel	Patrick	Astagob	Castleknock	6	M	Co Dublin	Scholar
Niel	Peter	Astagob	Castleknock	11	M	Co Dublin	Scholar
Niel	Mary	Astagob	Castleknock	2	F	Co Dublin	
Niel	Julia	Astagob	Castleknock	35	F	Co Dublin	House keeper
Obrien	Margret	Astagob	Castleknock	13	F	Co Dublin	Scholar
Obrien	Julia	Astagob	Castleknock	12	F	Co Dublin	Scholar
Obrien	Christina	Astagob	Castleknock	19	F	Co Dublin	Garden Workers
Obrien	Alice	Astagob	Castleknock	17	F	Co Dublin	Garden Workers
Obrien	Bridget	Astagob	Castleknock	7	F	Co Dublin	Scholar
Obrien	Timothy	Astagob	Castleknock	62	M	Co Dublin	Labourer
Obrien	Bridget	Astagob	Castleknock	40	F	Co Dublin	
ONeill	Michael	Astagob	Castleknock	50	M	Co Dublin	Market Gardener
ONeill	Anne	Astagob	Castleknock	45	F	Co Dublin	Housekeeper
Poynton	Edward	Astagob	Castleknock	66	M	Co Dublin	Agricultural Labourer
Poynton	Alise	Astagob	Castleknock	64	F	Co Dublin	
Powell	Margaret	Astagob	Castleknock	60	F	Blnchstowm	Market Gardener
Poynton	John	Astagob	Castleknock	38	M	Co Dublin	Groom
Poynton	Ester	Astagob	Castleknock	70	F	Co Dublin	
Reilly	Mary	Astagob	Castleknock	54	F	Co Dublin	Field Worker
Russell	Anne	Astagob	Castleknock	58	F	Co Dublin	Cooke
Russell	Richard	Astagob	Castleknock	57	M	Co Meath	Labourer
Saunders	Mary Anne	Astagob	Castleknock	34	F	Co Dublin	House Keeper
Scully	Gertrude	Astagob	Castleknock	14	F	Co Dublin	Scholar
Scully	Brigid	Astagob	Castleknock	26	F	Co Dublin	Barmaid
Scully	Julia	Astagob	Castleknock	50	F	Co Dublin	Market Gardener
Scully	Francis	Astagob	Castleknock	21	M	Co Dublin	Farm Labourer
Scully	Julia	Astagob	Castleknock	12	F	Co Dublin	Scholar
Scully	Anne	Astagob	Castleknock	54	F	Co Dublin	House Keeper
Tobin	Patrick	Astagob	Castleknock	5	M	Co Dublin	Scholar
Tobin	Mary Anne	Astagob	Castleknock	14	F	Co Dublin	Farmers Daughter
Tobin	Francis	Astagob	Castleknock	8	M	Co Dublin	Scholar

Tobin	Mary	Astagob	Castleknock	44	F	Co Kildare	Domestic Servant
Tobin	Ellen	Astagob	Castleknock	11	F	Co Dublin	Farmers Daughter
Tobin	Michael	Astagob	Castleknock	17	M	Co Dublin	Groom
Tobin	Catherine	Astagob	Castleknock		F	Co Dublin	
Tobin	John	Astagob	Castleknock	4	M	Co Dublin	Scholar
Tobin	Rose	Astagob	Castleknock	0	F	Co Dublin	
Tobin	Lucey	Astagob	Castleknock	9	F	Co Dublin	Farmers Daughter
Tobin	Elizabeth	Astagob	Castleknock	18	F	Co Dublin	Farmers Daughter
Tobin	Ellen	Astagob	Castleknock	39	F	Co Dublin	Farmers Wife
Tobin	Patrick	Astagob	Castleknock	49	M	Co Dublin	Farmer
Walsh	James	Astagob	Castleknock	2	M	Co Dublin	
Walsh	Patrick	Astagob	Castleknock	14	M	Co Dublin	Scholar
Walsh	William	Astagob	Castleknock	12	M	Co Dublin	Scholar
Walsh	Mary	Astagob	Castleknock	5	F	Co Dublin	
Walsh	William	Astagob	Castleknock	39	M	Co Dublin	Labourer
Walsh	Lawrence	Astagob	Castleknock	7	M	Co Dublin	Scholar
Walsh	Bridget	Astagob	Castleknock	35	F	Co Dublin	
Walshe	John	Astagob	Castleknock	45	M	Co Dublin	Labourer Farm
Walshe	Anne	Astagob	Castleknock	40	F	Dublin	
Walshe	James	Astagob	Castleknock	14	M	Co Dublin	Scholar
Ward	Christfor	Astagob	Castleknock	14	M	Co Dublin	Garden Labourer
Ward	Ester	Astagob	Castleknock	2	F	Co Dublin	
Ward	Dennis	Astagob	Castleknock	7	M	Co Dublin	Scholars
Ward	Eliza	Astagob	Castleknock	9	F	Co Dublin	Scholars
Ward	Kate	Astagob	Castleknock	34	F	Co Dublin	
Ward	John	Astagob	Castleknock	11	M	Co Dublin	Scholars
Ward	Patrick	Astagob	Castleknock	0	M	Co Dublin	
Ward	Patrick	Astagob	Castleknock	37	M	Dublin	Garden Labourer
Weldon	Teresa	Astagob	Castleknock	23	F	London	
Weldon	Mary	Astagob	Castleknock	25	F	Co Dublin	
West	Joseph	Astagob	Castleknock	45	M	Co Dublin	Market Gardener
West	George	Astagob	Castleknock	59	M	Co Dublin	Market Gardener
West	Eliza	Astagob	Castleknock	54	F	Co Dublin	Assi?g in General
West	Simon	Astagob	Castleknock	64	M	Co Dublin	Farm Market Gard Wine
West	Patrick	Astagob	Castleknock	49	M	Co Dublin	Market Gardener
West	Teresa	Astagob	Castleknock	47	F	Co Dublin	
Williams	Elizabeth	Astagob	Castleknock	55	F	Co Dublin	Licensed Publican
Williams	John L	Astagob	Castleknock	31	M	Co Dublin	Shop Assistant
Woods	Robert	Astagob	Castleknock	58	M	Co Kildare	Labourer
Young	Cathcrine	Astagob	Castleknock	60	F	Co Kildare	Out Door Work

Astagob 1911

Surname	Forename	Townland	DED	Age	Sex	Birthplace	Occupation
Byrne	Bridget	Astagob	Castleknock	71	F	Carlow	Farm Servant
Carroll	Michael	Astagob	Castleknock				
Carroll	Anne	Astagob	Castleknock	5	F	Co Dublin	Scholar
Carroll	Elizabeth	Astagob	Castleknock	3	F	Co Dublin	
Carroll	James	Astagob	Castleknock	9	M	Co Dublin	Scholar
Carroll	James	Astagob	Castleknock	80	M	Co Dublin	Ex Gardiner
Carroll	Jane	Astagob	Castleknock	14	F	Co Dublin	Scholar
Carroll	Kathleen	Astagob	Castleknock	13	F	Co Dublin	Scholar
Carroll	Margaret	Astagob	Castleknock	48	F	Co Dublin	
Carroll	Margaret	Astagob	Castleknock	16	F	Co Dublin	Scholar
Clarke	James	Astagob	Castleknock	60	M	Co Dublin	Market Gardner
Clarke	John	Astagob	Castleknock	24	M	Co Dublin	Labourer
Clarke	Margaret	Astagob	Castleknock	21	F	Co Dublin	
Clarke	Rose	Astagob	Castleknock	51	F	Co Dublin	
Clarke	Rose	Astagob	Castleknock	27	F	Co Dublin	
Clarke	Teresa	Astagob	Castleknock	12	F	Co Dublin	Scholar
Clarke	Thomas	Astagob	Castleknock	19	M	Co Dublin	Labourer
Clarke	William	Astagob	Castleknock	25	M	Co Dublin	Carter
Clarke	Winfred	Astagob	Castleknock	14	F	Co Dublin	Scholar
Coffey	Alice	Astagob	Castleknock	3	F	Co Dublin	
Coffey	Catherine	Astagob	Castleknock	44	F	Co Dublin	
Coffey	Edward	Astagob	Castleknock	6	M	Co Dublin	Scholar
Coffey	John	Astagob	Castleknock	42	M	Co Dublin	Groom Servant
Coffey	John	Astagob	Castleknock	9	M	Co Dublin	Scholar
Coffey	Julia	Astagob	Castleknock	12	F	Co Dublin	Scholar
Coffey	Kathleen	Astagob	Castleknock	4	F	Co Dublin	Scholar
Crofts	Eileen M	Astagob	Castleknock	2	F	Yorkshire E	
Cunningham	Ellen	Astagob	Castleknock	17	F	England	
Curran	James	Astagob	Castleknock	65	M	Co Dublin	Labourer
Donnelly	Annie	Astagob	Castleknock	10	F	Co Dublin	Scholars
Donnelly	Catherine	Astagob	Castleknock	24	F	Co Dublin	
Donnelly	Catherine	Astagob	Castleknock	12	F	Co Dublin	Scholars
Donnelly	Ellen	Astagob	Castleknock	57	F	Co Dublin	
Donnelly	John	Astagob	Castleknock	33	M	Co Dublin	Market Gardner
Donnelly	John	Astagob	Castleknock	58	M	Co Dublin	Dairy Proprietor
Donnelly	Joseph	Astagob	Castleknock	17	M	Co Dublin	Civil Assistant
Donnelly	Mary	Astagob	Castleknock	19	F	Co Dublin	
Donnelly	Mary	Astagob	Castleknock	49	F	Co Wexford	
Donnelly	Mary Ellen	Astagob	Castleknock	20	F		

Donnelly	Michael	Astagob	Castleknock	33	M	Co Dublin	Dairy Man
Donnelly	Thomas	Astagob	Castleknock	47	M	Co Dublin	Civil Assistant
Doyle	Edward	Astagob	Castleknock	23	M	Co Dublin	Groom
Doyle	Ellen	Astagob	Castleknock	28	F	Dublin City	
Doyle	James	Astagob	Castleknock	25	M	Co Dublin	Garden Labourer
Doyle	Joseph	Astagob	Castleknock	22	M	Co Dublin	Labourer
Doyle	Margaret	Astagob	Castleknock	64	F	Queens Co	
Dunne	Mary	Astagob	Castleknock	41	F	Co Dublin	General Domestic
Dunne	Mary	Astagob	Castleknock	9	F	Co Dublin	Scholar
Dunne	Michael	Astagob	Castleknock	12	M	Co Dublin	Scholar
Ennis	Agnes	Astagob	Castleknock	25	F	Co Dublin	School Teacher
Ennis	Hugh	Astagob	Castleknock	20	M	Co Dublin	Market Gardner
Ennis	James	Astagob	Castleknock	23	M	Co Dublin	Market Gardner
Ennis	Margaret	Astagob	Castleknock	27	F	Co Dublin	
Ennis	Mary	Astagob	Castleknock	51	F	Co Dublin	
Ennis	Veronica	Astagob	Castleknock	17	F	Co Dublin	Scholar
Feehan	Anne	Astagob	Castleknock	49	F	Co Dublin	Market Gardener
Fegan	Mary	Astagob	Castleknock	46	F	Inchacore	Seamstress
Flanagan	Mary	Astagob	Castleknock	56	F	Co Dublin	Field Worker
Galligan	Ann	Astagob	Castleknock	8	F	M Hospital on 2: 4: 11	
Galligan	John Joseph	Astagob	Castleknock	1	M	Co Dublin	
Galligan	Mary Jane	Astagob	Castleknock	38	F	Co Dublin	
Galligan	Mary Jane	Astagob	Castleknock	6	F	Co Dublin	
Galligan	Michael John	Astagob	Castleknock	3	M	Co Dublin	
Galligan	William	Astagob	Castleknock	36	M	Co Dublin	Labourer
Geraghty	Patrick	Astagob	Castleknock	40	M	Co Louth	Labourer
Glover	Agnes	Astagob	Castleknock	67	F	Co Dublin	
Glover	Eva Elizabeth	Astagob	Castleknock	41	F	England	
Hackett	Elizabeth	Astagob	Castleknock	64	F	Co Dublin	
Hackett	James	Astagob	Castleknock	68	M	Dublin	Gardner Domestic
Hynes	Bridget	Astagob	Castleknock	10	F	Co Dublin	Scholar
Hynes	Esther	Astagob	Castleknock	40	F	Co Dublin	
Hynes	Mary	Astagob	Castleknock	0	F	Co Dublin	
Hynes	Michael	Astagob	Castleknock	4	M	Co Dublin	Scholar
Hynes	Patrick	Astagob	Castleknock	12	M	Co Dublin	Scholar
Hynes	Patrick	Astagob	Castleknock	49	M	Co Dublin	Agricultural Labourer
Kiely	William	Astagob	Castleknock	15	M	Co Dublin	Labourer
Moore	Mary Eliza	Astagob	Castleknock	49	F	Co Dublin	
Moore	Rose Mary	Astagob	Castleknock	16	F	Co Dublin	Scholar
Moore	William	Astagob	Castleknock	61	M	Co Dublin	Engine Smith
Murray	John	Astagob	Castleknock	26	M	Co Dublin	Labourer

Murray	Joseph	Astagob	Castleknock	19	M	Co Dublin	Labourer
Murray	Mary	Astagob	Castleknock	64	F	Co Dublin	House Keeper
O'Neill	Elizabeth	Astagob	Castleknock	2	F	Co Dublin	
O'Neill	Frank	Astagob	Castleknock	8	M	Co Dublin	Attending School
O'Neill	James	Astagob	Castleknock	46	M	Co Dublin	Carpenter
O'Neill	Joseph	Astagob	Castleknock	13	M	Co Dublin	Attending School
O'Neill	Julia	Astagob	Castleknock	42	F	Co Dublin	
O'Neill	Julia	Astagob	Castleknock	4	F	Co Dublin	
O'Neill	Mary	Astagob	Castleknock	11	F	Co Dublin	Attending School
O'Neill	Peter	Astagob	Castleknock	20	M	Co Dublin	Labourer
O'Neill	William	Astagob	Castleknock	6	M	Co Dublin	Attending School
Obrien	Alice	Astagob	Castleknock	26	F	Co Dublin	
Obrien	Christina	Astagob	Castleknock	28	F	Co Dublin	
ONeill	James	Astagob	Castleknock	18	M	Co Dublin	Labourer
ONeill	John	Astagob	Castleknock	56	M	Co Dublin	Market Gardener
ONeill	Michael	Astagob	Castleknock	64	M	Co Dublin	Market Gardener
ONeill	Peter	Astagob	Castleknock	54	M	Co Dublin	Labourer
Powell	Margaret	Astagob	Castleknock	73	F	Co Dublin	
Poynton	Alice	Astagob	Castleknock	73	F	Co Dublin	
Poynton	Edward	Astagob	Castleknock	75	M	Co Meath	Agricultural Labourer
Russell	Richard	Astagob	Castleknock	70	M	Co Meath	Market Gardner
Sansom	Annie	Astagob	Castleknock	5	F	Co Dublin	Scholar
Sansom	Margaret	Astagob	Castleknock	30	F	Co Kildare	
Sansom	Robert	Astagob	Castleknock	36	M	Co Dublin	General Labourer
Saunders	Marianne	Astagob	Castleknock	46	F	Co Dublin	
Scully	Ann	Astagob	Castleknock	72	F	Co Dublin	
Scully	Francis	Astagob	Castleknock	31	M	Co Dublin	Labourer
Scully	Julia	Astagob	Castleknock	22	F	Co Dublin	
Scully	Julia	Astagob	Castleknock	61	F	Co Dublin	Market - Gardener
Tobin	Ellen	Astagob	Castleknock	49	F	Co Dublin	
Tobin	Ellen Margt	Astagob	Castleknock	21	F	Co Dublin	Domestic Servant
Tobin	John Joseph	Astagob	Castleknock	14	M	Co Dublin	Farmers Son
Tobin	Joseph	Astagob	Castleknock	9	M	Co Dublin	Scholar
Tobin	Lucy Agnes	Astagob	Castleknock	19	M	Co Dublin	
Tobin	Patrick	Astagob	Castleknock	61	M	Co Dublin	Farmer
Tobin	Patrick	Astagob	Castleknock	15	F	Co Dublin	Farm Servant
Tobin	Rose Margt	Astagob	Castleknock	10	F	Dublin	Scholar
Walsh	Anne	Astagob	Castleknock	56	F	Co Dublin	All Work
Walsh	James	Astagob	Castleknock	22	M	Co Dublin	Mill Worker
Walsh	John	Astagob	Castleknock	60	M	Co Dublin	Gardner Assistant
Weldon	Teresa	Astagob	Castleknock	34	F	Dublin	

West	Elizabeth	Astagob	Castleknock	64	F	Co Dublin	Managing Business
West	Joseph	Astagob	Castleknock	57	M	Dublin	Market - Gardening
West	Patrick	Astagob	Castleknock	61	M	Dublin	Market - Gardening
West	Teresa	Astagob	Castleknock	59	F	Dublin	House Keeping Sister
Williams	Elizabeth W	Astagob	Castleknock	65	F	Co Dublin	Licensed Publican
Williams	John Charles	Astagob	Castleknock	41	M	Co Dublin	No Profession

Chapter 9

EMPLOYMENT

There was a wide range of employment available to the people in the Strawberry Beds. Firstly this was, and is, an agricultural area, so all the large estates needed labourers, skilled workmen, ploughmen, blacksmiths, gardeners (the Brooke family employed eight gardeners), grooms, dairymen, woodmen, shepherds, huntsmen and gamekeepers. Bailiffs would also be needed to protect the fishing rights that the large estates owned, but I suspect they came from 'out of town'. Poaching of pheasant, duck, grouse or rabbit was a problem, so gamekeepers were employed. Rabbit warrens were farmed on the large estates, so the gamekeepers would protect this meat supply for the main house.

Domestic servants, ladies in waiting, cooks, butlers, cleaners, governesses, child minders and nursing assistants were required within the houses. It is also noted that many domestic servants and those employed within the house were brought in from England or Northern Ireland. There was mistrust amongst the large houses of hiring local staff, as they would be of the wrong religion as far as the household was concerned. There is also the fact that these jobs were specialised in nature and qualified persons would apply for the posts. Butlers, senior cooks and governesses would fall into this category. Such skilled persons would have been trained to fill these posts.

Gardeners maintained the grounds while also producing for the kitchens. Walled gardens were always a feature of the large houses. Green houses were a necessity to provide fresh vegetables all year around for the main house. Apples, pears and plums would also be part of the garden. Raspberries and of course early season strawberries. Wild fruit would also be picked when in season; blackberries, sloes, haws, crab apples, mushrooms and so on. Luxury fruit and vegetables were also cultivated. Grapes, figs, dates, aubergines, cucumbers, could be grown in the green house along with other exotic fruits, herbs and vegetables. Again, the growing of these foods would be of a specialised nature, so the gardeners would learn their trade and pass the training on to their juniors. The cooks and gardeners formed the link from within the house to the outside.

Mr Cooper was the Head Steward in Somerton and resided with his family in this home. Buildings such as this were a classical structure of the twenties and thirties. The grass is overgrown as this photograph was taken after Mr Cooper had passed away.
(Courtesy Mrs.Caroline Corballis)

Both women and men would labour on surrounding farms. For the men employment would hope to be all year long, whereas for women it might be seasonal. Men would be involved in the preparing and sowing seasons. The heavy burden of fertilising the field for the seed fell to the men. The seasonal labour would be of a harvesting nature, picking potatoes, beans, apples, or whatever fruit or vegetable was in season. This would be a commercial endeavour and the produce sold in the city markets. The hay making was a man's affair and generally a time of fun and play for the children as they rode the bogey back to the fields after the cock of hay had been left in the haggard. The heavy work of pitching the trams into the barn was done by fork and only the fittest and hardiest did this work. Hay was the main fodder for the animals so it was vital to save it correctly. The rate of pay at the time, mid-eighteen hundreds to early nineteen hundreds, was 8/- shillings a week. One such farm that employed women on a seasonal basis and men on a permanent basis was Lynam's farm in Astagob.

This family was descended from Thomas Warren Esq., who was dispossessed in 1692 of lands in Corduff that were forfeited to their Majesties. The Warrens and also the Burnells were large farming families in the area at the time of the eight Baron of Castleknock, Hugh Tyrell (1600s). When the Warrens were dispossessed of their lands, they then succeeded to portions of the Carpenter lands in the townland of Carpenterstown for a fee of £4 per acre payable to a Mr. Locke and the economy of St. Patrick's Cathedral. They subsequently moved to farm in Astagob and Porterstown.

Mixed farming predominated at these times in order to produce for one's own needs and sell the surplus to the Dublin market. Tillage farming for oats, wheat and barley was undertaken. Oats were grown particularly for the horses and ponies and the straw could be used for thatching. Straw from the other corn crops is not as suitable as oaten straw. Grasslands abounded for beef cattle and sheep that were exported from the city quays to England and often for armies fighting in foreign fields. Agriculture thrived in Ireland during wartime because the country was not engaged in the conflict and the combatants were too involved fighting to be able to grow or produce their own food. The English saw Ireland, with its ability to grow corn, as a breadbasket for themselves. It was an accepted practice of the time, for work-hands to take home some milk, vegetables or other produce for their families. This was a part payment arrangement between the farm hand and the landowner. It would also have been part of a community spirit.

Manure was a vital ingredient and every year's produce depended on its availability. Large mounds of manure, which came from the dairy herds, would be gathered in wintertime. These mounds required turning two or three times a year to ensure it decomposed correctly. A farmer would place a gate beneath the developing mound of manure, which would only be exposed when the mound was turned correctly. This trick was to prevent short cuts by the labourers. All work on the farm was labour intensive at the time, but wages were low and workers plentiful, so the system was economically viable for the landlords. Manure was essential to the market gardeners of course; they would have to purchase the fertiliser to grow their produce. In bygone times one's wealth was measured in the size of the 'dung heap' one had, but without the manure nothing would grow. Manure was not a waste product even to the biggest estate.

Horses thrived on the limestone rich soil, consequently good grooms, stable hands, riders and horsemen were essential. It must be remembered that the Crown forces, with horse cavalry for example, were resident in the Phoenix Park, so a tradition for horsemanship existed locally. Racehorse training evolved in the area due in part to the good grasslands, the limestone rich soil and the proximity of racecourses. The Curragh, Leopardstown, Phoenix Park, Fairy House and Punchestown were all within the range of the trainers.

An Epsom Derby winner was bred in Somerton in 1913. This colt, named Aboyeur, won the controversial race when two women from the suffragette movement were killed as they brought down the King's horse by running onto the track. The filly Blue Wind, winner of the 1000 guineas in 1978, was also bred at Somerton. While racehorses were bred at Somerton and Abbey Lodge it is interesting that other nearby estates did not pursue this endeavor. Estates around Clonsilla, however, were extensively involved in horse breeding, but Knockmaroon and Luttrellstown were not. These estates concentrated more on the grazing of cattle and dairy produce.

Aside from the racehorses, workhorses, hunters, ponies, and carriage horses demanded care and attention. Horses were, after all, the mode of transport up to the early 1930s. This would employ many men. Corn and feed was grown on the farms just for the horses. The Peelers, as the Royal Irish Constabulary were then known, would ride on horseback along the Lower Road from Chapelizod to Lucan during their patrols. The police were stationed in Chapelizod and their horses were stabled there also, so experienced handlers were needed to tend to the horses' care.

The Brooke family grew all their oats on Pickering Forest farm in Celbridge for their horses in Summerton in 1843. The Brooke families were ardent hunters, as indeed were the Laidlaw family who came after them, and followed the Kildare, Meath and Ward Union hunts. While hunting was a pastime for the wealthy, it still provided much employment. Care for the hunters, hounds, stags, the huntsmen and women was a full-time occupation. Hunts would meet twice or three times a week between the months of October and March. The grooms would ride the horses to the meet and the huntsmen and women would arrive by coach to collect their mounts. Sometimes two horses would be brought for one individual to ensure an injured animal didn't ruin the day. Preparing the horses meant an early rise for the grooms. Feeding, grooming, tacking-up and trotting the horses and ponies to a meet that could be six or more miles away by ten o clock in the morning would have required military precession and organisation. When the hunt ended at four in the afternoon the whole process was reversed and it meant a very long day's work for grooms and staff. A typical day could start at four in the morning and run to near midnight.

The Huntsman's House on the Strawberry Beds.

While hunting was labour intensive, an organised shoot on the estates was only moderately less so. Again an early start was necessary, preparing the many guns for the shooters, organising the beaters who would raise the pheasants and drive them onto the guns, and preparing the gun dogs to retrieve the fallen birds. The shooters would simply arrive, possibly unaware of the effort that had gone into the preparation of the day. At the end of the evening, all the birds would be collected, gun dogs cared for, guns retrieved, cleaned, and prepared for the next shoot. The staff did these chores, of course, and again another long day's work was required to finish the task.

The mills on the river provided local employment, Hills mills for woollen products, Anna Liffey for flour, New Holland for wire and later cotton and the Palmerstown mill for corn. Those families who lived closest to these establishments worked these mills. Families who worked in the mills would see to it that their children would become employed there when they reached the appropriate age. Little is new in this practice; it ensured continuity and loyalty to the employer. From Woodlands Cottage to the Glen, this 'middle ground' was agricultural and market gardening, whereas either end of the valley was more industrial.

THE HIGHER THE HILL THE BETTER THE VIEW

— and viewing the panorama of Irish suitings — cheviots, tweeds, serges, whipcords, flannels, gaberdines, hopsacks and worsteds, from Hills of Lucan, there is no finer range in sight.

Other enterprises that offered employment throughout the ages came and went. One such example was the Lord Annaly brickworks. The brickworks was started on the estate in 1843 to make bricks from the surrounding soil in Luttrellstown. This suitable soil would harden under heat to form the usable brick. Lord Annaly also had a lead mine on the estate. Seams of this ore, along with zinc, were known to exist running from Diswellstown to Luttrellstown since the 1200s. Both of these projects offered work for the local men, but following a landslide, the brickworks was covered over, the machinery destroyed, and so the work ended. The mining venture ended at the same time. The un-mined seams of lead ore and zinc were meagre and their exploitation was too expensive for the small deposits. Disputes over the ownership of the ore and the right to extraction were also a factor between the two estates.

There were a number of private entrepreneurs, of course; a blacksmith could be found at the bottom of Tinker's Hill and shops flourished on the road, such as the Wren's Nest, Tobin's, Gertie Murrays, and May Weldon's. The produce on sale in the shops varied widely. Some had all the stores needed for a family, while some only served ice cream or strawberries and cream in summertime.

While there may have been many 'sheebeens' on the Lower Road in bygone times, the public houses at the Wren's Nest, in existence since the sixteenth century, the Strawberry Hall, owned by Mrs. Williams, and the Anglers Hotel, owned by Mr. Gibney, were the licensed establishments.

The Kavanagh brothers, who lived near Knockmaroon Hill, were boot makers and cobblers of great talent and are described as 'Master Cobblers' in the Census of 1901. They held the contract for St Vincent's School in Castleknock for the footwear of the tutors and students such was their skill and talent.

The Anglers Rest Hotel was built in the late 1800s. A sheebeen existed prior to the building of the public house. In the Census of 1911 Michael Doyle was the vintner of the establishment.
(Courtesy National Library)

The ferrymen, Coady and Treacy, made a living by ferrying workers, shoppers and travellers across the River Liffey at the bottom of Knockmaroon Hill. Both are described in the Census of 1901 as 'land contractors'. The boat was also used to dredge sand from the riverbeds, which was used in construction. Mr. Tracey sold the sand for 3s / 6p per ton. A lot of dredging would be needed to harvest a single ton of sand from the riverbed. Many houses on the Lower Road were built with this sand, as was Farmleigh, home to the Guinness family.

In the late 1800s the local council in Palmerstown suggested the building of a bridge to span the River Liffey at the foot of Knockmaroon. The project was priced at £3000, a considerable sum, and was ruled unjustifiable. The Council then approached Lord Moyne (Guinness family) and sought to use the iron bridge which linked the Guinness Estate at Knockmaroon with the Harris land on the south bank. Lord Moyne declined this request as he had just purchased a new boat for Mr. Tracey for use as a ferry. To allow the public to use the bridge would ruin Mr. Tracey's business so the request was denied. The ferry continued in operation up to the 1960s. *The Ferryman*, written by Pete St. John, one of Ireland's finest song writers refers to the many ferries that criss-crossed the Liffey similar to the one owned by Tracey. The first line of the chorus is "Where the Strawberry Beds sweep down to the Liffey."

With the range of work available and the variety of agricultural produce it is unlikely that the famine of 1843–46 would have had the same impact on the people as in other poor areas of the country. As mentioned previously there was no great population change in the Strawberry Beds at this time. True, the potato harvest would fail through blight, but stores were in existence for the purchase of alternative goods. This was not possible in the west and south of Ireland, where reliance on the potato was total. Stores were very sparse in remote rural areas even if the starving people had the money, which unfortunately they did not. Furthermore, the population had exploded on the back of repeated successful potato crops that meant division and sub-division of holdings until they were no longer viable. Prior to the disastrous famine, the Irish were considered in European terms to be a fit, hardy and large stature people. The potato had provided well for the Irish. The growing of strawberries and flowers for markets in Dublin would have been incomprehensible to the starving in 1843.

****

Chapter 10

MARKET GARDENING

The Strawberry Beds, by its name, was known for its cultivation of this fruit. The original berry itself was a pale variety and not the most attractive to the eye. It was, however, a most succulent berry and its excellent sweet taste made it wonderful to eat. It was also suitable for jam making. The production for the markets probably started in the 1700s. The large houses of the area would have grown strawberries for their own use prior to their commercial sale. The berry itself, not being native, would have been brought in from abroad, similar to the potato, for cultivation in Ireland. However, the Strawberry Beds variety, with its pale colour, would eventually find it difficult to compete with the scarlet-coloured varieties from the Channel Islands when transport improved. The improvement in sailing and the advent of steamships meant produce for the Dublin market could now be transported quicker and with reliability. Later on, in keeping with the times, market gardeners would cultivate varieties that had a better appearance with great taste. Today, unfortunately, further crossbreeding has meant that an attractive appearance far outweighs the taste of the berry.

The growing season was generally early in the Beds and the inevitable goal was to get to the market first for the highest prices before the surplus hit. The early strawberries were called 'soldiers'. These were a small hard succulent fruit and much sought after. Strawberries were not the sole produce from the Strawberry Beds of course. As the season progressed, peas, french beans, onions, broadbeans, cabbage, lettuce, gooseberries, blackberries, cherries, and apples were picked for the market, which was situated behind the Four Courts as it is today.

Produce had to arrive before six o'clock in the morning on Tuesdays and Thursdays. This meant an early start for the workers to get the fruit to the market. At four in the morning the workers would set out on the five mile trek, either walking or travelling by pony and trap. Women did most of the carrying, one basket on their head and one on either arm. The trip would pass along the Lower Road, up Knockmaroon Hill through the Phoenix Park and out at Park Gate Street. Because the Phoenix Park has a commercial restriction, passes were needed to carry produce through the park if going by pony and trap. After the ponies and traps had served their use, the car and van arrived on the scene.

All families grew some produce on the hillsides for their own use or for selling. The 'lazy bed' was utilised. This was similar to a conventional drill except wider, about 3 feet wide, and it ran vertical up the hillside. Because the drill goes vertically up the hill there is no soil erosion or washing away in heavy rainfall. The remains of 'lazy beds' still exist on Higgins hill today. This was an efficient form of cultivation and allowed for fertilising, irrigation and fruit picking in an easier manner.

Some families specialised in market gardening such as the Wests, Lovelys, Weldons, Nashs, Carneys, Donnellys, Tobins, Lanigans, Scullys and Doyles. The West family, who cultivated many of the hills, used to employ men from Benburb Street for the fruit picking and also used young boys to set off clappers that scared the birds away from their fourteen cherry orchards. The clappers would start at four in the morning. Picked fruit would be brought for sale and Mr. West would give the women a glass of whiskey on their arrival in the market with their load.

Harvest time was seasonal with long hours that involved working late into the night to get the picking done. When the strawberries died back, then the turn came for flowers, beans, or whatever. A particular flower was the 'pink', which gave off a wonderful scent and sold for 6d a bunch in the early 1900s. The scent from these flowers would permeate the whole valley and added to the attraction for the travellers to the Strawberry Beds. The whole season was eight months of toil; springtime for sowing, summer and autumn for harvesting, certainly not much time for rest. The workers on the land of others still had to toil on their own holdings when they arrived home.

Manure for fertilising came from whatever animals a family had or was purchased from the local estates. Most families kept a cow and reared calves. The advent of bagged potash and lime must have been a great relief. Watering and irrigation of crops was also a laborious task. Up to the year 1960 there was no mains water supply on the road. Rainfall might be adequate, but flowers, lettuce, strawberries and peas require lots of water to develop fully.

All households and gardeners would draw water from the pumps along the road. These were placed to serve a number of houses, generally five or six households, in the near vicinity. The pumps were placed accordingly. The first pump was at the end of the Rugged Lane, another at the bottom of Somerton Lane, two pumps near the Strawberry Hall, and two

The Strawberry Beds

on Knockmaroon Hill. Water was also available through streams, one on the Silver Hill, one at Murray's / Scully's hill, the gripe at Tobin's shop, and the Glen also has a stream which never dries even in summer time. In wintertime locals were aware that many springs on the hills would start up and become a nuisance with too much water.

The pump on Knockmaroon Hill. Originally there were two such pumps, serving all the households on the hill. There were five pumps placed along the three miles of the Strawberry Beds, which drew the water from deep wells. In wintertime the pumps were wrapped in a sugan, or straw rope to prevent the effects of frost.

The River Liffey was a supply, of course. There were few drawing points unfortunately. One was directly opposite the Wren's Nest pub at the entrance to the New Holland mill. Another was directly opposite the Strawberry Hall, the site of a river ford. Water was taken from wherever the river could be accessed. Horse-drawn carriages were used to ferry barrels of water to the plot of land. Some families were able to sink their own wells, but the task of ferrying water from the river up the hills to irrigate vegetables or fruit must have been tremendous. A pumphouse did exist at the back of the Strawberry Hall to bring water from the river to the high ground, but I believe this served the Somerton farm only.

Smallholdings on the Strawberry Beds were leased from the estates at £8 to £10 per acre, per year, in the late 1800's. This was a considerable levy per annum. The cost of passage to America in 1846 was just £5. This valuation showed the potential and productivity of the land in the Strawberry Beds. Wages were around 7/- (shillings) to 12/- (shillings) a week in the late 1800s for workmen. Boys and girls got 6d (pence) a day.

The single most important land reform legislation took place in the mid- to late 1800s. This legislation followed the Land War in pursuance of the 3Fs (Fair Rent, Fixity of Tenure and Free Sale) with Charles Stewart Parnell, Michael Davitt and William O'Brien as leaders. Various Acts of Legislation were passed, but in 1903 the Land Purchase Act allowed Irish Tenant Farmers to buy out their 'freeholds', which has never been possible in the United Kingdom. By 1914, 75% of tenant farmers all over Ireland were buying out their holdings. With security of tenure, investment and devolvement was now possible with confidence.

****

Chapter 11

TRANSPORT

The Strawberry Beds has always been a difficult place to get out of. There are hills in every direction and of course the river acts as another boundary. Prior to modern transportation it was considered that one lived one's life in a radius of thirty miles. This was the distance a horse could travel in a day. This would mean that work, meeting your future partner, falling in love, marriage, homebuilding, raising a family and death could be expected to happen within this radius. This was also true of the people in the Strawberry Beds, which after all was a typical rural community with the added advantage of being only six miles from the center of Dublin. Many families married into each other and so are related through long lines.

In the 1800s travel was by pony and trap, or horseback, or by walking. The Lower Road was a dirt track at the time, dusty in summer and muddy in winter. The lanes off the road were Tinker's Hill (St John's Hill), Rugged Lane, Somerton Lane, or Knockmaroon Hill. The roads were passable to a greater or lesser extent given the weather conditions. The Rugged Lane that runs up to Lynam's on the Porterstown Road, alongside the castle wall, was initially just a track. Mr. George Greene, who lived on the Lower Road, offered on commission, to make it a usable roadway. He set about this task using dynamite to remove the rock. He managed for several yards to advance the roadway but progress was too slow and the task too great for him so the local council took over from him to finish the work.

Many 'Mass paths' existed in the area. These paths are marked on the maps of 1836 up to 1936. These 'shortcuts' for those on foot, can be found all over the country. Landowners understood the reason for their existence and often were powerless to extinguish the right of the people to use them as they had become legitimate through long use. One such pathway runs from Woodlands Cottage at the corner of Luttrellstown Castle up to the top of the Rugged Lane. A shortcut, not long, but appreciated none the less.

Many pathways crossed Somerton lands to the church in Porterstown. One such pathway led from the Strawberry Hall public house, up past their teahouse into 'Lovely's Field' (opposite Somerton's main entrance). A swing bridge crossed Somerton Lane from Lovely's Field onto the terrace - a pathway that bounded the southern edge of Somerton. The terrace then led to the 'moat field' where it joined another pathway coming up from the Lower

Road. This second pathway started at the Huntsman's house and crossed the 'moat field' and then passed on to the church. The swing bridge was taken down in the 1960s but it had been in use for over one hundred years. Another pathway was the 'slip', which ran off Somerton Lane just where the Doyle family used to live and ran down to the Lower Road.

The Glen at the west end of Knockmaroon Estate linked the Sandpits with the Lower Road. Until recent times this was a well-used pathway. All these paths existed to help the people from the Lower Road travel the shortest way to the surrounding villages, churches, shops or work. Living in the valley always meant an uphill trek.

The Dublin to Galway road was the main artery to the west and to reach this the river had to be crossed. Several houses had rowing boats to do just this. The Plunkett family (Rose Plunkett) would ferry people across the river, who would then make their way up to the main road crossing the Hermitage Estate by a right of way. Here they would get the tram to Dublin. On their return they would retrace their steps to the riverbank, shout across the river to get the attention of Mrs. Plunkett and get ferried back over.

Rose Plunkett ferrying across the river. The riverbank is without the heavy vegetation that we see today. The thatched house in the background is on the Rugged lane, home of the Geraghty family.
(Courtesy Rose Blackburn)

Other families had rowing boats, of course, to cross the river, or for fishing and pleasure. These were the Greene family, the Ennis family, the Scully family and others. These boats were both recreational and for purpose and a keen knowledge of the current and flow of the river was vital, especially when used in wintertime. It was easy to get carried downriver and possibly washed over a weir. They were used in fishing excursions as well as a Sunday pleasure trip with the family.

Trams arrived in Lucan in 1881. The early trams were powered by steam and could carry forty-two passengers. This was a very successful enterprise and in 1887 they carried 135,117 passengers. In 1890 there were six double-trips from Dublin to Leixlip a day. The fare to Lucan was 10d. and the trip took 50 minutes. The electric tram arrived in March 1900 and ran at 45-minute intervals and often jarvies met the trams at the Lucan terminus to pick up passengers and carry them onwards by road. On one occasion, Mr. Hill of Hill's Mill, a pompous man by all accounts, attempted to board the tram in Lucan, which was full. He was refused by the conductor, to whom he replied, 'Do you know who I am? I am the Hill of Lucan'. The conductor replied, 'I don't care if you are a 'mountain of Mourne', you are still not getting on'. The trams ran until April 1940 when double-deck buses took over.

The tram at Lucan terminus. The jarvies, as seen in the photograph, would meet the tram and carry the passengers onwards to their destination. (Courtesy Mrs. Mary Shackleton)

Shackleton Mills had drays moving in and out of Dublin carrying corn or other necessities for the mill. At times there would be fourteen drays travelling per day. Women travelling to town would get lifts on the empty drays. The horses would always go by Lucan, as this was a less steep hill for them. Those who lived at the Knockmaroon end of the valley would simply walk to Chapelizod to catch the trams.

In late 1940, a bus service started to run from Aston Quay in the city to Luttrelstown gates. It was the number 80 bus and it became an oddity in the Dublin bus service. The locals considered it almost a private service. It could be boarded at the top of the Rugged Lane, Somerton Cross, the Glen or at College Cross. It ran every two hours although often less frequently. It had a conductor and driver and was known as the 'arm chair' by the bus workers. This wasn't an onerous route! The locals were well known to the drivers, who knew the routines of the locals so well that the bus might wait for certain passengers. At times it might go off route to drop off 'Bridget the cook' to Somerton on a dark wet night. It was known on occasions to travel up the Carpenterstown Road at the Sandpits to drop off passengers. On one occasion the bus travelled down Somerton Hill and turned at the Wren's Nest to drop my mother to the gate. It was probably raining at the time. She was mortified at the event and tried to keep her head lowered in case she was seen. Of course everyone knew; news would travel faster than the bus itself. Secrets were difficult to keep on the 'Beds'. Going off route for a bus was a breach of duty, of course; however, the bus drivers were kind and considerate to the local people.

All local news was swapped between neighbors on the bus, relationships blossomed or faded, and school goers caused ructions at the back of the bus. Fare dodging on the bus was impossible, as the drivers knew the ages of all the teenagers. The drivers had grown up with the families of the Lower Road. Retirement parties were given for the drivers in the local community centre in appreciation for their care of the community. The bus route lasted for 40 years and ended, due mostly, to the proliferation of the motorcar.

While not every family had a car at their disposal, getting lifts from those who had cars was acceptable. The bicycle was essential for any worker. While always reliable, pushing it uphill was the chore. However, for those who lived on the Lower Road, it was just part of life. The motorbike, in particular the Honda 50, was a wonderful asset for any family to have. Certain families had particular styles of motorbike. Willie Hands had an old BSA and Johnny O'Rourke had a Henkle, while the Martins, Raymond and Peter, favoured the Honda.

Chapter 12

STRAWBERRY BEDS IMPROVEMENT ASSOCIATION

Up to the 1950s there were few services on the Lower Road. This was a rural community, a distance of six miles from the capital, surrounded by villages such as Lucan, Chapelizod or Clonsilla. All services would initially go to the areas with a greater concentration of people. The Strawberry Beds lay between these villages and the intention of the association was to tap into the services that served these villages. In the 1940s there was no mains water supply. There was no public transport on the road, there was an inadequate electricity supply, there was no telephone service, no refuse collection on the road and the nearest medical service or doctor was in Castleknock. There were no sewerage facilities despite the fact that a sewerage pipe ran through the valley from Peamount Hospital to the sea. This sewerage pipe was laid down in the 1940s. Most houses had septic tanks, although there were many houses without any sanitary facilities. A pleasant note about the sewerage pipe construction was that Michael Kavanagh, who worked on the line, met and married Shelia Scully, who was of course born and reared on the Strawberry Beds.

A committee known as the Strawberry Beds Improvement Association was formed in January 1953 with the aim of improving the services on the road. It would be naive to believe that this was the first such association to come together to improve the living conditions of their community. Unfortunately, no information is to hand on previous associations. However, documentation does survive on the above association and their efforts to enhance the living standards of the residents of the Strawberry Beds.

The first committee elected to the Strawberry Beds Improvement Association was as follows:

Chairman	Brendan Ellis
Secretary	James Troy
Treasurer	Desmond Cummins
Members	William Dumbrell
	Patrick Tobin
	Peter Carney
	Jimmy Buggle

Ms. C. Weldon
Ger. Lanigan
Ms. Peg Clarke
Peter Martin

A minute exists to co-opt Mr. Skeen, a solicitor, who lived on the Rugged Lane, onto the committee, if it was considered necessary. Meetings were held in the schoolhouse, although the minutes mention one meeting held in Mrs. Murray's tearooms. The meetings were well attended by the locals according to the minutes. Many topics also came up for discussion. All community committees are subject to disagreements from within and without and this Association was similar in this regard. However, their success was notable in that they did achieve many of their goals.

Correspondence between the Association, the various Government Departments, the Lord Mayor's office, local representatives (councilors and TDs), churches, and local landowners was prolific.

The committee had initial success with the Electricity Supply Board in that transformers were erected, enhancing the power supply. In the late 1940s the electricity supply was unreliable, insufficient in power and available for only a few hours a day. The association pressed the Electricity Supply Board for an improved service. The ESB erected transformers at strategic points in the valley to strengthen the power output and to lessen the power breaks. This was a significant success when one considers that the two dams on the River Shannon and Liffey had only been constructed in the 1940s and many parts of Ireland were seeking supply for the first time or to have their supply enhanced.

The next project for the Strawberry Beds Improvement Association was to get a phone line for the residents. The Strawberry Beds is an isolated area and calling for a doctor or an ambulance was a worry for people. Similar to other rural areas in times of need, someone had to go and get the doctor, which in this case involved travelling to Castleknock. However, the committee failed to get the telephone kiosks they sought. The answer from the General Post Office was that telephones could be placed privately in the public houses and used by the locals. The cost of kiosks on the road was considered by the General Post Office to be too expensive. Eventually private houses and the public houses did install phones, but the service was appalling all through the sixties. It was not unusual for locals to suffer an absence of service for six months or more.

> OIFIG AN AIRE POIST 7 TELEGRAFA.
> (OFFICE OF THE MINISTER FOR POSTS AND TELEGRAPHS)
> BAILE ÁTA CLIAT
> (DUBLIN).
>
> Aibreán, 1954.
> 12.
>
> A Chara,
>
> I am desired by the Minister for Posts and Telegraphs to refer to your letter of the 23rd March and to say that the request for a public telephone kiosk at the Strawberry Beds has been carefully reconsidered.
>
> As already intimated, the position is that it is the settled policy of the Department to provide kiosks only at places where the revenue is likely to cover at least the cost of erection and maintenance; the Department could not afford to provide kiosks at every point where one would be useful to cater for occasional calls without regard to the cost involved. In fact, kiosks are generally not installed in towns of less than 1,500 inhabitants.
>
> Having regard to the population, number of houses etc. in the Strawberry Beds area, it is most unlikely that a kiosk would pay its way at present. Passing traffic during the Summer would not affect the position materially. In the circumstances, I have to confirm with regret that it is not possible to meet your wishes in the matter.
>
> It should be added that the suggestion in regard to some resident renting a telephone was made to try to find a solution to your needs in this matter on the assumption that the residents would be sufficiently interested to share the rental (£2.10s. per quarter; with Coin Box 10s.6d.) which would be a small charge among a number of residents. It is regretted that no abatement of this rental could or is ever conceded. This course was suggested in the hope that the positioning of the Coin Box would not interfere with the privacy of any individual.
>
> The Minister has asked me to make it clear that the whole financial structure of the Telephone Service would be imperilled if Kiosks, whose maintenance and capital charges are over £40 per annum, were installed in the number that would be required. The Coin Box, on the other hand, has been the acceptable solution in a great many similar communities.
>
> Mise, le meas,
>
> Rúnaí Aire.
>
> James P. Troy, Esq.,
> Secretary,
> Strawberry Beds Improvement Association,
> "Ardmore,"
> Strawberry Beds,
> CO. DUBLIN.

Proposals that the Lower Road be incorporated onto the refuse collection run in Lucan, which was already in place, was refused because of the sparse population on the Strawberry Beds and the distance to be travelled. This service would eventually arrive in the 1970s. The suggestion of getting public transport on the road was rejected by Corus Iompair Eireann, as the roadway was considered too narrow. This was a long running battle and really did not cease until a school bus run was put on the road to carry the children to Castleknock school in 1971. Only the Luttrellstown bus, the number 80, which travelled on Porterstown Road, offered a service. Success was achieved with a mains water supply, public lighting, sewerage access and, finally, a telephone service. Most of these latter achievements came in a staggered fashion during the sixties and seventies.

A dispensary was sought for the 300 people who lived on the Lower Road and surrounding area. The doctors for the area lived and had their surgeries in Chapelizod, Castleknock or Lucan. Compassionate requests to the Dublin Board of Assistance on behalf of the people of the Strawberry Beds for a weekly dispensary service were unfortunately rejected. The presence of an ambulance on the road was rare during these years, but the sight or sound of one was generally sinister.

> "ARDMORE"
> Strawberry Beds,
> Chapelizod,
> Co. Dublin.
>
> 22nd June, 1953.
>
> The Secretary,
> Dublin Board of Assistance,
> 1, James Street
> DUBLIN.
>
> <u>Strawberry Beds Improvements Association</u>.
>
> Dear Sir,
>
> I am directed by my Committee to request the provision of a weekly Dispensary service at The Strawberry Beds.
>
> There are about 300 families located on this (the Lower Road) and due to the natural hilly roads on all sides, and to the fact that there is no public telephone or transport available, you will appreciate there is particular hardship on those needing medical assistance. The nearest doctor available lives in Castleknock, a distance of 2½ miles approx.
> The majority of the people live in rather strained circumstances and cannot afford to pay for private medical attention.
>
> I am to point out that suitable premises for a dispensary are available.
>
> In the circumstances, therefore, I shall be glad if you will give the matter your kind consideration and advise me as soon as possible.
>
> Yours sincerely,
>
> Secretary.

> Telefón: 52205
>
> Freagra go dtí an Runaí
> Reply to Secretary
>
> Faoi Uimh. Thag.
> Quoting Ref. No.
>
> **BORD CÚNAIMH BHAILE ÁTHA CLIATH**
> DUBLIN BOARD OF ASSISTANCE
>
> SRÁID SAN SÉAM
> JAMES'S STREET
>
> BAILE ÁTHA CLIATH
> DUBLIN
>
> 25th June, 1953.
>
> Mr. John P. Troy,
> "Ardmore,"
>   Strawberry Beds,
>   CHAPELIZOD.
>
> Dear Sir,
>
> I have to acknowledge your letter of the 22nd June, 1953, with regard to the provision of a weekly dispensary session at the Strawberry Beds, and to inform you that the matter is having attention.
>
> Yours faithfully,
>
> [signature]
> DEPUTY SECRETARY
>
> fe/dw.

In 1954 flooding from the River Liffey was severe and it entered many homes and caused much damage. The committee sought flood relief from The Lord Mayor's relief fund. Households had their furniture destroyed, families had to vacate their homes and move to neighboring houses on higher ground. Market gardeners had their livelihood jeopardised. Following correspondence with the Lord Mayor's office, the committee was successful in getting compensation. Names of those persons most affected were forwarded and all received £5 as compensation.

"Ardmore",
Strawberry Beds,
Co. Dublin.

3rd May 1955.

Alderman A. Byrne, Esq., T.D.,
Lord Mayor of Dublin.

Dear Alderman Byrne,

Referring to recent interview in regard to flood damages, I submit as agreed, a list of householders who I think should receive allowances. (All addresses Strawberry Beds, Co. Dublin).

(a) <u>Cases where allowance of £5 has already been given.</u>

James Doyle, Mrs. Galligan, Mrs. G. Murray, Frank Scully, Senr., Mrs. J. Murphy, Miss M. Tobin, Matthew Plunkett, Miss E. Lawless, Miss Peg Clarke, Mrs. P. Tobin, William Dempsey.

(b) <u>Cases where no previous allowance has been given.</u>

Miss Mary Byrne, Mrs. E. O'Neill, William Lennon, Anthony Halpin.

I will recommend the first <u>two</u> of these be granted £5 each and the later <u>two</u> £6 each (market gardeners) to agree with similar amount given to the others.

There are other cases at the Millbank area (Messrs. Pierce, Kelly, Doran, Somers, O'Neill) with which I am not familiar. Perhaps you could at some future date let me have a list of all cheques issued for agreement with my records. You can issue cheques to the above with the usual recommendation.

I hope now all cases have been dealt with and again desire to express my admiration for the prompt and courteous manner in which you have handled this matter, and also the attention and consideration of your son Patrick in this matter.

Yours respectfully,

JAMES P. TROY (SECRETARY)

Strawberry Beds Improvements Association.

P.S.
I have omitted P. Carney's name from above list, as you will recollect, his cheque for £3 was handed to Senator V. Carton.

Chairman: Alderman Alfred Byrne, G.C.S.S., T.D., Lord Mayor, Alderman John Belton, T.D., Councillor Charles J. Haughey, B.Comm., B.L., A.C.A. Councillor Eugene Timmons, P.C., Councillor Peadar Cowan, Councillor Thomas Cosgrave, Councillor Gilbert Hughes, Councillor John Joseph Phelan Councillor Denis Larkin, T.D., Councillor Mrs. Lillie O'Shea-Leamy, P.C., Senator Victor Carton, Alderman Tom Byrne, T.D., P.C.

LORD MAYOR'S RELIEF FUND

MANSION HOUSE

DUBLIN

1st March, 1955.

James P. Troy, Esq.,
Ardmore,
Strawberry Beds,
Chapelizod,
CO. DUBLIN.

Dear Mr. Troy,

Following your recent telephone call [conversation] regarding the question of Flood Relief for residents of the Strawberry Beds, I am now directed by the Lord Mayor to forward for your information a list of persons who have now received Grants of £5 each, on the recommendation of the County Dublin Branch, Irish Red Cross Society.

As I explained to you on the phone, funds are limited and only the really distressing cases can be dealt with. The question of compensation for loss of property and damage to furniture, loss of earnings, etc., is primarily a matter for Judge Lavery's Committee or some other form of Public Assistance. Further, the Red Cross Society List was submitted to us as a comprehensive list of persons throughout the county area most deserving of assistance and it would be unfair to persons in other areas to make a large number of additions to the list in respect of the Strawberry Beds at this stage. If, however, your Committee is aware of a small number of householders (not exceeding say 8 or 10) whom you can fairly recommend for special assistance the Lord Mayor will be prepared to sanction special Grants for them.

> 2.
>
> I am sure you will understand the position and that you will appreciate the great difficulty of satisfying the large number of applicants with whom we have to deal.
>
> I am,
> Yours sincerely,
>
> *Patrick J Byrne*
>
> Enc.

Letters documenting the struggle faced by the committee show the determination and resilience of the people to better their way of life. Credit also has to be granted to the various bodies for the courteous and frank manner with which matters were dealt with and decisions made.

The Feehan Family who used live in Mrs. Nash's house on the Strawberry Beds. Mr. and Mrs. Feehan sit in the front row, while Simon West is standing in the back row on the left. His wife is seated in front of him and Jack Lovely is the baby on the woman's lap.
(Courtesy Mr. Michael Harford)

Gretta Higgins, Ronnie Condron, Paddy Condron and Alida McGuiness in the community centre.
(Courtesy Eileen Troy)

Johnny O Rourke with friends.
(Courtesy Gerard O'Byrne)

My father Jimmy Troy on his wedding day in 1952. In the photograph are Mrs. Scully and Gertie Murray outside their cottage. The cottage was covered in roses, which had a wonderful fragrance.
(Courtesy Shelia Kavanagh)

Chapter 13

THE SCHOOLS

There were a number of schools surrounding the Strawberry Beds in the 1800s, although the education system favoured the Protestant section of the community. There were schools in Chapelizod, Lucan, Clonsilla, Porterstown, Blanchardstown and Castleknock. The two nearest schools to the Strawberry Beds were in Porterstown and Castleknock. These two schools catered for children of the Established Church (EC) or Church of Ireland and for some Catholic children.

Porterstown School had been built by Lord Annaly of Luttrellstown in the townland of Kellystown. It catered predominately for Church of Ireland children and a small number of Catholic children. Disputes arose however, between the Catholic priest Father Dungan, and the Protestant rector Dr. Sadlier, as to the religious education of the children. In 1852 the partnership ended and Father Dungan built a Catholic school, the Clonsilla National School on the banks of the Royal Canal, in 1853. Its ruin can still be seen and it was in use up until the nineteen sixties, but it was in very poor condition by this time. It is said that the building, which was never an attractive structure, could be seen from every window in Luttrellstown Castle to spite Lord Annaly.

A Church of Ireland school existed in Castleknock from 1720. This school had a large population as many of the military personnel that lived within and without the Phoenix Park sent their children to this primary school for their education. This school was also supported by the large estates that surrounded Castleknock as most of the estates were in ownership by families of the Church of Ireland.

The earliest school for the education of the children in the Strawberry Beds was established in 1822. The school was situated next to the Strawberry Hall on the Lucan side. The remains of the fireplace of this building can still be seen in a car park area beside the public house. Col. Thomas White of Luttrellstown owned the land on which it was built and it was leased to John McNeill (Griffiths Valuation 1843). The rent payable on this lease was £1 per year. Funding for the building and servicing of the school was collected from the local residents of the Lower Road.

The school consisted of one large room measuring 32 feet by 14 feet with a single source of heat, the open fire mentioned above. It had four 'ten-foot' forms and four 'five-foot' forms. These forms had to seat up to seventy pupils if all were in attendance. How the seating arrangement was settled is open to speculation; it may have been a case of early risers got the best seats or perhaps the older and bigger children pressed their needs on the smaller children. This was a non-vested school, in essence a private school, and fees of one penny per week or 1s 1p per quarter was payable to the schoolteacher by the children.

The National School Board was formed in 1831. The aim of the Board was to improve the standard of education for primary school children in the country. Schools that met certain educational standards would have the teacher's salary paid, a house provided for the teacher, and the children would also have free education. According to Charles and Mary Hulgraine, authors of St. Mochta's Church, the Lower Road School applied for acceptance to the National School Board and was accepted. Unfortunately the standard of teaching was poor under Mr. Joseph Coady and his wife Catherine Fagan and it was removed from registration in 1834.

The National School Board accepted it back into registration in 1836. Mr. Key was now the primary school teacher. However, the educational standard was little improved and registration was lost for a second time. Joseph and Elizabeth Lynch succeeded Mr. Key in August 1838. However, the school closed in 1839 due to the poor standard of education. It reopened in 1844 under the tutelage of John and Margaret Jessop.

It is obvious that the ability of the teachers was poor at this time. The education of the children was a private affair and a means of income for the teachers. An inspector for the National School Board noted that one teacher could only teach the alphabet and knitting to the children. The education of the teachers themselves was obviously poor. Joseph Coady, who is mentioned as the first teacher when the school opened, was most likely of the same family that operated the river ferry. He is mentioned in Griffiths Valuation as residing at the Knockmaroon end of the valley. Over the next fifty to sixty years the teaching and education continued to an indifferent standard. The condition of the school building deteriorated over time and there are reports of gaping holes in the roof, damp rooms, poor sanitation and certainly unhealthy teaching conditions at its end. The National School Board had to persistently impress on one teacher to light the fire for the children, who were in bare feet.

In 1904, sixty-eight pupils were recorded in the school register (Register 4201), forty girls and twenty-eight boys. The teacher was Anne F. McDonnell. The largest class, infants, had twenty-four pupils. There were six standards of education as the child progressed up the years. However, the fall off was always considerable. At this period in time only two or three pupils would stay on until the fifth or sixth standard. Primary school education was often the sole formal education a child would receive in their lifetime, so parents, with the foresight and the means to extend the students tuition to the final standards, gave the children a significant advantage in future years.

The registers in 1906 show a seventy-eight percent attendance rate. A school inspector, Mrs. Taaffe at the time, visited the school quite often. One task the inspectors had, besides maintaining educational standards, was to pursue non-attendees and inform families of their duties to send the children to school. Children could not leave school before the age of fourteen. However, a child could leave school at the age of eleven onwards only if he or she showed proficiency in reading, writing and elementary arithmetic. This was set in Statute.

Clonsilla National School - 1853

Old National School, Porterstown.

(Sketch)

Chapter 14

IRISH EDUCATIONAL ACT 1892

The Irish Educational Act 1892 was enacted to ensure compulsory education for all children between the ages of six and fourteen years. The Act was a wonderful piece of legislation when one considers that on mainland Europe no such compulsory educational programmes existed. In England, in the year 1870, a similar Educational Act was passed. It contained the same objective of ensuring children had an appropriate education up to their eleventh year. The Act was only partially effective in England by the year 1903, but became fully enforced by 1916. The reason for the delay in implementation the Act was due to pressure on the educational system by industrialists who wished to continue to use children as a source of cheap labour in their factories and mills.

Child labour in the woollen and cotton mills was extensive during late nineteenth and the early part of the twentieth centuries. Children as young as four were often forced into labour through the need of the family. Their significant use was that they were small enough to crawl beneath the looms and extract the smallest particles of cloth and dust. Their duty was to minimise the risk of fire in the mills and to ensure the looms worked without cloth particles clogging the moving parts. They preformed their tasks as the machinery continued just above their head. Deafening noise, dangerous moving parts of the loom, and choking conditions were the lot of the poorer children in Britain. Irish children were spared these dreadful work conditions during this period because Ireland was, in general, less industrialised than England. The mills in Ireland were not able to compete with the larger operations in England. Irish mills were coming to the end of their usefulness and child labour was not as relevant in the Irish context. The Irish economy was based more on agricultural production and the Irish Educational Act 1892 took note of this difference in the drafting of the Bill.

The Act of 1892 made it an offence for any employer to work a child unless that child was over fourteen years of age and had a certificate of proficiency in the three subjects, reading, writing and elementary arithmetic. This was a least fourth year standard. A child could get the certificate at the age of eleven if he or she reached this standard. The certificate was issued by the principal teacher and forging, issuing, or counterfeiting a certificate could mean imprisonment.

Extracts from the Irish Education Act 1892.

Sections 1, 2, 9, and 14 and schedules 1 and 2.
Compulsory Education

(1)

(a) In everyplace to which this section applies, the parent of every child not less than six nor more than fourteen years of age shall cause the child to attend school during such number of days in the year for such time on each day attendance are as prescribed in the First Schedule of this Act, unless there is reasonable excuse for non-attendance.

(b) Provided that a child over eleven years of age shall not be required to attend school, if the child has received such certificate of his proficiency in reading, writing, and elementary arithmetic as is prescribed in the Second Schedule of the Act.

(c) Any of the following reasons shall be a reasonable excuse for non-attendance of a child namely,

(d) That there is not within two miles, measured according to the nearest road, from the residence of the child any national school or other efficient school at which the child can attend, and to which the parent does not object, on religious grounds, to send the child;

(e) That the child has been prevented from attending school by sickness, domestic necessity, or by reasons of being engaged in necessary operations of husbandry or the ingathering of crops, or giving assistance in the fisheries, or other work requiring to be done at a particular time or season, or other reasonable unavoidable or reasonable cause;

(f) That the child being under seven years of age, lives at too great a distance from any national school which he can attend, even though that distance is less than two miles;

(g) That the child is receiving suitable elementary education in some other manner.

(2)

(1) a person shall not, except as in this Act mentioned, take into his employment in any place to which this section applies, any child except for the setting or planting of potatoes, hay-making, or harvesting –
   (i) who is under the age of eleven years; or
   (ii) who, being of the age of eleven years or upwards, and less than fourteen years of age has not attained such certificate of his proficiency in reading, writing, and elementary arithmetic, as is prescribed in the Second Schedule to this Act, unless the child is employed and is attending school with the Factory and Workshops Acts, 1878 to 1891, but no employer shall compel a child to attend a school to which its parents objects on religious grounds.

(2) If any person acts in contravention of this section, he shall be liable on summary conviction to a fine not exceeding forty shillings.

(9) The Commissioners may make regulations as to the registers to be kept by school attendance committees and by the teachers of national schools, and as to the inspection thereof, and every school attendance committee shall comply with such regulations.

(14) If any person forges or counterfeits any certificate which is by this Act made evidence of any matter, or gives or signs any certificate which is, to his knowledge, false in any material particular, or, knowing any such certificate to be forged or counterfeit, makes use thereof, or makes or knowingly uses any false entry in the register kept in pursuance of this Act, he shall be liable on summary conviction to imprisonment for a period not exceeding three months, with or without hard labour.

FIRST SCHEDULE

The number of attendances for the purpose of the first section of this Act shall be seventy-five complete attendances in each half-year ending respectively the thirtieth day of June and the thirty-first day of December at any national or other efficient school.

SECOND SCHEDULE

A certificate of proficiency for the purposes of this Act shall be a certificate issued by the principal teacher of the school which the child has last attended of such proficiency in reading, writing, and elementary arithmetic as is now prescribed for the fourth class in the programme of instruction of the Commissioners, or such higher proficiency as may hereafter be prescribed by them.

****

Non-attendance at school was monitored. The legislation set out the times and reasons that absence from school was acceptable. Children could be absent at harvest time due to ingathering of crops, assistance at fisheries, or other seasonal work. Should a child live more than two miles from a school then they could receive education at home or attend a similar school nearer. A child under seven years, living a distance from the school, but less than two miles could also be excused as a round trip of four miles was thought to be too long for a child of six years. It should be remembered that most children were still walking in bare feet at this time. An attendance of seventy-five complete attendances in each half-year was required within the Act.

A copy of this Act was placed inside every school register on the first page for the teacher's awareness. The thought of hard labour for the teachers, as set down in Section (14) of the Act, must have been an attractive idea for some of the pupils. It should also be said that there was some leniency within the Act where children would, or would not, be sent to school. This fact is evident when the school rolls are examined where it is apparent children, for whatever reason, missed multiple days. Perhaps not all parents saw the value of education for their children.

The health of the children was also of importance. Dental clinics were introduced in 1913 in all primary schools. Public health doctors would also make visits to the schools and hearing, sight, stature, and physical health and development was examined. This health screening for the children was a progressive undertaking to ensure the good health of the Nation. School inspectors from the National School Board visited to ensure that educational standards were met and that good governance of the school was present. The Act combined the physical and educational needs of the children.

The Irish Educational Act 1892 incorporated the needs of the family, the needs of the children, the society in which they lived, and the future of the country. The Act,would eventually lay the foundation for an educated people that would lead the country to Independence.

Chapter 15
LOWER ROAD SCHOOL

Schools were built all over Ireland from 1900 onwards to fulfill the requirements of the legislation. These new primary schools were of a similar design and were constructed within reach of the children they were expected to educate. The schools were positioned to serve an approximate radius of two miles. The new Lower Road School opened on the 16th day of August 1910 at a new site at the bottom of Somerton Hill. All the children were transferred from the old school beside the Strawberry Hall to the new premises in August 1910. Simon West, according to the Census 1901, owned the land on which the new school was built. There is no knowledge of the leasing or purchasing arrangement for this land and the school would ultimately become the property of the Catholic Church, its patron. Ms. Eliza Williams, owner of the Strawberry Hall public house, retained ownership of the land on which the old school had been built.

The building and playground area of the new school was standard for all the new buildings. It consisted of one large room, thirty feet by fourteen feet, divided by a partition to make two smaller rooms. For seating it had twenty three-foot forms and four ten-foot forms. It had an open fire for each room although a pot-bellied stove was introduced later when only one room was required to cater for the number of pupils. Two small cloakrooms ran off the main rooms. There were two outside dry toilets, boys and girls at opposite ends of the schoolyard. The schoolyard measured 562 square yards and served as a play area for the children during break time. The school, being Catholic in ethos, was the responsibility of the parish priest in Blanchardstown.

When the Lower Road School opened on Tuesday 16th August 1910 forty children were in attendance, twenty-one boys and nineteen girls. The school register (4201), in which each pupil had a specific school number, continued in use from the old school to the new premises. This continued use of the register meant that there was continuity in the identity of the children transferring. The transfer took place after the summer break. The teachers on the opening day were Mary Doyle, who had become principal in the old school in 1906, and Anne Keating as assistant teacher. Ms. Keating began teaching in 1909, just prior to the transfer.

In January 1914, children coming to the school for the first time were entered in a new school register. The new register was numbered 16026, as was granted by the National School Board. The numbering sequence commenced at number one. The honour of being 'number one' was given to Annie Roche for the girls and John Roche for the boys. The principal was Mrs. Mary Roche (nee Doyle), so this privilege was bestowed on her own children. This was fitting as Mrs. Roche spent her whole career teaching the children of the Lower Road School. The Lower Road School had the official status of a two-teacher school. The number of pupils determining its status had to be greater than forty. This attendance figure, as it dropped, would eventually herald the school's closure in 1971.

****

Chapter 16
THE TEACHERS

Anne F. McDonnell, the teacher prior to Mary Doyle, signed the school rolls in the earliest register that is available. This roll dates from 1904. She had beautiful handwriting and kept the roll in exemplary fashion; her last signature is in October 1905. She is not recorded in the census lists of the time so nothing is known of her. Mary Doyle was her assistant teacher in 1904 and was made principal in 1906. Following this, Anne Keating became the assistant teacher in 1909. Both Mary Doyle and Anne Keating, who had started teaching in the old school, would duly oversee the transfer of the children between the schools. Given the dilapidated condition of the old school, the newly built school must have been greatly welcomed. Both teachers continued to teach until after 1931. Mary Doyle had married to become Mary Roche while Anne Keating married to become Anne Byrne.

Of the teachers in the old school generally little is known. The registers for the period 1822 to 1904 have not been found. Perhaps they lie in the basement of the National School Board, the predecessor to the Department of Education, as rolls have been returned there in the past. However, the returned rolls are not cataloged, simply stored, so until they are cataloged it is not known if they actually exist. Reports from the inspectors of the National School Board continually complained about the inadequate standard of teaching so the keeping of appropriate rolls may also have been haphazard or totally absent. However, the names of teachers that are recorded are Joseph Coady and his wife Catherine Fagan, Mr. Key, Joseph and Elizabeth Lynch and John and Margaret Jessop.

The following are the teachers from 1904 onwards:

1904–1905	Annie F. McDonnell
1905–1931	Mary Roche
	Anne Keating
1931–1936	Missing register. With the retirement of Mary Roche and Anne Keating in 1931, or thereabouts – the exact date is unknown – a number of substitute teachers may have been employed. Perhaps this is the reason for the register becoming mislaid.
	From 1941 onwards all children and teachers had to record their names in Irish. While in most cases the translation from the English version to the Irish version was appropriate, in some names there is no exact translation for a name originating in England. Imaginative translations were often used in the school rolls.
1941–1947	Teresa Mac Suibhne
	Maigread nic Suibhne
	Trasna bean Mac Aoid
	Caitlin ni Stiopain
	Caitriona ni Seighin
	Maire Bean ni Breaglaoic, who got a contract in 1946, did not teach in the Lower Road for any period of time.
1947–1968	Eimile ni Briain
1968–1970	Teresa Beirne

Between the years 1941 and 1947 there were seven teachers in the school. All were female and all record their name in Irish. This period covered the Second World War, a time of uncertainty and unrest. However, nothing is known of six of these teachers.

Mrs. Roche with her school in 1922. Mrs. Roche was the longest serving primary school teacher in the Lower Road School. She started teaching in the old Lower Road School in 1905. The pupils that are recognized are as follows:
Back Row, left to right, Lizzie Neil, Brigid Greene, Brigid Gannon, Tommy Kelly, ?, ?
Middle Row, Christy Lawless, John Gannon, Jack Galligan, Stephen Gannon, Peter Moore, Michael Galligan.
Front Row, Peggy Kelly, May Lennon, Kitty Nolan, Ester Lawless, ?, ?, Willie Cording, Paddy Galligan, James Duffy and Birdie Scully, Shelia Scully, Owen Scully sitting down in front. The principal was Mrs. Roche standing on the right, and the name of little boy standing on the left is not known.
(Courtesy Shelia Kavanagh)

In 1947 Eimile ni Briain (Emily O'Brien) was an assistant teacher, but later became the principal. As principal she taught in the Lower Road for the next twenty-five years. A contract of employment was signed by Ms. Eimile ni Briain on the 24th March 1948 and was counteredsigned by Father Liam O'Rourke SC on behalf of the patrons, the Catholic Church, and by Cormac Brady on behalf of the Department of Education.

No assistant teacher was sanctioned for the school from 1947 onwards. The school now had the status of a 'one teacher school'.

Employment contract of Eimile ni Briain signed in 1947.

In 1968 Ms. Emily O'Brien retired and a series of substitute teachers followed her retirement. Their names are unknown, however. The teachers of the Lower Road School were all female. In the older school the names of three men are on record, Mr. Key, Mr. Jessop and Mr. Coady, but none in the new school. Ms. Teresa Beirne was appointed as principal in 1970 and it was Ms. Beirne who oversaw the transfer of the last pupils from the Lower Road School to St Bridget's Primary School in August 1971, bringing to an end one hundred and fifty years of schooling in the Strawberry Beds.

The Lower Road School. (Sketch)

Chapter 17

THE SCHOOL REGISTERS

After the closure of the Lower Road School in 1971, the whereabouts of the rolls became a mystery. Initially it was thought they were stored in Blanchardstown parochial house. This proved to be false and an enquiry of the Department of Education was equally fruitless. Finally they were unearthed in the attic of St. Bridget's Primary School in Castleknock. The children had been transferred to this primary school in Castleknock. The last teacher in the Lower Road School, Ms. Beirne, brought the rolls there in August 1971. This newly built school was warm, had indoor toilets, a gymnasium, several teachers, male and female, and a number of other facilities not available in the old Lower Road School.

The school rolls date back to 1904 and account for all years up to the closure of the school. Unfortunately, one roll is missing - that of the five years 1931 to 1936. However, as most children attended school for eight years or more, few names should be absent. The rolls that exist are:

>   1904–1908
>   1908–1913
>   1913–1919
>   1919–1925
>   1925–1931
>   1931–1936 (missing)
>   1936–1944
>   1945–1965
>   1965–1975

The roll recorded the name, age at which the child registered in the school, school number, daily attendance, the total numbers of days attended in the last quarter and the school fees paid. All children are recorded as being free in the registers because, for the years the rolls exist, the school was registered with the National School Board, or the Department of Education. The roll also denoted the religion of the child.

The Lower Road School was Roman Catholic in ethos. Nevertheless, several children from the Established Church, i.e. Irish Church or Church of Ireland, attended the school during its existence. Families, such as the

Webbs, Sansoms and Trenchs, sent their children there. While it may have been expedient to send the children to the school for a short period, where a father had taken up temporary employment for example, the above families completed their studies in the school. In all, eight families from the Church of Ireland and one atheist family are recorded as sending their children to the Lower Road School.

Extracts from the school rolls are recorded below. All pupils that attended the schools from 1904 to 1973 are recorded. The year 1904 names all the pupils in the school, 73 pupils in all. Thereafter only those children who joined the school in the relevant year are recorded. Some children spent ten years in education while some names are only recorded for a few months. The records show the name of each pupil, their registered school number, and the year they enrolled in the school. In the full registers, the age of each pupil is given. However, these may not be correct as many children started school at the age of three or so. These children were 'granted' a few extra months to bring them up to four years of age, the earliest a child could go to school. Registering a child early was helpful in protecting the school from closure. The school would forward the predicted number for the coming year to the Department of Education. The threat of closure against one, or two teacher schools, was always present throughout the country as a whole.

YEAR 1904

	School number
	BOYS
Carroll James	226
Clarke Thomas	150
Coffey John	224
Donnelly Joseph	176
Doyle Joseph	169
Dunne Michael	208
Emmett Thomas	167
Fegan Bernard	204
Fegan John	172
Geraghty Patrick	225
Gough James	256
Halpin Edward	212
Halpin Francis	194
Hanlon James	218

Hanlon William	219
Keely William	221
Maiden George	222
Maiden Joseph	220
McCarthy Michael	211
Murray Joseph	156
Neill Francis	217
Neill James	162
Neill Joseph	195
Neill Laurence	189
Neill Patrick	175
Tobin Francis	186
Tobin John	205
Tobin Patrick	191
Walsh James	206
Walsh Laurence	181
Ward Denis	112
Ward Elias	184
Ward Patrick	223

GIRLS

Carroll Jane	199
Carroll Kathleen	214
Carroll Maggie	198
Carroll Mary	197
Clarke Annie	191
Clarke Maggie	161
Clarke Teresa	211
Clarke Winnie	194
Coffey Julia	237
Coffey Mary	236
Cunningham Agnes	176
Cunningham Ellen	190
Cunningham Rose	209
Dardis Alice	210
Dardis Claire	223
Dardis Kathleen	204
Dardis Norah	205
Donnelly Annie	234
Donnelly Kathleen	215
Donnelly Mary	184

Donnelly May	181
Doyle Lizzie	183
Dunne Mary	235
Gallaghan Annie	239
Geraghty Christina	222
Geraghty Rose	202
Halpin Angela	196
Hanlon Mary	230
Jacob Josephine	201
Maiden Kathleen	232
McAuley Maggie	229
McCarthy Kate	218
McCarthy Mary	219
Neill Mary	213
O Brien Bridget	192
O Neill Annie	216
Tobin Lucy	182
Tobin Rose	231
Walsh Mary	206
Ward Esther	233

All the children registered in 1904 are recorded. This roll applied to the old schoolhouse.

YEAR 1905

BOYS

Emmett Joseph	190
Hurley Harry	228
Hynes Patrick	229
Lynam James	231
McDermott John	230

GIRLS

Doolan Ellen	244
Doolan Maggie	242
Geraghty Josephine	245
Halpin Ellen	240
Halpin Margaret	238
Hurley Maggie	241
Hynes Bridget	246

Hynes Esther	247
Hynes Margaret	229
McHugh Mary	243

Five boys and ten girls were enrolled in 1905.

YEAR 1906

	BOYS
Byrne Patrick	232
Doolan Joseph	233
Tobin Joseph	226
Walsh Joseph	234

	GIRLS
Byrne Annie	249
Doolan Winnie	250
Moore Rose	195
Walsh Elizabeth	252

YEAR 1907

	BOYS
Feeney James	235
Neill William	236
Sherry Christopher	237
Sherry John	239
Sherry Joseph	231
Sherry Michael	240

	GIRLS
Carty Teresa	254
McCarthy Agnes	217

YEAR 1908

	BOYS
Anderson William	246
Byrne Christopher	241
Byrne Richard	240
Geraghty Christopher	243

	GIRLS
Anderson Mary	260
Carroll Annie	261
Carty Mary	258
Gallaghan Mary J	256
McDermott Nora	259
O Neill Mary	251

YEAR 1909

	BOYS
Coffey Edward	247
Ennis Christopher	251
Ennis William	252
Gough Thomas	253
Griffen Thomas	253
Hoey George	209
Hynes Michael	249
Muldoon John Patrick	254
Sutton Nicholas	244
Sutton William	245
Ward Charles	248

	GIRLS
Griffen Annie	264
Griffen Katie	265
Ennis Veronica	207
Lynch Annie	263
Lynch Marcella	268
Madden Marcella	262
McMahon Annie	267
McMahon Mary	266
Muldoon Mary Elizabeth	269

Twenty children enrolled in 1909, which was the largest number of pupils to enroll in any one year. The new school would open the following year in August 1910.

YEAR 1910

	BOYS
Dunne Joseph	210
Gallaghan Michael	257
Geraghty Peter	255

	GIRLS
Clarke Mary J	211
Coffey Kathleen	270
Sansom Margaret Annie	271

YEAR 1911

	BOYS
Geraghty Matthew	258
Cleary Thomas	259

	GIRLS
Coffey Alice	273
Green Mary J	275
Kavannagh Annie	277
Kavannagh Kathleen	276
Neill Julia	276
Powell Alice	279
Carroll Lizzie	274
Clarke Mary Bridget	272
Cleary Esther	275
Cleary Kathleen	278

YEAR 1912

	BOYS
Boyd John	260
Geraghty Joseph	261
Halpin Joseph	264
Halpin Thomas	263
McDermott William	262
Walshe William	266

	GIRLS
Cleary Eva	290
Gahan Sarah	285
Harney Bridget	284
Harney Margaret	?
Kane Bridget	?
Lawlor Daisy	282
Lawlor Eva	283
Power Mary	286
Reilly Margaret	?
Walshe Bridget	289

In 1913 the new School Register was introduced. Eva Cleary was the last girl to be registered with a school number of 290, while William Walsh, the last boy was registered at 286.

YEAR 1913

	BOYS
Roche John	1
Byrne Paul	2
Gallaghan John	265
Gannon Stephen	4

	GIRLS
Roche Annie	1
Byrne Bridget	6
Byrne Mary	5
Gannon Mary	3
Green Bridget	2
Neill Lizzie	4

YEAR 1914

	BOYS
Flynn Nicholas	8
Gallaghan Patrick	9
Hartin John	11
Wall Joseph	10
Wall Peter	7
Wall Richard	5

	GIRLS
Gannon Fanny	9
Geraghty Bridget	13
Hynes Mary	10
Troy Mary	8
Wall Agnes	12
Wall Annie	11

YEAR 1915

	BOYS
Blake John	21
Bowe William	13
Cahill Michael	18
Cahill William	16
Cunningham James	19
Green Fred	20
Kavannagh Patrick	10
Kelly Joseph	15
Kelly Patrick	14

	GIRLS
Coffey Christina	18
Geraghty Maggie	16

The war years did not appear to have a great impact on the number of children enrolling in the school.

YEAR 1916

	BOYS
Devoy PJ Thomas	24
Duffy James	26
Gannon John	25
Green William	240
Plunket Barton	23

	GIRLS
Bannon Patricia	20
Brennan Margaret	23
Devoy Margaret	21
Lennon Mary	22
Plunket Julia	19
Roche Eileen	26

YEAR 1917

	BOYS
Duffy Francis	28

	GIRLS
Fay Julia	27
Kavannagh Gladys	25
Keogh Bridget	24

YEAR 1918

	BOYS
Lovely James	31
Lovely John	30
Scully Owen	32

	GIRLS
Roche Mary	30
Gammell Eva	31
Gannon Bridget	29

YEAR 1919

	BOYS
Duffy Andrew	38
Redmond Patrick	33
Lawless Christopher	37
Lennon William	36
Redmond John	34

	GIRLS
Redmond Kathleen	33
Redmond Margaret	32
Scully Bridget	35
Geraghty Margaret	37
Lawless Esther	34
Pessagno Annie	36

YEAR 1920

	BOYS
Kelly Thomas	40
Emmett Desmond	39
Feehan Joseph	261

	GIRLS
Kelly Margaret	39
Lovely Mary	39
Geraghty Martha	38
Burns Annie	40

YEAR 1921

	BOYS
Judge Michael	47
Judge Patrick	48
Kelly Albert	44
Cording Enda	42
Cording George	43
Cording Robert	45
Nolan John	46
Nolan Thomas	50
O Brien Joseph	42

	GIRLS
Nolan Annie	21
Nolan Kathy	50
Nolan Mary	46
Scariff Margaret	49
Clarke Mary	51

Buggle Mary	43
Lennon Theresa	47

YEAR 1922

BOYS

Cassidy Gerard	51
Halpin Leopold	53
Hughes Frank	52

GIRLS

Roche Teresa	57
Scully Sheila	23

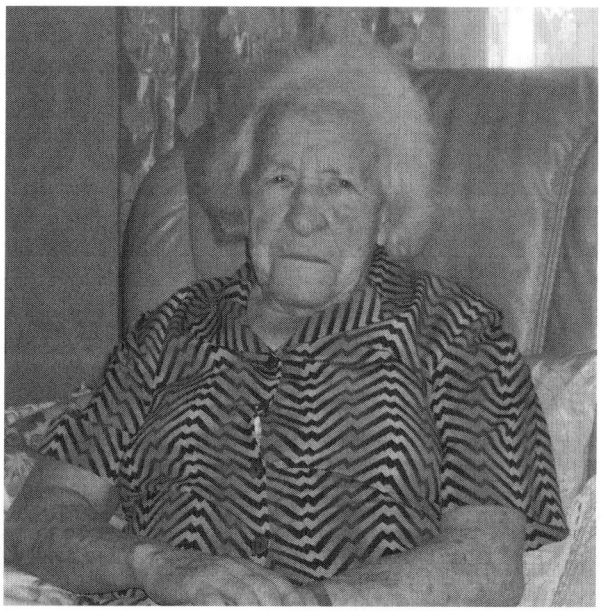

Shelia Kavanagh (nee Scully) registered in the Lower Road School in the year 1922.

YEAR 1923

BOYS

Davis Christopher	58
Kavannagh John	57
Meehan Christopher	54
Meehan John	56
Roche Michael	59

GIRLS

Lovely Esther	54

YEAR 1924

	BOYS
Bridges William J	67
Cassidy James	60
Cording William	66
Melia Patrick	65
Melia Peter	64
Nolan William	61
Smith Paul	63

	GIRLS
Nolan Kitty	7
Hughes Annie	57

YEAR 1925

	BOYS
Roche Patrick	68
Scully Frank	69
Byrne Francis	67
Clarke John	78
Curry Patrick	71
Lennon George	70
Meehan Philip	72

	GIRLS
Roche Lizzie	48
Green Annie	7
Curry Lily	59
Tobin Ellen	60
Tobin Mary	61

YEAR 1926

	BOYS
Halpin Anthony	74
Kelly James	15
Madden Thomas	78
Mole Bernard	75

		GIRLS
Kelly Eileen		62
Mole Ellen		63
Fagan Madge		65
Gainey Mary		65

YEAR 1927

		BOYS
Ferguson Robert		83
Greene Alfred		79
Greene Patrick		80
Meehan Joseph		82

		GIRLS
Stirrup Kathleen		66
Ferguson Mary		67

YEAR 1928

		BOYS
Byrne John		81
Clarke James		84
Golding James		85
Lynch Nicholas		87
O Hara Patrick		86

		GIRLS
Stirrup Ellen		68

YEAR 1929

		BOYS
Lanigan Gerard		88
Lennon Thomas		90
Lynch Patrick		93
Murray James		91
Plunket Joseph		89
Roche Thomas		92

	GIRLS
Meehan Kathleen	73
Mole Bridget	78
Murray Joan	75
Murray Kathleen	71
Murray Mary	72
Tobin Kathleen	77
Delaney Nora	76

School photograph of all the girls in the Junior School taken 1929.
From left to right are
Back row Kitty Newcombe, ?, Maureen Tobin, Annie Doran, Kitty Murray, Mary Byrne, Nelly Mole, Betty Gill.
Middle row Shelia Scully, Eileen Kelly, Theresa Roche, Essie Lovely, Mary Murray, ? Doran
Front row Patricia Clarke, Kathleen Stirrup, Rose Clarke, Theresa Tobin, ? Mole, Kathleen Tobin, Philomena Roche, Ita Murray, Joan Murray.
(Courtesy Shelia Kavanagh)

YEAR 1930

	BOYS
Cullen John	97
Cunningham John	94
Newcombe John Joseph	95

	GIRLS
Cunningham Eileen	79
Cunningham Margaret	81
Cunningham Mary	80

The school rolls for the intervening years of 1931 to 1936 are unfortunately missing. The full school population for the year 1936 are entered below, 34 pupils in all.

YEAR 1936

	BOYS
Barton Michael	115
Byrne Thomas	108
Dempsey Timothy	113
Dennis George	117
Donnelly Maurice	109
Doyle Desmond	100
Dunne William	114
Flood James	111
Gill Patrick	107
Greene Kevin	99
Newcombe Thomas	104
Plunket John	106

	GIRLS
Byrne Annie Teresa	96
Byrne Julia	97
Byrne Mary	74
Byrne Philomena	88
Byrne Rita	98
Carroll Una	108
Dempsey Elizabeth	106
Dennis Annie	105
Doran Annie	84

Doran Emily	92
Flood Theresa	104
Gill Elizabeth	93
Jenkinson Mary	90
Lyons Maureen	107
Lyons Olivia	103
Molloy Mary	99
Newcombe Kathleen	94
O Neill Agnes	100
O Neill Alice	101
Roche Philomena	91
Scariff Eileen	107
Tobin Teresa	86

YEAR 1937

YEAR 1938

The years 1937 and 1938 saw only three girls enrolled and two boys.

YEAR 1939

	BOYS
Newcombe Patrick	120

	GIRLS
Dunne Carmel	113
Lanigan Mary	112
McDermott Maureen	115
McDermott Patricia	116
Plunkett Kathleen	117
Webb Sylvia	114

YEAR 1940

	BOYS
Lynn Trevor	118
McDermott John	121
McDermott Joseph	122

	GIRLS
McCormack Pauline	120
Poole Madge	119

In the early forties a directive from the Department of Education instructed all primary school teachers to record the pupils name in their native tongue of Irish.

Lower Road School photograph around the year of 1939. From left to right are Back row ?, ?, ?, Paddy Tobin, ?, Tommy Byrne, John Gill, ?, ?, ? Dunne Middle row Mary Byrne, Philomena Roche, Brigid Byrne, Kitty Newcombe, Emily Doran, Betty Gill, Joan Murray Front row Alice O Neill, Una Carroll, Letty Dempsey, Rita Byrne, Roseleen Plunkett, Kathleen Plunkett, ?, Mary Lanigan, Sylvia Webb, ?, ?. (Courtesy Shelia Kavanagh)

YEAR 1941

	BOYS
Poole Feardorca	123
O Fearagail Sean	124

	GIRLS
Lynn Patricia	121
Donnelly Maire	123
West Mairin	124
Buggle Kathleen	122

YEAR 1942

	BOYS
Carroll Thomas	127
O Neill Patrick	126
Curry Joseph	125
	GIRLS
Buggle Marian	125
Donnelly Anne	126
McDermot Nuala	127

YEAR 1943

	BOYS
O Naidoig Eamon	128
	GIRLS
Buggle Nuala	129
Dunne Mairead	128

YEAR 1944

	BOYS
Buggle Matthew	131
Poole John	129
Fagan Sean	130
Curry Patrick	131
	GIRLS
McDermott Kathleen	130

YEAR 1945

YEAR 1946

There were no children enrolled during the years 1945 and 1946. This was the start of the decline of pupil numbers. The fall off in numbers would last for twenty years.

YEAR 1947

	BOYS
Buggle Michael	137
Martin Brian	134
McCorcaig Brian	136
Somers Luke	135

	GIRLS
Somers Betty	137
Carty Rose	135
Buggle Phillis	138

YEAR 1948

	BOYS
Baker Noel	140
Baker Patrick	141
Foy Noel	138
Kelly Sean	139

YEAR 1949

	BOYS
Martin Raymond	144
Murphy Dermot	142
Somers Eamonn	143
Vaughan Joseph	142

	GIRLS
Lyons Marie	139

YEAR 1950

	BOYS
Clifford Patrick	145

	GIRLS
Baker Aine	140

YEAR 1951

	BOYS
Ballisty Peter	146

	GIRLS
Buggle Olive	144
Dunne Florence	141
Greene Brid	142
Ryan Patricia	143

YEAR 1952

	BOYS
Telford Thomas	147

	GIRLS
Martin Irene	146
Telford Peggy	145

YEAR 1953

	BOYS
Baker Oliver	149
Dunne Liam	150
Scully Thomas	151
Somers Patrick	148

	GIRLS
Kavanagh Marie	147

Lower Road School with Ms. Emily O'Brien as Principal. Ms. O Brien became Principal in 1947 so this photograph probably dates from around 1952. From left to right in the back row are: Matthew Buggle, Patsy Clifford and Tom Carroll. The partly hidden child is unknown and the two girls are thought to be Phillis Buggle and Eileen Somers. First in the middle row is Luke Somers, the next girl is unknown, Emily O'Brien, unknown girl and Irene Martin. The front row has Eammon Somers, Derry Murphy and Michael Buggle.
(Courtesy Eileen Troy)

YEAR 1954

BOYS

Coyne Martin	167
Martin Seamus	155
Telford Sean	154
Thornton Alice	148
Thornton Christopher	152
Thornton Robert	153

GIRLS

Bardon Eileen	149
Coyne Maureen	151
Foy Marie	150

YEAR 1955

	BOYS
Kavanagh Chris	152
Moore Michael	156

	GIRLS
Foy Angela	153

YEAR 1956

	BOYS
Coyne Phillip	157
Martin Peter	158

YEAR 1957

	BOYS
Clarke Paul	159
Ellis Gerard	162
Hands Noel	160
Troy Patrick	161

	GIRLS
Troy Helen	154

YEAR 1958

	BOYS
Coyne Eamonn	164
Smith Jimmy	163

	GIRLS
Dunne Maria	155
Quigley Teresa	156

Back Row, Seamus Martin, Eileen Bardon, Raymond Martin, Maria Dunne, Ms. Emily O'Brien, Bridie Fagan
Front Row, Irene Martin, Helen Troy, Peter Martin, Patrick Troy, Tommy Scully, Noel Hands, Gerry Ellis, and Martin Moore. The home of Gerry Ellis can be seen on the hillside while a rose bush covers the gable end of Jack Scarrifs house.

YEAR 1959

	BOYS
Crefin Thomas	165
Troy Denis	166

	GIRLS
Lanigan Bernie	157
Lanigan Geraldine	158

YEAR 1960

	BOYS
Conroy Anthony	161
Conroy Martin	170
Malone Noel	172
Conroy Alan	168
Conroy Patrick	169

The pupils of the Lower Road School in the late fifties. From left to right are Back row Bridie Fagan, Irene Martin, Eileen Bardon, Noel Hands, Maria Dunne, Thomas Scully, Seamus Martin, Ms. Emily O'Brien. Front row Paul Clarke, Phillip Coyne, Helen Troy, Martin Coyne, Patrick Troy, Michael Moore, Peter Martin.
(Courtesy Eileen Troy)

YEAR 1961

	GIRLS
O Rourke Marie	159
Troy Catherine	160

YEAR 1962

	BOYS
Fortune Eilis	161

YEAR 1963

	GIRLS
O Rourke Rita	163
Russell Fiona	164

YEAR 1964

	BOYS
Brown Desmond	180
Byrne Bernard	174
Russell Pauric	179
Troy Ciarin	173
O Rourke Alan	178
O Rourke Ralph	177
Tone Matthew	175
Tone Frank	176
	GIRLS
Higgins Gwen	166
Tone Ita	165

YEAR 1965

	BOYS
Troy Maurice	181
	GIRLS
Brown Maria	167

YEAR 1966

	BOYS
Byrne Michael	183
Comiskey Joseph	186
Higgins John	182
Lanigan Martin	184
	GIRLS
Comiskey Siobhain	171
Brown Patricia	170
O Rourke Stella	169
O Rourke Una	168
Russell Paula	172
Troy John	185

YEAR 1967

	BOYS
Convery Martin	187

	GIRLS
Fagan Brenda	173

YEAR 1968

	GIRLS
Convery Philomena	178
Higgins Angela	174
Lanigan Anne	177

YEAR 1969

	BOYS
Troy James	188
Murphy Derek	189
Fagan Larry	190
Martin John	191

	GIRLS
Higgins Margaret	176
Martin Siobhain	183
Tobin Ellen	181
Murphy Sharon	179
Martin Elizabeth	180

YEAR 1970

	BOYS
Murphy Trevor	192

	GIRLS
Comiskey Derbhla	182
Tobin Anne	184

The last two children to enroll in the school were Anne Tobin with a school number of 184 and Trevor Murphy with a registered number of 192.

PATRICK TROY

The final photograph of the school children in the Lower Road School taken in 1968 with the Principal Ms. Emily O'Brien.
Back row Gwen Higgins, Lucy O Rourke, Rita O Rourke, Ciaran Troy, Geraldine Lanigan, Fiona Russell, Denis Troy, Bernard Byrne, Bernadette Lanigan, Ita Tone, Joseph Comiskey, Martin Lanigan, Maria O Rourke, Susan Comiskey, Catherine Troy.
Front row Angela Higgins, Michael Byrne, James Troy, Brendan Fagan, Martin Convery, Philomena Convery, Ms. Emily O'Brien Principal, Pauric Russell, Patricia Byrne, Maurice Troy, Stella O Rourke, John Troy, Paula Russell, John Higgins.
(Courtesy Eileen Troy)

Chapter 18

ATTENDANCE

In 1904 there were 68 pupils attending the old school beside the Strawberry Hall in what must have been very cramped conditions. The available seating space in the one-room school added up to sixty feet. So in essence sixty children would have one-foot upon which to sit. Obesity was not an issue in the early twentieth century! Perhaps it was a case of 'first up best dressed' and sitting on the floor, probably dirt, was the last option. Forty children transferred to the new school and the numbers rose to sixty between the years 1912 and 1914. Seventy-eight percent attendance was recorded in the school rolls at this period in time.

By 1926 there were sixty-five pupils on the register. This appears to have been the maximum number ever to attend the school and in 1935, a mere nine years later, the number had dropped to thirty-three. Reasons for the fall in number are varied and can only be surmised. Birth rates go in cycles, so peaks and troughs are normal, but external influences may have had an effect.

Perhaps the First World War, which ended in 1919 with a massive loss of young men in England and Europe, may have offered opportunities for employment abroad. Men left Ireland to join the British army during both wars, some never to return again. The formation of the Labour Trade Unions under Jim Larkin in 1913 and the Great Lockout, which lasted eight months, certainly gave rise to men enlisting. Coupled with this is the fact that Ireland had gained Independence from Britain in 1922 and a Trade War was in place between the two countries. The Trade War effected the agricultural output and production with heavy tariffs. This was Ireland's main source of income and also the income for the people of the Strawberry Beds. Whether any of the above influences had any effect on the population of the Strawberry Beds is not known, but the school attendance dropped by half in just nine years.

Boys were most likely not to feature in the fifth or sixth standard. Looking at the rolls it is predominantly girls at this level of educational standard. It is thought that boys would become employed in manual occupations to generate income for the family or they may not have enjoyed their studies as much as the girls and simply left their schooling. Some boys, according to a past pupil of the thirties, became too strong for the female teachers and were sent to a male teacher, Daniel O'Leary, in Castleknock Primary School, to 'put manners on them'. This would be a drastic measure because it would deplete the numbers of the Lower Road School while enhancing that of Castleknock Primary School. Boys did not feature in the top grades until the nineteen fifties and sixties.

From 1939 to 1943 the numbers dropped further to the mid-twenties. By 1947, just post war, only high teens were recorded to be in attendance at the school. In the year 1966 there were only twelve pupils on the record with ninety percent attendance. This is the lowest number of children ever to be registered at the school. A pupil's absence could hardly go unnoticed and in essence this was a privileged and private education from Ms. Emily O'Brien and the educational standard was high. Ms. Emily O'Brien retired in 1968, ironically two years later the numbers began to rise again. Three years later, 1971, there were thirty-one pupils registered in the school, a threefold increase, with further growth predicted.

School inspectors visited regularly to examine educational standards and to ensure good governance in the school. The teacher was responsible for the expenditure and budget for the school as well as teaching. All roles were also subjected to scrutiny. The National School Board, the school patron, or the Department of Education in later years, frequently required reports. Mrs. Mary Taaffe SAO (School Attendance Officer) was the Inspector on record from 1904 to 1926. There are many recordings of her visits in her twenty-two years. The school principal would inform the inspector of any child absent from school without adequate explanation. Mrs. Taaffe would then call to the family to investigate the circumstances of the absence. Mrs. Taaffe would have known the families in the Strawberry Beds quite well and certainly had a role in the transfer of the schools.

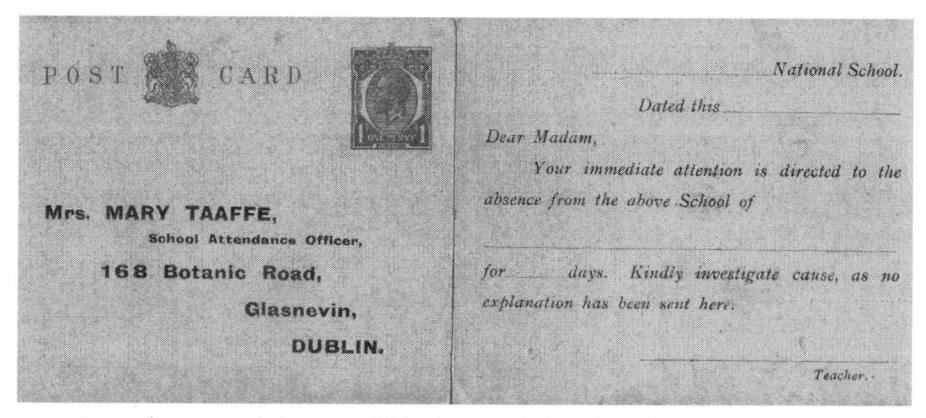

Attendance card that would be forwarded to the school inspector for investigation.

In 1933 Mr. Thomas O'Neill was the inspector appointed to replace Mrs. Taaffe. The school, up to 1946, still retained two-teacher status, despite the number of pupils, and there are several entries in the rolls of his visits. Thereafter, school inspections from the Department of Education Inspectors became less frequent. Perhaps they concentrated on the larger schools in the parish with the knowledge that good governance had always existed in the Lower Road School. The priests in the parish overseeing the schools often carried out visits and the Catechism became the primary subject of examination. Perhaps this was because of their familiarity in that subject. The monthly salary for a teacher in 1939, was twenty pounds for the principal and ten pounds for the assistant. By 1956 the principal salary had risen to sixty-four pounds per month.

****

Chapter 19
THE LOWER ROAD SCHOOL CLOSES

Following the formation of the Free State and the Department of Education, legislation was enacted in 1929 (Amalgamation of Schools Act) (ref), which deemed that forty pupils was the minimum number for a school to remain viable with two teachers. When the legislation was drafted, the Lower Road School had more than sixty pupils registered, so it was not in any danger of closure. However, demographics in Ireland were changing, there was internal migration to the larger cities, and emigration to other countries. This shift in populations would effect the number of children going to the local schools. Motorised transport was becoming more common, so the clause in the Irish Educational Act 1892. referring to the two-mile radius between school and home was becoming redundant. As these changes continued, more and more schools would suffer a fall in their numbers and the forties and fifties were particularly severe in this context. With a fall in pupil density the status of a one teacher school was determined and amalgamation became inevitable. The Lower Road School fell into this category around 1947.

Between 1967 and 1971 correspondence between the School Committee for the retention of the Lower Road School and the Department of Education was plentiful. The Department initially proposed that the school children would be sent to Clonsilla School, an imposing two-storey building built in 1853. There were many objections to this suggestion. Firstly the school was in a dilapidated condition and was certainly in a poorer state that the Lower Road School. The Clonsilla School was an older building by nearly fifty years and was under the treat of closure itself. The Lower Road School was maintained and repaired by local men when required. It was in a reasonable state of repair. Furthermore, children attended the Lower Road School from the Knockmaroon end of the road; the distance they would now have to travel, if going to Clonsilla, was increased by two to three miles on foot, as there was no bus service that was convenient. The school in Clonsilla did close in 1968, ending this suggestion. Further proposals made by the Department to educate the children in Lucan or Chapelizod (other parishes) were considered to be unacceptable and against the best interests of the children. The children would possibly have been divided up along a regional basis; that is those living closest to Lucan would attend the primary school there while the remainder would go to Chapelizod.

Finally, agreement was reached and a transfer to St. Bridget's School in Castleknock was accepted but only when the new proposed school was built. The existing primary school (St. Bridget's) was also in poor condition. It was situated on the main road from Castleknock to Blanchardstown. It had been built in 1867, thirty years earlier than the Lower Road School, but after one hundred years of tuition it had served its purpose and was worn out. It was to this school that some boys were sent when they became 'too strong' for the female teachers in the Lower Road School. A letter written by the then Minister of Education, Donnacha O'Malley, on the 8th March 1968 to my father agreed that the children of the Lower Road School would only be transferred on completion of the new school building. This is possibly the last official letter the minister signed for he died two days later on Sunday 10th March 1968.

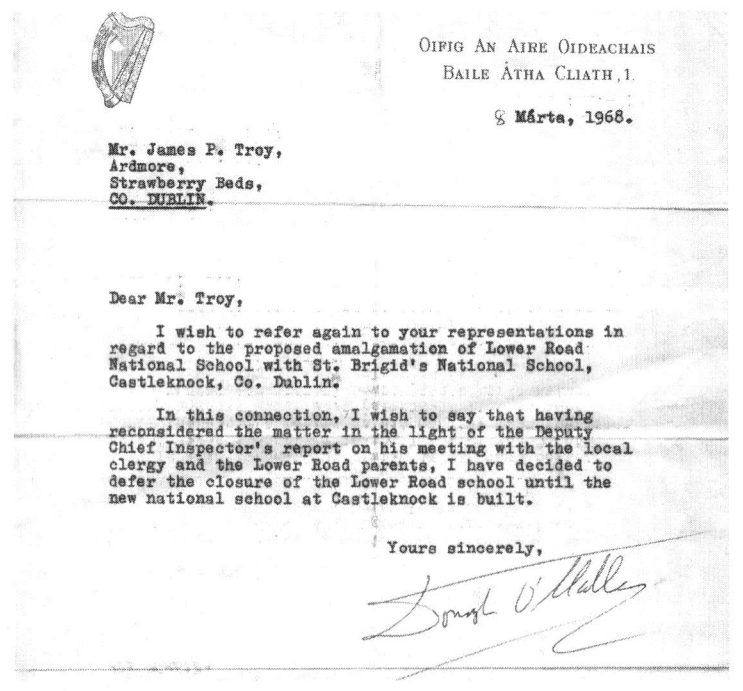

Letter from the Minister of Education, Donnacha O Malley, written in March 1968 agreeing to remove the treat of imminent closure of the Lower Road School until a new modern school was built in Castleknock.
(Courtesy Eileen Troy)

The following photographs were taken at the retirement presentation held in the schoolhouse on July 19th 1968 for the Lower Road School principal, Ms. Emily O'Brien, after twenty-two years of service to the children.

Ms. Emily O'Brien receives a gift from Mr. Kevin Boland, Minister for Local Government.

Ms. O Brien acknowledges the thanks from the community.
Seated at the table are, left to right,
Father O Brien, brother of Emily O'Brien, Mr. J Moriarity Department of Education, and Ms. Emily O'Brien retired principal, James Troy BA. Chairman, and Mr. Kevin Boland, Minister for Local Government.
(Courtesy Eileen Troy)

*Past and present pupils singing at the presentation for Ms. Emily O'Brien.
(Courtesy Eileen Troy)*

*An appreciation of her teaching effort and years of contribution was
acknowledged by all the community. There were many past pupils and parents
at the final presentation to their tutor and mentor.
(Courtesy Eileen Troy)*

The newly appointed school principal, Ms. Therese Beirne, was greeted to the post with a reception in the schoolhouse in 1970.

The final teacher of the Lower Road School Ms. Therese Beirne receiving a presentation from my father. Father Crowe was the Parish Priest and patron to the school at the time of the school closure.
(Courtesy Eileen Troy)

Ms. Therese Beirne the new principal, Father Morgan Crowe Parish Priest, Mrs. Joan Lanigan, James Troy and Ms. Emily O'Brien, the retired principal, at the presentation to Ms. Beirne.
(Courtesy Eileen Troy)

Welcoming and parting gifts were presented on the day Ms. Beirne was appointed principal of the Lower Road School. Mrs Lily Martin and Paula Russell look on as a gift is presented to Ms. Emily O'Brien.
(Courtesy Eileen Troy)

Chapter 20
THE COMMUNITY CENTRE

With the closure of the school the residents of the Strawberry Beds, through the community committee, approached Father Crowe, parish priest in Blanchardstown, seeking the building for use as a community centre. The building had been an integral part of the Lower Road for all of its existence. On many occasions money had been raised from the community to upgrade or maintain the building when it was in use as a school. This request was granted and so began a new phase of activity on the road.

The main aim of the centre and the elected committee was to concentrate on the needs of the older residents, the youth and the local people of the Lower Road. This new community spirit and committee was a follow-on from the Strawberry Beds Improvement Association of the 1950s. Many of the committee members of the original committee would now serve on the Strawberry Beds Community Centre Committee, nearly twenty years later.

The project was a community effort, so over the next twenty-five years men and women gave their time and effort in maintenance, construction, painting, cleaning, and exercising appropriate governance of the building. Additional rooms for catering were constructed, as were suitable toilets and a sewerage system. During the construction of the toilets local men, under the guidance of Peter Martin, dug a trench from the main sewerage line in the middle of the field opposite the school to the roadside. This was a deep trench and took significant effort with pick and shovel. Unfortunately, when the roadside was reached an already existing pipe was discovered. This branch had been put in place when the main line was being set down in 1947. The men realised that all their hard work for many weeks had been wasted. Still they continued with the original task of having proper sanitation in the hall. New floors were laid as the old planks were worn by the passage of pupils. Loans were raised for the various projects and paid off promptly and this rectitude was commended by Father Crowe.

The centre became the focus of the Lower Road. In December 1968 the first Old Folks Christmas party was held. Preparation would be intense for weeks beforehand as all the food was cooked and prepared by the women on the road. The prepared food would then be brought to the centre on the night of the function. Music was supplied by a local band or entertainers. A census of the elderly and youth was held prior to invitations going out, lest anyone be forgotten. Initially the numbers locally were adequate. However, with the passage of time, the elderly residents became fewer and the boundaries grew. Tentative association with the Strawberry Beds was all that was necessary to be invited to the parties. One tragic night, at an Old Folks Christmas party, Owen Scully passed away as he attended the dinner. The Scully family were one of the oldest families on the road, dating back to before 1843 where they are recorded in Griffiths Valuation. Thankfully there were no other tragic nights.

The youths would serve the meals at the Christmas dinner and presents were given to all the elderly. Many old acquaintances would revisit stories of the past while everyone danced, drank, chatted and enjoyed the night. The Old Folks Christmas party was held in high regard by all who knew about it. Nearly forty years later this practice still continues, although no longer in the Old School House, the servers now being served.

The first Old Folks Christmas party took place in the school house in 1968. The following photographs taken on the night show the enthusiasm and fun that both servers and served had on these special occasions.

Jack Scariff who lived beside the schoolhouse is served his dinner by Gretta Higgins. (Courtesy Eileen Troy)

Christmas dinner is served. Mrs White and Gertie Murray are in the foreground, while Delia Murphy and Mrs Cooper are also seen.

Miss Pilgrim and Nell Doyle. Nell Doyle used light the fire in the school for the children every morning. The rooms were always warm when the children would arrive at nine o clock.

Mrs. Rose Plunkett with Ms. Byrne and Ms. Peg Clarke in the background. Shelia Doyle pours the tea for Mrs. Plunkett.

Dancing always followed the dinner. Detta Russell is in the foreground.

Listening to the children singing after the Christmas dinner was finished. Singing was, of course, taught in the school with a preference for Irish songs.

The room was crowded with the partygoers and the servers. Elderly residents might only meet once a year and that meeting would be at the Christmas party.
(Courtesy Eileen Troy)

The centre was also used for dances, parties, art exhibitions, historical exhibitions, auctions, flower shows, committee meetings and private functions. The hall could be requested for these purposes. Application was made to the committee for the facility of the hall giving all the details of the function. Security and cleaning up after the event were issues of constant concern to the committee. Irish dancing was held in the hall, lessons in ballroom dancing were given and these lessons also included the tango, salsa and learning how to jive. Unfortunately the dance teacher, Mrs. Roche, broke her leg soon after the start of the dancing tuition and this activity ceased, but the Irish dancing classes continued for many years.

Every friday night discos were held for the appropriate age group. Organisation of these by the youth was impressive with the procuring of the latest records in the charts, a disc jockey, suitable lighting, soft drinks only! and a supervisor to ensure all was in order. These discos were self-governed and while teenagers might travel to the venue, there was never any trouble. These discos became very popular because they were friendly, fun, and had great quality music. A big contingent from Clonsilla could be expected as these lads and lassies mixed together anyway. Strangers were few however, because all had to get home after the dance and this was generally on foot. The committee always stipulated that a member close the premises after the function, which could be two o'clock in the morning.

At Christmas time parties for the children would be organized, at which time Santa would visit. It always took place on a Sunday afternoon, the week following the Old Folks party. A local man would be inveigled to act as Santa although I believe on one occasion a woman acted the part as no suitable men could be found. The female Santa was Nora Cummiskey I believe. The party was an entirely local venture; even Santa lived somewhere on the Strawberry Beds. Food, cakes, beverages, presents from Santa, were provided by the community for the children. Even those children who no longer believed still came to the party because it was an entertaining day for the children and indeed the parents. Some mothers would sit on Santa's knee, ask for a present and kiss him, while having their photograph taken.

During wintertime the social centre was used for games. Billiard tablets were made locally by the skilled men, and provided excellent entertainment. Table tennis was played, push penny, chess, card games (whist and twenty-fives), draughts, all with a little music and the open fire in the background. This was the commitment to the youth of the area, made by the visionaries of the community centre. The idea was to provide a centre with youth activities, but it was such a success and attraction that both adults and teenagers competed on these evenings in all the events. Serious competitions were held just before Christmas to determine the best in billiards, table tennis or chess. The adults gave little quarter to the youth at this stage. Draws were made and broadcast locally in these knockout tournaments. Adults, and this means the men, generally dominated in the billiards while table tennis was the domain of the youth. Whole evenings would be spent in this fashion with the ending time often after midnight.

A Strawberry Fair was suggested in the summer of 1968. The first fair took place in the community hall. This arrangement lasted for three years, and in 1971 because of its growing success, it was held in the field opposite the centre, the field owned by my uncle Pakie. The Blanchardstown band played at the Strawberry Fair that year; their seats were the straw bales.

The fair was in keeping with the long tradition of selling strawberries and cream to travellers and day-trippers who journeyed out from the city. The first Sunday of July was picked as the most appropriate day. The reason for this was that the strawberries ripened at this time. Strawberries were picked locally for consumption; volunteers were sought to do the picking, but refusing was never an option. Stalls were set up for selling bric and brak, for games, for cake sales, a wheel of fortune and, of course, strawberries and cream served with tea and scones. Such was the growing success of the fair that after a few years it extended to the first two Sundays in July. This presented a further problem for the Garda in that the traffic would back up on the road despite the availability of car parking in the fields close by.

Many traditional games were resurrected, the sheaf-of-wheat, horseshoe throwing, pony rides, and wellington boot throwing. A Lord Mayor was nominated to oversee the day, meet guests, and lend authority to the proceedings. A tug-of-war was generally held and teams were picked to represent the public houses. The teams pulled for a trophy, a perpetual cup, which was presented by the Lord Mayor to the winning establishment. Wren verses Strawberry or Strawberry verses the Anglers, men verses men, women verses women. No one ever questioned the players on the team, why a man pulled for the Strawberry one year and the Wren the following year. Many women didn't drink at the time but could end up representing a public house. Indeed, anyone looking strong and available (mostly) would get called up. A few strong farmers generally decided the issue so enlisting them was a priority. The same farmers, used to tossing bales onto trailers, would invariably win the sheaf-of-wheat competition as well and take home the bottle of whiskey, which was always the prize.

The Strawberry Beds

It never rained on the Strawberry Fair, throughout the twenty-five years of its existence, or so it seemed.

The following photographs were taken when the Strawberry Fair was in its infancy. At this time the proceedings took place in the field opposite the community hall.

*A Cheile Band plays at the Strawberry Fair in 1974.
The Old School House is in the background.
(Courtesy Michael Daly)*

*The Ladies Tug-of-War competition. Mary Lynam, in front takes the strain
while Nora Comiskey, Joan Murphy are also on the rope.
This was a lightweight team by all appearances.
(Courtesy Michael Daly)*

The Men's Tug- of War, wearing runners was never a good option in this sport.
Colm Condron is the anchorman on this occasion.
(Courtesy Michael Daly)

The following photographs were taken when the Strawberry Fair moved from the field opposite the community hall, to land donated to the community by Mr. T. K. Laidlaw. The first year the fair took place in this field was 1977. The fair could now expand in its own, new surroundings.

The day of the Strawberry Fair in July 1986.
Mary Lynam, Peter Martin, Gretta Higgins and Pat Mannion.
(Courtesy Michael Daly)

*Shelia Doyle, Kathleen Byrne and Mary Skelly prepare the strawberries and cream.
Kathleen Byrne seems to be in great spirits.
(Courtesy Michael Daly)*

Shay Healy with a film crew chats with Kathleen Byrne outside the large tent that was always erected to protect the strawberries in case of rain, which never appeared to arrive.
(Courtesy Michael Daly)

Jimmy Troy and Caoilfionn Skelly as 'Honeymoon' couple at the Strawberry Fair in the Millennium year of 1988.
(Courtesy Michael Daly)

*Lillie Martin, Jimmy Troy and Caoilfionn Skelly arrive in style at the Strawberry Fair.
(Courtesy Michael Daly)*

*The late Brian Lenihan with Mary Eustace sitting in the sunshine at the Pony Bingo stall. The wire fencing in the background was erected to enclose a tennis court. The court was newer used to any extent.
(Courtesy Michael Daly)*

*Pony rides were a favourite for the small children.
Here Geraldine Lanigan leads the trail.
(Courtesy Michael Daly)*

*Celebrations in the Wrens Nest pub following the Strawberry Fair in the
Millennium year of 1988.*

A strong farmer generally won the Sheaf of Wheat competition at the end of the day. The weight was generally rushes or a heavy bag of straw. The crossbar was raised until only the finest, fittest and strongest could throw the sheaf over the top bar.
(Courtesy Michael Daly)

Chapter 21

THE SPORTS FIELD

Around 1975 representation was made to Mr. T. K. Laidlaw of Somerton to see if he would be agreeable to granting a field to the local community. The field in question lay at the bottom of the Rugged Lane and in some respects was distant from the main farm at Somerton. This was a four-acre plot of land that the West brothers used to lease from Somerton at the start of the 1900s and used for market gardening. Mr. T. K. Laidlaw granted the request and he also undertook to level and re-seed the field at his own expense, prior to its transfer to the community. Mr. Laidlaw did make a special request that a tennis court be laid in the field. Unfortunately while the court was laid down, it saw limited use.

The field was never formally named. It became known as the Community Field, the Sports Field or simply the Field. Initially it was used extensively; the annual Strawberry Fair now had a permanent home. Football competitions, Gaelic and Soccer, in the form of a weekend blitz were held there. An annual 7-a-side soccer competition was held every summer and cricket was played there on one occasion. It became home for the Strawberry Beds XI, an under-eleven soccer team made up of boys from the Lower Road. This team won its league in its first year under the tutelage of Peter Martin and narrowly missed success the second year. Unfortunately the team folded after the two years in the spotlight. However, its success could not go unnoticed.

In due course part of the field was set aside for use as a Pitch and Putt course. This new development was a wonderful success, and the local residents used it extensively. Budding golfers appeared from nowhere and with no little talent were soon masters at the game. The course became known as a very difficult one, running as it did alongside the river. A stray golf shot landing in the river and the ball was gone forever. Established Pitch and Putt teams from around the area would compete with the Strawberry Beds Pitch and Putt team, which was not without talent, and often went home defeated. A return match would then be arranged away from home. Some children had never witnessed their parents skill and competitive side and were impressed with their successes.

Mr. T.K. Laidlaw plants a tree in the field following its granting to the community. Mr. Peter Melia and Mr. Peter Martin, wearing the Lord Mayor's Chain of Office, are assisting in the planting.
(Courtesy Mary Eustace)

Christmas morning would see several men playing, possibly to stay out of the kitchens! Johnny O'Rourke, Ger Lanigan and Ollie Cummiskey would always meet for an early golf outing on the 25th of December. Records and scores for the year were kept and the best golfer of the year would be awarded the Laidlaw Cup. Mr. Peter Melia maintained the Pitch and Putt course. Peter was skilled at this chore as he worked in the Hermitage Golf Course just across the river. He rowed to work on a daily basis and a heavy flood on the river was no obstacle to Peter. Unfortunately after Peter Melia died in 1997 the course fell into disrepair. Without maintenance it became more and more feral and the golfing ceased.

Photographs of the inaugural day are shown below. The pitch and putt course was developed over two years with greens being laid down, tee boxes, bunkers, along with the necessary landscaping. The trees that were planted in 1986 are now nearly fully grown.

Peter Melia places a tee box marker while Mary Eustace, Winnie Barron, Eileen Troy, Marguerite Byrne, Stella O Rourke, Wally Barron, Jack Lovely, Ger Lanigan, Susan Comiskey and Ann Lanigan look on.
Mr. Laidlaw has his back to the camera.
(Courtesy Mary Eustace)

Ronnie Condron, Peter Martin and Jimmy Smith pose for the camera before they tee off. This photograph was taken in 1986.
(Courtesy Mary Eustace)

Mrs. May Telford, Jack Lovely, Essie Lovely and Peter Melia.
(Courtesy Mary Eustace)

*Jimmy Smith demonstrates his technique as he tees off
while Peter Martin and Ronnie Condron look on.
(Courtesy Mary Eustace)*

*The turn of Ronnie Condron to tee off under the watchful eye of her husband Paddy.
(Courtesy Mary Eustace)*

*Jack Lovely rests at the clubhouse while Ann Lanigan, Stella O Rourke, Pat Kane, and Eileen Troy wait to play.
(Courtesy Mary Eustace)*

Ger Lanigan plays onto the third green. The green cover in the background was to prevent the drive going onto the road!
(Courtesy Mary Eustace)

Maria O Rourke, Johnny O Rourke, Dervla Comiskey and Mary Eustace pose for the camera before they start their round of golf.
(Courtesy Mary Eustace)

Mary Eustace and Kit Martin check the scores. .
(Courtesy Mary Eustace)

Chapter 22
ALL THINGS CHANGE

The Strawberry Beds, like so many other areas, went through changes that would radically change a way of life. Outside forces often dictate these changes; a change in government policy, a global crisis, or a fortuitous windfall can have profound effects. Whether it is a fishing village, a mining town, or a farming area, all communities are susceptible to the winds of change.

The Strawberry Beds appears to have been stable from the nineteen century for a period of about eighty to ninety years. Prior to this large estates owned the land and tenant farmers worked the land. With the Land Act legislation of 1890s, tenants could purchase their farms freehold. Purchasing the land, which was done with enthusiasm, required finance. Those most able to afford the land price would succeed in the purchase. For this reason new families moved to the Strawberry Beds, while sitting tenant farmers, already in leasehold, would, if able, purchase their few acres. Hence, the area would now comprise of a stable community of new and old residents living and working side by side.

Agriculture was the mainstay of the community, the people were self-sufficient, employment was available and local markets, schools and shopping were within easy reach. But changes were underway from the start of the twentieth century; the First World War was on the horizon. The element of service to the large houses would drop considerably and with international political changes, the outlook of the Irish people became more self assured. Ireland was to become an independent state. This new political state would also impose its own burdens.

As the State developed, motorised transport became commonplace, electricity was generated and supplied nationwide, a national water supply was developed, the telephone, following its invention, would slowly and indeed very slowly become available all over the country. All of these new services contributed to the changes that were taking place. Market gardening as a living was hard, demanding work and fewer and fewer families in the Strawberry Beds came to rely on it as a way of life. By the nineteen seventies and eighties no more than two families continued in market gardening as their sole means of income. The strawberry itself was no longer cultivated extensively for the Dublin market but some produce, flowers in particular, continued to be grown before the market gardening industry petered out.

The closure of the Lower Road School was a significant factor in the changing appearance of the Strawberry Beds. The education of the children had gone abroad; the children made new friends and acquaintances. The isolation of the Strawberry Beds was breached. The children were now bussed to school in the morning and back in the afternoon. The children in the new schools knew the pupils from the Lower Road School as the 'Valley Kids'. Perhaps this derogatory term was meant to convey the belief that the children were 'slow' in some sense. Nothing could be further from the truth as they all continued to excel in the new schools as they had done in the past.

Another factor in the changing community was the ending of the Strawberry Fair. This once acted as a great gathering for the people, it maintained the community spirit, and all wished to be involved. The charm of the golf in the community field also passed, although it had lasted over twenty years. The social centre was used less and less until it was barely in use at all. Eventually, following a decision by the committee, the community hall was returned to the parish. A belief that the Church would give part, or all, of the proceeds of any sale of the hall to the community was poorly founded. This is not a reflection on the committee as the community in general realised that the centre had little future with the changing times. The schoolhouse is now a private residence.

The Old School House.

The generation of children born in the sixties and seventies spent much more time away from the Strawberry Beds at work or at college. There was less work locally in any event. The Honda 50 facilitated the exodus of the youth. Small changes occurred that went unnoticed, but they were changes nonetheless. The closing of Tobin's shop, Mrs. Murray's shop, or May Weldon's shop, which used to sell ice cream in the summer, meant that people travelled a little further to shop. The postman got a car; this cannot be denied to the man, as on a bad day he would have to climb thirty-three hills to deliver the mail. Still, human contact was lost.

The delivery of bread from Boland's Bakery, George was the driver. He once used the bread van to carry a sick child (Irene Martin) to the Harcourt Street Hospital for an appendix operation. The delivery of groceries from Toolan's, meat from Collins or Giltraps in Lucan, coal from the Malone family, groceries from Findlaters were regular services on the road up to the eighties. One by one they disappeared. The milk rounds of Mr. Spendlove and Hughes Dairies also ended. Milk was delivered in glass bottles in the early morning hours and was left outside the gate only for the crows or magpies to pierce the lid and drink all the cream. Many a mother would ask the deliveryman to cover the bottles to thwart the early birds. They would also leave a note to change an order or leave money as payment. Honesty and trust was notable. On Friday evenings, men from the dairies would also visit to collect payment. Unfortunately it became unprofitable to continue all of these services and they all faded away over time.

The biggest loss with the ending of these services was the communication and community contact that disappeared. Mothers now had to travel to Dublin to purchase their groceries and carry the heavy bags down from the Luttrelstown bus. They would alight from the bus at the top of the Glen, Somerton Cross or at Porterstown and lug their loads down to the Strawberry Beds. The valley was eventually bisected by the M50, a section of motorway that circumnavigated the city of Dublin. Initially the residents of the Strawberry Beds tried to object to its construction, as it would destroy the beauty of the valley. At a residents meeting in the community centre, the late Mr. Brian Lenihan T.D. informed the locals and neighbours that objections were futile and that it was going to be constructed. By and large, its presence goes unnoticed. Noise is created from high winds or from heavy traffic with a continuous din. It is unsightly and certainly spoils the view of some of the houses built high up on the slopes. There was one tragic incident where a woman jumped from the bridge and died. The incident was documented as one of self-harm.

The motorway as it crosses the Strawberry Beds.

As mentioned above, after twenty-five years of wonderful activity the Strawberry Fair ended. The last Strawberry Fair took place in 1995. The day was brought to a close following an insurance claim where a visitor hurt their arm. The cost of the insurance cover the following year was prohibitive as the total amount of money made on the day was only sufficient to meet the expenses of the parties at Christmas and maintain the social centre. Efforts to revive the Strawberry Fair were attempted but they fell short of the halcyon days of the seventies, eighties and nineties. This was not the fault of the organisers or those with a renewed vision. The original organisers, after a quarter of a century of effort had tired and perhaps time had just moved on for the Strawberry Beds.

Small cottages situated on the roadside that once raised large families were demolished. Planning permission would be granted to build a new house on condition it replaced an existing house. New comers with financial resources sought permission for large houses to be built at the top of the hills with long avenues. Electric gates, some with barbed wire on top, and laurel hedging seal these new families into their properties. This was never the way of life of the Strawberry Beds. While flooding was no longer a worry for these new residents, they now became isolated from the community and its richest asset – its people.

Some of the typical cottages of the Strawberry Beds still remain but many have been demolished and used as sites for the building of larger houses high up on the hillsides.

The Strawberry Hall as it is today, while below is a photograph of the public house when owned by Eliza Williams at the start of the twentieth century.

Ms. Eliza Williams is standing with some customers outside the public house. The men in question are reported to be Royal Irish Constabulary, who had travelled out on bicycles to the Strawberry Beds. Note that some of the men are wearing gaiters to protect their trouser legs when cycling. Cycling was of course a common means of travel for those going to and from the Strawberry Beds. (Courtesy The Strawberry Hall)

Throughout this period, a giant ash tree has stood witness to all the changes that have taken place in the Strawberry Beds. The tree, which stands near to where the primary school used be, is thought to be over 150 years old. This tree was growing before the independence of the State; it would have shadowed the visit of Queen Victoria's cortège as it passed along the Lower Road to her visit to Luttrelstown Castle in 1900. It would have witnessed the purchasing of the land and farms from the large estates following the Land Act Legislation. Given its age now, it would have a sapling at the time Queen Victoria passed by on the road.

The giant ash has seen the selling of the strawberries and cream; seen the large houses change hands; and seen the deaths, births and marriages of the families on the road. It has seen the road itself evolve from a dusty or muddy towpath to a raceway in the early morning and late evening time. It has seen many floods, few droughts, some snow, lots of rain, and perhaps a little sunshine. The tree has thankfully seen few tragedies and few fatalities in its existence. It has seen the schooling of all the children as they passed beneath its leaves and branches to get their education in the primary schools and move on. It offered shelter from the rain for the same children. No one shelters beneath it now as so few walk the road anymore.

'Man has never made a tree.'

The greatest change to the Strawberry Beds came with the passing of legislation that allowed Dublin County Council to designate the Liffey Valley as an area for recreation and tourism under the Special Area Amenity Order. This Order would eventually ensure the end of families that lived for generations on the Lower Road.

Under the Order strict restrictions in planning meant that sons or daughters of farmers, market gardeners, publicans and long time residents could no longer build locally and were forced to purchase outside the Strawberry Beds. Property was always valuable in the Strawberry Beds and only those with substantial resources could buy the houses that became available on the road. Local people were unable to compete with the stronger purchasing power of outside wealth. There are now only seven families on the road that can claim to have an unbroken line to their ancestors of sixty years ago. Perhaps four have a direct line extending back to their ancestors of one hundred years ago. It is now believed that even the robin or the wren would have difficulty getting planning permission to build its nest in springtime.

The Liffey Valley, with its beauty, uniqueness and richness, has been in existence since the start of time. The people have always tended to the Valley as they farmed and cultivated the land. It is because of these farmers and gardeners that the Strawberry Beds became the attractive place it is to live in or to visit. By conferring on it the Special Amenity Area status with its stringent legislation the keepers and carers of the valley have been selectively excluded from their role as guardians. There was never any need for such legislation as strict adherence to normal planning legislation would have been adequate. The vision of the legislators has not been realised, as there are now fewer visitors to the area than in the sixties or seventies. There are fewer amenities and services available now for travelers to the Strawberry Beds.

****

Chapter 23

REFLECTIONS

There are many, many memories and stories of the Strawberry Beds. The people remember different incidents, accidents, tragedies, celebrations, marriages, births or deaths, or just plain stories. These stories, with time, often become fables without a shred of truth to back them up. This is of all part of community living. To have stories is one thing; to carry the story requires effort. Public houses are the centre of this art and storytelling is just part of Irish life. Rambling houses, where people would meet late in the evening and pass the time chatting, playing cards, or knitting, are now a distant memory, but would have been common in the past. It was an honour to have your house picked as the rambling house. The honour would pass to another home the following night. Popularity could also be a nuisance of course. Gertie Murray was a wonderful source of current news and would visit certain houses to chat and carry the news of the day. She would visit during the daytime, drink tea, and chat to the wives while the husbands were at work. Often she might start a rumour or pass on a snippet of gossip, 'Mrs. Jones is on the way again!', which could be entirely untrue but it could always grow legs. She had a great heart, never said a bad word about anyone, and used her rambles in exchange for company with other neighbours.

I have recounted some stories and memories here and hope that these few stories will stimulate the reader to correct or add to what has been written. Perhaps they have a totally different version to a tale - equally incorrect. All memories and stories need to be told, to be remembered, and included at a future date in another publication. Perhaps the reader could remember his or her own story for inclusion at a later date.

The murder of Lord Cavendish, Chief Secretary in Ireland, and Thomas Burke Under Secretary, by the Invincibles took place in the Phoenix Park in May 1882. It is thought that the perpetrators escaped along the Strawberry Beds after the deed had been executed. The planning and meeting for the murder may have taken place in the Strawberry Beds. A large barn that lay between Higgins and Troys was thought to have been the meeting place prior to the murderous act and the horses used in the escape were stabled there. The River Liffey and valley was searched for the knives that were used in the murder. The use of knives, as opposed to guns, in the murder was considered particularly callous at the time. There have been other, more recent episodes of the police chasing criminals and offenders along the 'Beds' because the Lower Road could be used to escape a crime that was committed elsewhere. Car chases, with the ramming of the police cars happened from time to time and the fugitives even swam the river to escape their pursuers.

In 1960 University students from Trinity College, all in good spirits, late in the evening, were out driving along the Lower Road in a soft top Aston Martin car, which they drove through a small wooden gate into a field belonging to Johnny Plunkett. The small triangle-shaped field is at the junction between the Lower Road and the Rugged Lane. Nobody was injured in the crash and the revelers were actually laughing as they extracted themselves. The cause of their high spirits may just have been that – spirits. The car remained there for several days for all the locals to examine, parked as it was in Johnny Plunkett's lettuce patch.

In 1837, on the second of January, the trial of Peter Doyle took place on the charge of burglary and robbery. He was a resident of the Strawberry Beds, or the Lower Lucan Road, as it was described in the official Court transcript. The convict was transported to Australia. He was thirty-five years of age. The exact address, his occupation, whether he had a family or not, or who his people were, all remain a mystery.

The Wren's Nest public house dates back to 1588. A beam in the 'tap room' has the year 1588 burnt into it. The beam was uncovered during renovations and is the evidence needed to give the Wren's Nest public house the honour of being one of the oldest, if not the oldest, pub in the country still serving the public. The tap room, which got its name from the tapping of the barrels of porter, was the well-known sanctuary for talented musicians of all sorts. It was, and still is, a great venue for traditional music. The Dubliners played many times in the pub and they also posed for photographs for one of their albums on the Wren's Nest weir opposite the pub. Music would be played nearly every night of the week with different musicians, some talented and some not so talented. Frequently there might be two or three groups playing throughout the pub. Brendan Behan, the playwright and author, was a frequent visitor to the pub. Hugh Ennis (Hughie), the owner, had a love of classical and operatic music. While this type of music might not be the choice of the patrons, they would put up with this in the hope of getting extended drinking time. Occasionally as the night moved on, the patrons would move the hands of the clock back, to get more drinking time. When Hughie discovered this ploy all the revelers would be expelled, only to be back the following night.

*The Wrens Nest public house in the late 1800s.
The house in the background on the Silver Hill was home to the Ward family.
(Courtesy Michael Daly)*

Hugh Ennis had a donkey called Bessie that fell into a ditch on a Friday evening in wintertime. It became cast and couldn't get out. Locals were asked for assistance and many answered the call. Long discussions, much to Hughie's annoyance, took place in the pub as to how to save the donkey. Ropes, harnesses, oats and even tractors were considered. The task of getting the donkey out wasn't difficult of course, but it showed the concern that the local men had with their rapid response and the possibility of a drink or two! The baying of Bessie could be heard for miles around.

Christmas Day and Good Friday, the two days of temperance in the whole year, were days when men really needed a drink. They would walk slowly, very slowly, past the pubs on the road hoping to get a nod or signal from the pub that service was available. They would then sneak in and get the thirst off them. The Sparrow Doyle, one of two brothers who lived with their sister Nell at the bottom of Somerton Hill, would shelter beneath an ivy bush opposite the Wren's Nest and would wait for a sign. Annoyed wives would call the police, especially on Christmas Day, for the pubs to be raided to get the men home for the dinner. The men would run out the back, up the hill, through the nettles and briars and away home to avoid charges. Neither the public houses, nor the men were ever caught or charged. Sometimes the children would be sent to get their fathers home, not a pleasant experience for the child. The public houses on the Strawberry Beds had very strict rules when it came to underage drinking and women would only be served half pints of beer or stout as it was considered improper to serve full pints to female patrons. This practice continued up until the mid-eighties. This was the era of the Babycham, the Avocat, and the Sherry.

Many local people fished the river, as did others from abroad. Fishing rights, which were owned by the large estates, were never fully exercised on the section of river that runs through the Strawberry Beds. Frank Scully was a local fisherman who knew the river well. He could place the salmon as they rested in the rapids just below the weir before they continued upstream to eventually spawn. Frank was a great singer, a great voice always heard in the Wren's Nest, but salmon was his passion when they ran. The salmon season on the Liffey opens in January and Frank had great success with the rod. He also had a flat bottomed boat that he would row out to midstream and anchor it there. From there he could drift the fly beneath the overhanging trees where the salmon would lie. It was said that in the early fifties, one could shoot the salmon as they jumped the Wren's Nest weir, such was their numbers. Other species, such as perch, rudd, pike, roach, eels and elvers, were the fish caught by the amateurs. One man, certainly not an amateur, used to travel by motorbike, a gray 1950s Puch, to fish at the Wren's Nest weir. He never seemed to have any catch, but was always to be found on the bank. I don't know his name, but I remember he was a pleasant man to talk to and he gave little tips on fishing, a pastime I care little for.

Unfortunately there were some tragedies relating to the river. A man took his own life in the river back in the sixties. He had parked his car close to the Grand Lodge and it appears he entered the river at this point. His body was noticed about a mile downstream by some canoeists as it was caught in riverbank bushes. He had been missing for six weeks. The Fire Brigade and police were on hand to remove the body from the water at a point just opposite the bottom of the Rugged Lane.

More recently there has been two additional accidental drownings in the river. Both occurred at the Wren's Nest weir and both were girls. The girls were not local and would not have been familiar with the dangerous undercurrents that exist.

Two canoeists at Lucan Weir in the Liffey Descent of 1990. These were the days when helmets were not mandatory. The two heros are Collie Quinn and Fred Daly who appear to be enjoying themselves while another canoeist is in trouble in the background.
(Courtesy The Strawberry Hall)

One strange tale took place four years ago where a woman entered the River Liffey near Leixlip. She was a non-swimmer and the river was in heavy flood, although it was autumn. A local girl, at the Wren's Nest weir, saw the woman as she floated past. She had drifted three miles downstream at this stage being carried along in the flood. The girl informed the police and a full rescue operation took place with the Fire Brigade and an Air-Sea Rescue helicopter. The woman was eventually taken alive from the water at Palmerstown weir. Later it transpired that she was pushed into the river at Leixlip and was carried for five miles in flood waters, passed over four weirs, several rapids, and finally grabbed and hung onto a tree just above Palmerstown weir, where a canoeist saw her and went to her aid. This was a remarkable episode of survival for a non-swimmer.

In 1968 the Ward Union Hunt hunted a stag from the 'meet' in Dunboyne all the way to the Lower Road. The stag jumped into and swam across the river, as did some hounds and huntsmen. It happened at a point between Anna Liffey Mill and Lucan Bridge opposite the CPI (Concrete Products Ireland). The stag was 'put at bay' on the south bank and returned unharmed to end the hunt. This hunt was remembered for the chase, the speed, and the distance of the chase, which was over ten miles, and of course, the swimming of the river.

A house belonging to the Fagan family was carried away in a landslide in the early fifties. The house was situated on the steep banks of the Strawberry Beds between the motorway (M50) bridge and the Glen. Legend has it that it was Barney the sheep dog, who roused the house with his barking in the dead of night. The family arose and moved outside only to witness the house carried away in a landslide. The neighbours collected money and resources for the family until they were re-housed in Woodlands Cottage. In more recent years landslides have become more of a problem due to the construction of houses at the top of the hills. This disturbs the hill by allowing water to seep into the soil and form a slide plane. Thankfully they have only been minor.

In 1962 a cyclist in a road race, was killed on the Lower Road as they headed to a finish in the Phoenix Park. This accident took place at a bend near Woodlands Cottage when the race leader, John Dillon, trying to gain advantage, cut the corner. Tragically an oncoming car driven by a local man on his way to Lucan struck him. The failure of the lead-cars to warn motorists of the oncoming race would have contributed to the cyclist's death. The first cyclist to come onto the crash was Ian Gallagher of the Tealtain Club, who had also broken away from the peloton and was chasing down John Dillon. This tragedy is still remembered in cycling circles.

Another tragedy that happened was the death of Peter Proudfoot, who suffered an electrical shock while digging a trench. The accident happened in the nineteen sixties. The Proudfoot family had been living in the townland of Porterstown since the eighteenth century. Peter was born in 1911 according to the Census of 1911. He was one of seven children. My father was called to attend the scene of the tragedy, but Peter was not to recover.

Hay was made in the summer time in the fields that ran along the riverbank. This involved cocking or tramming the hay. Those with the 'know how' would pitch in and a fork was always left at the gate to entice help. Horse-drawn buck rakes were used to bring in the hay for the men to tram. Tractors were a sixties intervention and Lynam's had a Ferguson that did the job. One interesting field where hay was made was in Nash's field. This was on a hillside overlooking the river. This was not a field for tractors as it is a really steep hillside with a cliff style drop down to the road, the remnants of an old quarry. Finally, with all the hay made, the social aspect would prevail and all would adjourn to the pub where their payment was in beer.

THE STRAWBERRY BEDS

May Tobin lived in Somerton Cottage on Somerton lane. A kind, gentle woman who was always helpful in any way possible. She kept her cottage in pristine condition with the sweetest smelling rose bushes outside. This bouquet could be smelt from a distance. The roses were ancient and propagated from the 1800s. This cottage was the last thatched home in the Strawberry Beds. Mrs. Tobin worked for the Laidlaw family in Somerton in her earlier years. Members of the Laidlaw family would always make a point of calling in to visit when passing down the road. She always spoke most fondly of the three Laidlaw brothers, Thomas, Robert and David. She lived with her husband Joe in the cottage, who unfortunately died at home in the eighties. Joe Tobin passed away peacefully as he sat in his armchair beside the fire. His doctor attended him and his body was moved to Blanchardstown Hospital. Mrs. Tobin told me some time later that she would have liked to have had a wake for her husband in the cottage, but things happened so quickly it did not occur. But many, many locals paid their respects in visiting her cottage.

May Tobin with her dog Twink and Caroline Corballis (nee Laidlaw) in 1987. Caroline is showing her son James to Mrs. Tobin in the doorway of her cottage. (Courtesy Mrs. Caroline Corballis)

Mrs. Tobin lived next door to Mr. and Mrs. Horan. This lovely couple were equally friendly but they passed on in the nineteen seventies. Their small house fell into disrepair and was knocked down to make way for a new dwelling. The late Minister of Finance, Mr. Brian Lenihan, came to live here. Mr. Horan was known by the children in the area as Mr. Blackberry because he would pick the blackberries that grew on the brambles in August and September. He would sell the punnets of blackberries in the fruit market. However, the children would also eat the berries on their way home from school and they would attack the bushes like a swarm of locusts. Mr. Horan had a small rake, however, and could always reach the high fruit that would defeat the opportunists.

The home of Mrs. Tobin was known as Somerton Cottage, and she was adamant that only her cottage was entitled to this title. Many amateur and professional photographers, because of its attractiveness, photographed it. It was truly a classic Strawberry Beds cottage. Unfortunately it was burnt down soon after the death of Mrs. Tobin and with it went a distinguished part of the Strawberry Beds.

The cottage being re-thatched in 1987.
The Chestnut trees have been pruned and the leaves are gone from the trees, the daffodils are up and this was the month of April.
(Courtesy Mrs. Caroline Corballis)

A soccer team, the Strawberry Beds XI, comprised of boys from the Lower Road was formed by Peter Martin in the seventies and, as mentioned before, had a successful couple of years. However, a team called Somerton Rovers existed in the twenties and thirties and had their grounds on lands donated to them by Mr. Laidlaw. Somerton Rovers were the predecessors to St Moctha's Football Club, which was formed in 1947. In most cases boys would travel to the nearest team to play as all travel was by walking or cycling, and when one team folded the players would simply move on. St Moctha's, prior to getting their permanent grounds, also had their grounds in Somerton, initially in Lovely's field, opposite Somerton gates, and laterally where the yellow barns used to stand. The hay barns, often used by lovers late at night, have now been replaced by sheds for the golf course.

Somerton Rovers, team photograph in the early thirties. The eleven players from left to right are, Back row Andy Wade, Jim 'nigger' Kelly, Michael Galligan, Tommy Dumbrell, Frank Duffy, and Albert Kelly. Front row Andy Duffy, William Greene, Billy Kelly, Peter Melia, Paddy Dumbrell and Towser was the team mascot.
(Courtesy Mary Eustace)

The players came from both ends of the road, the Kelly family from near the Wren's Nest and the Dumbrells from Knockmaroon. The training pitch for Somerton Rovers was an area of flat ground that lay between Martins house and the Wren's Nest pub on the Silver Hill.

The Guinness iron bridge, which was initially used by the Guinness family to bring goods to and from Hughes land on the south side of the river, was also used by locals for pleasure. This was trespass of a kind. Boys, during summer time would jump off the bridge into the river below. This is a not insignificant drop of 30 to 40 feet. One 'hero' called Red Ned from Palmerstown would drink a bottle of wine along with some cider and then dive from the top most point into the river below. He survived childhood, adolescence, and even made it into adulthood. He subsequently went to the UK to become a wealthy builder and gave up drinking altogether.

Local people would also use the bridge in a respectable fashion and cross it when it was fully boarded out. There was a stroll along both riverbanks. Because of the dangerous practice of lads jumping off the bridge the flooring was lifted and the bridge was sealed at both ends. This happened in the late seventies and it has fallen into disrepair since. Discussions between Fingal County Council, South County Council and the Guinness family to reopen the bridge failed. It is in a poor and rusty state now.

Red Ned from Palmerstown would jump from the top most point into the river below.

In Lucan Dick Fallon who had a hardware outlet, informed me that in 1930s his father used to carry out a milk run along the Strawberry Beds. His father used to collect the milk from the Harris dairy. The land on the southern bank opposite the iron bridge belonged to Peter Harris. It is rumoured that Peter Harris might indulge a little too much and too often to carry out the milk run. Dick informed me that his father, Jim Fallon, would collect the milk at three in the morning, drive across the iron bridge, onto the Lower Road and make the deliveries to the houses. Later on Hughes Dairies or Spendlove Dairies delivered the milk.

The church that most locals from the Strawberry Beds attended was Porterstown. There were two Masses on a Sunday - the eight o'clock and the ten-thirty Mass. As most people, prior to the eighties walked to the chapel, it was imperative to reach the top of the Rugged Lane before the bell sounded or else you were going to be late. Initially the Mass was said in Latin with overnight fasting and altar boys who had been picked from the local primary schools. Later on the Mass was said in the English language and girls were incorporated into the serving of the Eucharist. My sisters thought this was a much fairer arrangement. However, the change happened too late for them to participate. The ten o'clock Luttrelstown bus on Sunday, which coincided with the Mass, was always delayed by cars parking at the chapel and often wouldn't make it to the terminus at the Castle gates. The priest would announce from the altar that cars were blocking the bus, but generally the bus stayed stuck until the Mass ended.

The priests were part of the community to a great extent. They lived next door to the chapel and could be called upon for assistance by a troubled family or a needy member of their congregation. They perhaps had greater contact with the people than they do now. Their tenure of office appeared so much longer years ago. The church was also the place where the locals would say 'goodbye' to one of their own. In general, when a local died, the deceased would be removed to the church the night before, usually around six o'clock to facilitate workers, and a large congregation would turn out to pay their respects. The following day the interment would take place in the local cemetery. On one occasion the church was so full that many had to stand out in the cold. Just as the service finished, the large bell above the door rang out, giving everyone a terrible fright. The most elderly looked about to see if anyone else had dropped. The graveyards of Mulhuddart, Clonsilla and Esker in Lucan were the most commonly used for the people of the Strawberry Beds.

Clonsilla Graveyard is where many of the older families are interred. Although a Church of Ireland chapel, Catholics and Protestants lie side by side. A feature of some of the head stones is that they identify the deceased as being 'late of Strawberry Beds'. The Scully family, who were first noted in Griffiths Valuations 1843, has a large tombstone in the graveyard. It reads Owen Scully died 1856, as the first of its inscriptions. Agnes Nash (nee Halpin) is laid beside the church door. She died in 1974. The Lovely family is represented with Catherine 1903, Simon and John. The families of Shackleton, Ennis, Galligan, Pilgrim and Tobin are also buried in these grounds. Gertie Murray (nee Scully) is buried with her husband John Murray, who died in 1949. The Greene family also has a tombstone in the yard with the Greene family inscriptions. Fred Greene put it in place in 1934. Perhaps there are other families from the Strawberry Beds buried there but the headstones have aged too much to make out the details.

Music always had a strong base on the Lower Road. All three public houses had music and singing as entertainment on weekends. Traditional music in the Wren's Nest, country or melodies in the Strawberry Hall and pop music in the Anglers Rest. Each pub had its own loyal clientele and the music might not vary from week to week. The Strawberry Hall has a resident pianist. The Wren's Nest attracted a wide variety of musicians. It was unpredictable as to what instruments might emerge. Guitar, violin, flute, mouth organ, accordion and even the harp could be heard if one was fortunate enough. The order of the day was a full house, drink, smoking, music and song and possibly, only possibly, a drink after hours.

Further back in time, musicians would sit on the mile-markers opposite the public houses to entertain the passing travellers. This was a weekend occupation for these fiddle and squeeze box players. The Anglers Rest was the first venue and then along to the Strawberry Hall. Strawberries and cream, tea and scones, possibly a few pints of porter went with the music.

Music wasn't confined to the public houses. Within families there were talented singers and musicians. Bands were formed from these musical families. From the 1960s onwards four such bands originated from the road. Perhaps there were others prior to this time but they are not remembered. The Martin family, in particular, played a large part in two of these bands as the boys and only girl were very musical. The Somertons was a folk band, which had Irene Martin, Paul Ward, Brendan Phelan, Pat Armstrong, and Tina Armstrong as their members. They played in the folk clubs all around Dublin. The next group was The Craft. This group had Raymond Martin, Seamus Martin, Peter Martin, Brendan Connolly and Ben Fagan. They were more of a show band and often acted as the support group to the big show bands of the day. They were a very talented group. They would play mid-week or at weekends in the National Ballroom or the Crystal Ballroom - big venues in the sixties. It was forbidden during Lent to hold dances so the band would have forty days and nights of rest!

The next band was the Symbolics. This group had Peter Martin, Noel Malone, Brendan Connolly and Denis Troy. Peter was the drummer, Noel was the organ player and Brendan played the lead guitar. The bass player, Denis, who couldn't in fact play the instrument, and never plugged it in, was only brought along to chat up the girls in the clubs. The organ player covered the total lack of ability of the bass player. Success was limited with the girls by all accounts and if ever a team carried a player! However, they supported and backed some big groups during their three-year lifespan.

The last band to originate from the Lower Road was from the next generation. It was known as the New Hollande Band after the original name for the Wren's Nest public house. Its members were John Mooney, Maurice Troy, Martin Lanigan and Michael Byrne. They could be heard practicing in the community hall every Friday night. This band became quite accomplished and produced their own music. They are best remembered for the concert they gave on the riverbank at the Wren's Nest weir. The date, the 18th July 1982, is still remembered. A large crowd had congregated from all around the parish, and despite there being no official policing for the event, there was no trouble at all. Fortunately no-one drowned in the river, which continued well into the early hours.

New Hollande Band on their record cover.
(Courtesy Maurice Troy)

Picking strawberries for the market in the seventies was still possible for students as summer work. These workers would work alongside full-time gardeners, in my case Patsy Clifford and Noel Hands, both of whom worked for Ger Lanigan. Sometimes pickers, when bored, might indulge in a little strawberry throwing if the opportunity arose. Hitting a colleague on the backside with an over-ripe strawberry always left its mark. This was an infrequent happening because the 'boss' would also be picking. However, sometimes a picker might slacken or daydream and might receive an unripe berry on the backside to wake them up, as I did on one occasion. Only a colleague picking behind you could throw such a berry. This shot did not come from an amateur. There were only two pickers behind me on that day - I think Patsy Clifford was innocent, perhaps the 'boss' could be a deadly shot when he needed to keep a dozing worker up to his task!

George Brooke, who lived in Somerton, was a keen huntsman and was master of the North Kildare Hunt. He bred his own hounds, known as Brooke's Harriers, for this purpose and had kennels built in the 'moat field' up from the Huntsman house (Owen Scully's old house). The kennels were built under the supervision of a local stonemason, John Neill; the remnants of these kennels were present up until the sixties.

When George Brooke became a Baronet in 1903 the locals gathered outside the large gates of Somerton. A fire was lit and George and Annie Brooke were invited to come out for the celebration. A speech on behalf of the people was given by George West congratulating the Brooke family and wishing them well in the future. A footman then brought out drinks and a party ensued for most of the night. The Brooke family was touched by the thoughtfulness of the local people.

The Lower Road School was a nursery of kinds. The children could go home for lunch provided they were able to run home and be back in time. Children used to bring sticks to school, or cipini, as they were known as in Irish. Mrs. Doyle, the caretaker from next door to the school, used these to light the fire for the teacher in the morning. The school was always warm in the morning. One prized job in the school was to be the stoker of the boiler in the main room. This was always a boy's task. Noel Hands was the stoker at one stage and I managed to acquire the job after him. One could avoid awkward questions if one was busy putting coal into the boiler. A favorite trick was to make the boiler glow with heat to force substitute teachers to the back of the room out of fear it might explode. The heat generally sedated them. But this ploy did not work on Ms. Emily O'Brien.

A kettle was always heating on the boiler and on one occasion when a school inspector arrived he was impressed that the school mascot, a boxer dog called Hennesy, understood Irish. Ms. Emily O'Brien simply said 'Amach' to the dog and he got up and left the room. What the inspector did not see was that Ms. O'Brien had lifted the kettle and the dog understood the prompt. Hennessy would spend all day at the school mostly lying on the granite step at the front door.

All subjects were taught in Irish, which was unusual as the school was not a designated Gaelscoil. When the pupils went to the secondary schools they always had a good foundation in the language. I did not realise that subjects such as science or history could be taught in another language until I arrived in secondary school. The school was also well known for the knitting and sewing lessons. Boys and girls had to take these lessons and this skill was written about in a national newspaper of the time. Schooling ended with the sitting of the Primary Certificate examination. There was a fear amongst the pupils that you couldn't leave primary school if you failed this state exam and that you would have Ms. Emily O'Brien for the rest of your life.

The schoolyard was used for football by the boys or for 'tag' with all running and screaming around the yard. The screams could be heard for a distance and any neighbor within earshot could set their watch by it, such was the accuracy of the school day. On occasions the teacher might be sick or unable to get to the school due to snow or ice. Then the lessons would be cancelled. Ms. Emily O'Brien would telephone our house, as we were one of the few houses that had a phone at the time, we would have to pass the news along the road to the other twelve to fourteen children that were registered. This news was passed with delight. Unfortunately snow never lasted too long on the Strawberry Beds.

Denis and Paddy Troy at school in 1962.
All children in the school were taught a correct pose for the photographs.
(Courtesy Eileen Troy)

After school, which ended at three o clock, the children would run home, change out of their school clothes and play cowboys and indians for hours on the hills or football in a field. In summertime the weir at the Wren's Nest was a favourite haunt. Swimming, climbing the old mill, throwing the moss that grew on the weir at each other or fishing for eels were some of the sports that went on. Apart from this there were trees to be climbed, stones to throw – which was not appreciated – rambling through the fields, robbing orchards, picking daffodils or going for a cycle for those that had bicycles. The days were long and full of energy.

Some children went to piano lessons with Mrs. Ratcliff who lived with her husband Paddy beside Tobin's shop. Nearly all children went to learn the piano and she was an excellent and formidable teacher. The most talented would be sent forward for examinations and moved up the grades.

Paddy Ratcliff with his wife Shelia Ratcliff on the day of their marriage.
Standing in the background are Paddy's brother and Vera Murray.
The name of the other woman is unknown.
(Courtesy Hugh O Connor)

Stephen Galligan came to live on the Lower Road in the 1960s. His uncle Paddy Galligan lived with his dog Bran in the house next to the community centre for many years. Paddy Galligan was known for the Morris Minor car he drove and his generosity for giving lifts to the locals. Few people had cars in those days. The Galligans were living on the road in 1911 according to the Census. There were four brothers in the family, Paddy, Jack, Michael and John. Stephen had a great passion for motorbikes and used to race them in Skerries, Northern Ireland, the Isle of Man, Fore in County Westmeath and elsewhere. His preference was for the sidecar. Frequently he would test the bike on the Lower Road, which had an enormous roar as it raced up and down. This was a tuning exercise for the bike and always happened on Saturdays, Stephen's day off work. Tragically, Stephen was killed in a race in Northern Ireland following a crash. His son was the pillion passenger in the race. He was injured but thankfully survived.

Stephen Galligan is driving while his son Arron is the pilot in a race. (Courtesy James McGuigan)

The Dunne family lived on Somerton Lane. Mrs. Dunne, who was born as Rosie Moore, had two children Carmel and Billy. The Moores are recorded in Griffiths Valuation in 1843. Carmel trained as a nurse and worked in the UK and in Blanchardstown Hospital. She unfortunately developed rheumatoid arthritis in later years and the neighbours, to help her condition, purchased a special bed for her. Her brother Billy served in the Irish army and was sent overseas to the Congo with the Irish Peacekeeping forces in the nineteen sixties. This was the first peacekeeping mission sent overseas from Ireland. Unfortunately it was on this tragic mission in the Congo where several Irish soldiers were killed. Billy died a premature death with a neurological condition.

The Strawberry Beds gardening club generated a lot of energy and enthusiasm. Sid and Marie Neill were enthusiastic growers and a real driving force of the gardening club. They were originally from England but lived on the Lower Road for many years. Growing Dahlia's was their specialty but their produce was varied. The flowers, shrubs, cuttings and displays were put on show and for sale in the community hall on an arranged Sunday in summer. Gardeners from Castleknock would also bring their produce for showing. This generated a friendly rivalry between the two groups. Maria used to give the children in the school small books about flowers that could be found in the wild. There were many other amateur growers of no little skill selling and showing their achievements.

Trips were also organised for the two groups to visit the wonderful gardens of Ireland. Dr. Haldane Nelson was President of the Castleknock Club and he organised visits to Almont, Rossborough, Beechpark, owned by Mr. Dick Shackleton, and many other gardens. Finally the two clubs joined, which was a practical arrangement as numbers of members began to dwindle. Dr. Nelson was also the family physician to many families on the road of course. As a physician he was held in very high regard.

The Lower Road School has lost scholars before their time. They must be remembered because their untimely deaths are within living memory. The memory of Raymond Martin, Ann Lanigan, Noel Hands, Martin Convery, Ellen Tobin, Lucy O'Rourke and Niamh Russell must not be forgotten. All these lives shortened by tragic circumstances left family and friends with a great loss. There are many, many more, of course, as the school was open for seventy-five years. The oldest living scholar from the Lower Road School is Shelia Scully who was a pupil in the 1920s.

In 1984, while working as a doctor in Jervis Street Hospital I came across a neighbour from the Lower Road with whom I had been in school with. Raymond Martin, who was only a few years older than me, was a patient who unfortunately had a serious illness that would eventually take him away. Raymond was a very kind and obliging man, well liked by everyone because he had a very friendly demeanor, and as we chatted he made a remark I have always remembered. He said in all truth

> *'No bowsie has ever come from the Lower Road'*

These are just a small number of memories of incidents that come to mind. There may be inaccuracies; I recently had the names of the dogs on the road corrected by Irene Martin, who has a wonderful memory for such detail. Every person will have their own reflections on the years gone by and hopefully they will be recorded in the near future.

It is with great sadness that, as this book neared completion, four elderly residents of the Strawberry Beds passed away. All four had contributed greatly. They were Eileen Troy, Ger Lanigan, Michael Harford and Shelia Kavanagh (Scully).

Since this book was published in 2013 two more elderly residents have passed away. Jim Higgins who was instrumental in the acquiring the sports field on behalf of the community and Maureen O'Rourke (nee. Tobin) who was the proprietor of The Wren's Nest pub following the death of her uncle Hugh Ennis in 1973.

May their memory and all those who have gone before be forever remembered, and thanked for the richness they gave to the Strawberry Beds.

****

Chapter 24
APPENDIX

1 Map 1870.
2 Map 1907.
3 Houses in Townland of Astagob 1901 and 1911.
4 Census Details for the Townlands of:
a Annfield   1901 and 1911
b Broomfield   1901 and 1911
c Part Castleknock   1901 and 1911
d Diswellstown   1901 and 1911.
e Porterstown   1901 and 1911.
f Woodlands   1901 and 1911.
5 Amalgamation Schools Act 1929.

****

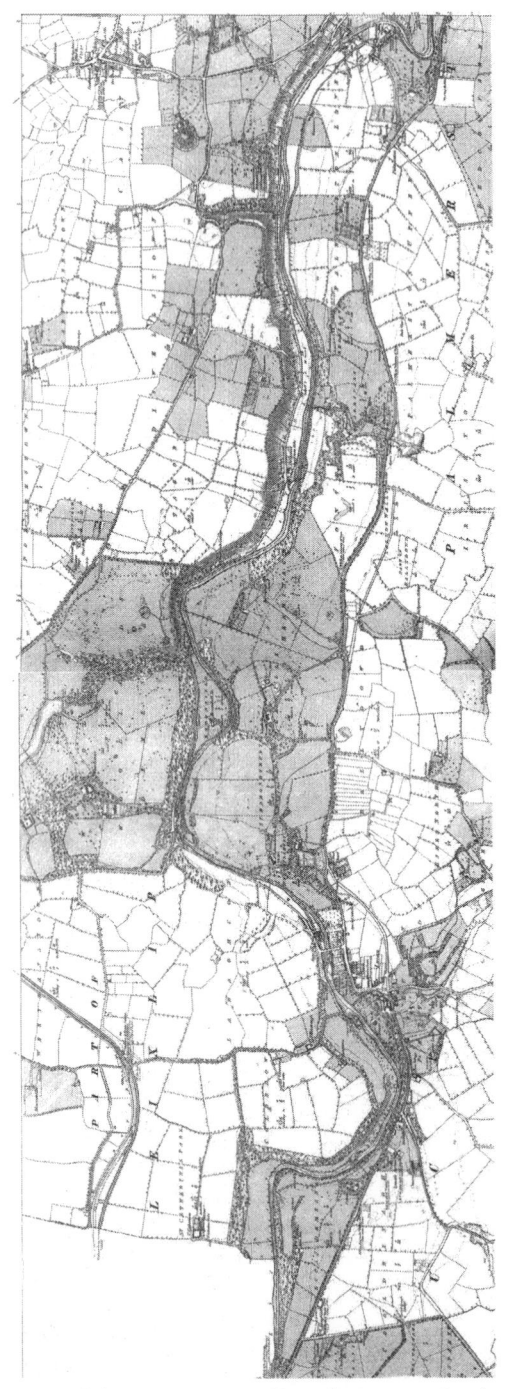

The Lower Road from Lucan to Knockmaroon in the year 1870.

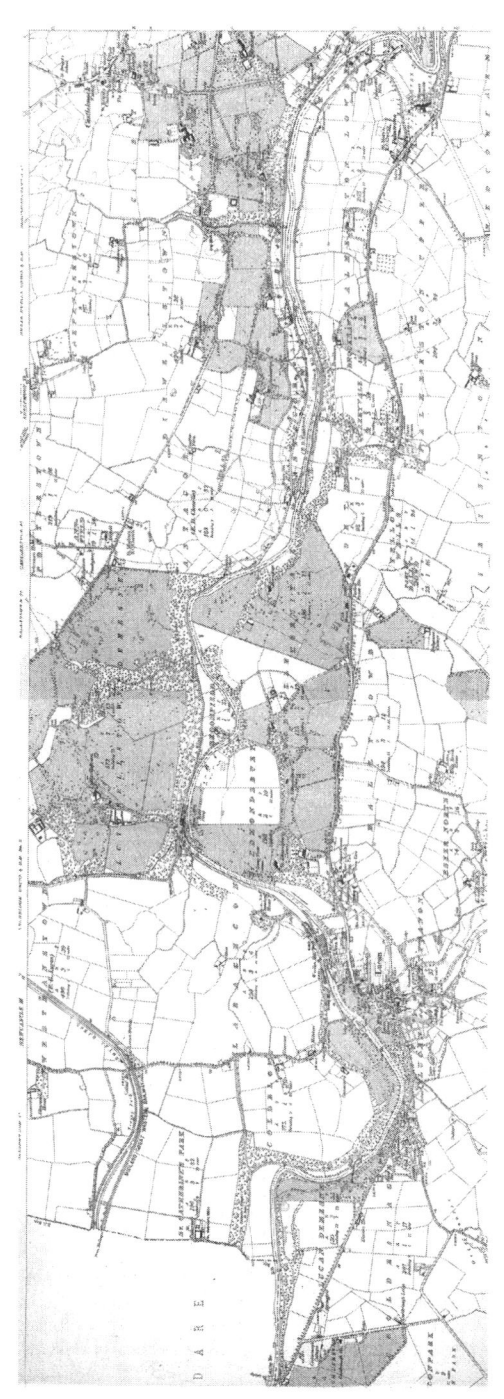

The Lower Road from Lucan to Knockmaroon in the year 1907.

HOUSE ORDER IN ASTAGOB IN 1901 AND 1911

The order in which the houses lay in the Astagob townland is not evident from the census lists of 1901 or 1911. This addendum lists the houses as they appeared in these lists. House number 1 is not always possible to identify and hence the sequence of the remaining houses is often difficult to follow. Families who have lived in the same house for over one hundred and twenty years will be able to identify their home. For example, the Warren (Lynam) family lived in 'House 1' Astagob (Clonsilla) in 1901 and 'House 1' in 1911. The Ennis family, however, lived in 'House 1' Astagob (Castleknock) in 1901, but in 'House 3' in 1911. As the townland starts at this point, the houses on the Silver Hill may account for this number change. As can be seen, there were often many families or surnames residing in the same house. These names could relate to domestic staff, fostered children, relations or boarders. Boarding was quite common at this time. The lists give an idea as to how families moved around and when they moved to the Strawberry Beds, or more accurately the townland of Astagob.

Astagob Castleknock House Number	1901 Surnames in House	Astagob Castleknock House Number	1911 Surnames in House
1	Ennis	1	Doyle
1	Halpin	2	Poynton
1	Tobin	3	Ennis
2	Obrien	4	Hynes
3	Lynam	5	Coffey
3	Reilly	7	Hackett
4	Costello	7	Saunders
4	Neill	8	Curran
5	Byrne	8	Scully
5	Hegarty	9	Sansom
6	Walsh	11	Galligan
7	Poynton	12	Walsh

7	Ward	13	Carroll
8	Poynton	13	Carroll
9	Butler	14	Moore
9	Cunningham	15	Tobin
9	Day	16	Russell
9	Judge	17	Carroll
9	Saunders	19	Flanagan
9	Woods	20	Crofts
10	Curran	20	Cunningham
10	Scully	20	Feehan
11	Guidon	20	Powell
12	Murray	21	Murray
13	Geraghty	22	Geraghty
14	Halpin	23	Weldon
15	Jones	23	West
16	Walshe	24	Glover
17	Doyle	24	Williams
18	Carroll	25	Doyle
19	Russell	25	Kiely
20	Moore	25	O Brien
21	Neill	25	O'Neill
22	Tobin	26	Clarke
23	Cranny	28	Donnelly
23	Galligan	30	Dunne
24	Cunningham	31	Fegan
24	Feehan	32	O'Neill
24	Powell	33	O'Neill
25	Mooney	34	Byrne
26	Byrne	34	Scully
26	Seully	35	Donnelly
26	Young	37	Lovely
27	Weldon	37	McKay
27	West		

28	Glover
28	McNeill
28	Williams
29	Doyle
29	O Brien
29	O'Neill
30	Clarke
30	Higgins
31	Flynn
31	Hetherington
32	Donnelly
33	Niel
34	Brogan
34	Downey
35	Carroll
36	Donnelly

Astagob Clonsilla House Number	1901 Surnames in House	Astagob Clonsilla House Number	1911 Surnames in House
1	Doyle	1	Dunne
1	Flanigan	1	Gill
1	Kearney	1	McGovern
1	Warren	1	Warren
2	Fagan	2	McKeon
3	Neill	3	Fagan
4	Doyle	4	West
5	West	5	Geraghty
6	Clinton	6	Curtis
7	Coates	7	Byrne
7	Gauntlet	10	Shea

7	Hollywood	11	Walsh
8	Kellaghan	13	Greene
9	Madden	14	Kelahan
9	Malone	16	Armstrong
10	Curtis	16	McDermott
11	Geraghty	17	Clinton
12	Byrne	18	Long
13	Greene	19	Balfe
14	Raby	19	O Callaghan
15	Fullerton		

The following are the Census of 1901 and 1911 details for the townlands that surround The Strawberry Beds. These townlands are Annfield, Broomfield, part Castleknock, Diswellstown, Porterstown and Woodlands.

Annfield 1901

Surname	Forename	Townland	DED	Age	Sex	Birthplace	Occupation
Daly	Mary	Annfield	Castleknock	21	F	Co. Dublin	Domestic Servant
Marmion	Margaret	Annfield	Castleknock	24	F	Co Meath	Domestic Servant
Morgan	Rose	Annfield	Castleknock	24	F	Co Meath	Governess
Rooney	Jane	Annfield	Castleknock	41	F	Dublin	
Rooney	Ethel	Annfield	Castleknock	3	F	Co. Dublin	
Rooney	Eileen	Annfield	Castleknock	4	F	Co. Dublin	
Rooney	Margaret	Annfield	Castleknock	10	F	Co. Dublin	Scholar
Rooney	Christopher	Annfield	Castleknock	41	M	Co Meath	Grazier
Rooney	Mary	Annfield	Castleknock	15	F	Co. Dublin	Scholar

Annfield 1911

Surname	Forename	Townland	DED	Age	Sex	Birthplace	Occupation
Connor	John	Annfield	Castleknock	10	M	Co. Dublin	Scholar
Connor	Christopher	Annfield	Castleknock	47	M	Co Meath	Ag Labourer
Connor	Bridget	Annfield	Castleknock	40	F	Co Meath	
Connor	Kate	Annfield	Castleknock	9	F	Co. Dublin	Scholar
Connor	Christopher	Annfield	Castleknock	20	M	Co Meath	Ag Labourer
Connor	Annie	Annfield	Castleknock	16	F	Co. Dublin	
Connor	Claire	Annfield	Castleknock	14	F	Co. Dublin	Scholar
Connor	Joseph	Annfield	Castleknock	4	M	Co. Dublin	Scholar
Connor	Patrick	Annfield	Castleknock	1	M	Co. Dublin	

Doyle	Frank	Annfield	Castleknock	24	M	Wexford	Groom Servant
Maxwell	Alicia	Annfield	Castleknock	34	F	Co Kildare	General Servant
Purcell	Richard	Annfield	Castleknock	22	M	Wexford	Groom Servant
Ringwood	Arthur G	Annfield	Castleknock	38	M	Co Tyrone	Farmer

Broomfirld 1901

Surname	Forename	Townland	DED	Age	Sex	Birthplace	Occupation
Byrne	John S	Broomfield	Clonsilla	12	M	Co. Dublin	School Boy
Byrne	Jeremiah	Broomfield	Clonsilla	29	M	Co Wicklow	Coachman
Byrne	William J	Broomfield	Clonsilla	0	M	Co. Dublin	
Byrne	Julia	Broomfield	Clonsilla	30	F	Co Meath	House Keeper
Byrne	Mary Jane	Broomfield	Clonsilla	8	F	Co. Dublin	School Girl
Byrne	Mary Anne	Broomfield	Clonsilla	27	F	Wicklow	
Byrne	Chris	Broomfield	Clonsilla	37	M	Co Meath	Store-Clerk
Costello	Bridget	Broomfield	Clonsilla	22	F	Co Meath	Cook Servant
Flynn	Patrick	Broomfield	Clonsilla	14	M	Dublin	Gardener
Furlong	Anne	Broomfield	Clonsilla	67	F	Co Carlow	House Keeper
McNamee	Francis	Broomfield	Clonsilla	73	M	Dublin	Gardener
McNamee	Fanny	Broomfield	Clonsilla	60	F	Dublin	
Mooney	Denis	Broomfield	Clonsilla	60	M	Co Kildare	Blacksmith
Mooney	Eliza	Broomfield	Clonsilla	59	F	Carlow	Blacksmith
Shackleton	Jane C	Broomfield	Clonsilla	22	F	Co. Dublin	Millers Daughter
Shackleton	J. Wigham	Broomfield	Clonsilla		F		Wife
Shackleton	J. Fisher	Broomfield	Clonsilla	69	M	Co Kildare	Flour Miller
Whelan	Julia	Broomfield	Clonsilla	28	F	Co Kildare	Maid Servant

Broomfield 1911

Surname	Forename	Townland	DED	Age	Sex	Birthplace	Occupation
Byrne	Chris	Broomfield	Clonsilla	50	M	Meath	Store Clerk
Byrne	Mary	Broomfield	Clonsilla	17	F	Dublin	
Byrne	William	Broomfield	Clonsilla	10	M		Scholar
Byrne	Julia	Broomfield	Clonsilla	44	F	Meath	
Byrne	John	Broomfield	Clonsilla	21	M	Lucan	Lab. Flour Mill
Byrne	Joseph	Broomfield	Clonsilla	9	M	Porters'tn,	Scholar
Kelly	Patrick	Broomfield	Clonsilla	30	M	Lucan	Lab.Flour Mill
Kelly	Catherine	Broomfield	Clonsilla	26	F	Margarets	

Castleknock 1901

Surname	Forename	Townland	DED	Age	Sex	Birthplace	Occupation
Behan	Hannah	Castleknock	Dublin	2	F	Co. Dublin	-
Behan	Mary	Castleknock	Dublin	9	F	Co Kildare	Scholar

Behan	Mary	Castleknock	Dublin	29	F	Co Cork	Dressmaker
Manning	Mary	Castleknock	Dublin	55	F	Co Cork	-
Behan	Daniel	Castleknock	Dublin	6	M	Co Kildare	Scholar
Carty	Teresa	Castleknock	Dublin		F	Co. Dublin	-
Carty	Joseph	Castleknock	Dublin	44	M	Co. Dublin	Electro typist
Carty	Hannah	Castleknock	Dublin	36	F	Co Cork	-
Carmichael	Francis	Castleknock	Dublin	6	F	Co. Dublin	Scholar
Coffey	John	Castleknock	Dublin	8	M	Co. Dublin	Scholar
Clarke	Maggie	Castleknock	Dublin	5	F	Co. Dublin	Scholar
Clarke	Annie	Castleknock	Dublin	15	F	Co. Dublin	Scholar
Clarke	John	Castleknock	Dublin	45	M	Co Meath	Labourer
Clarke	Patrick	Castleknock	Dublin	12	M	Co. Dublin	Scholar
Clarke	Thomas	Castleknock	Dublin	8	M	Co. Dublin	Scholar
Clarke	Anne	Castleknock	Dublin	40	F	Co. Dublin	-
Drake	Mary	Castleknock	Dublin	7	F	Co. Dublin	-
Drake	Evea	Castleknock	Dublin	12	F	Co. Dublin	-
Drake	Michael	Castleknock	Dublin	30	M	Co. Dublin	General Labourer
Drake	John	Castleknock	Dublin	3	M	Co. Dublin	-
Drake	Kate	Castleknock	Dublin	30	F	Co Meath	-
Fegan	John	Castleknock	Dublin	24	M	Co. Dublin	Tailor
Fegan	John	Castleknock	Dublin	1	M	Co. Dublin	-
Fegan	Mary	Castleknock	Dublin	21	F	Co. Dublin	-
Kieran	Eveline	Castleknock	Dublin	3	F	Dublin City	-
Kieran	Mary	Castleknock	Dublin	11	F	Dublin City	Scholar
Byrne	Emma	Castleknock	Dublin	31	F	Dublin City	Domestic
Kieran	Peter	Castleknock	Dublin	38	M	Dublin City	Artist, Engraver
Kieran	Arthur	Castleknock	Dublin	9	M	Dublin City	Scholar
Kieran	Philip	Castleknock	Dublin	12	M	Dublin City	Scholar
Kieran	Frederick	Castleknock	Dublin	8	M	Dublin City	Scholar
Kieran	Margaret	Castleknock	Dublin	38	F	Co Louth	-
Breen	Anna M	Castleknock	Dublin	9	F	Co. Dublin	Scholar
Breen	Nora Maud	Castleknock	Dublin	8	F	Co. Dublin	Scholar
Breen	Margaret R	Castleknock	Dublin	10	F	Co. Dublin	Scholar
Breen	Mary E J	Castleknock	Dublin	13	F	Dublin City	Scholar
Heffernan	Mary	Castleknock	Dublin	22	F	Co Kerry	Telegraphist
Heffernan	Ellie	Castleknock	Dublin	19	F	Co Kerry	Telegraphist
Breen	Timothy	Castleknock	Dublin	15	M	Co Kerry	Scholar
Breen	Gerald E	Castleknock	Dublin	2	M	Co. Dublin	-
Breen	William E	Castleknock	Dublin	4	M	Co. Dublin	Scholar
Breen	Nora	Castleknock	Dublin	42	F	Co Limerick	Post mistress
Clarke	Mary	Castleknock	Dublin	1	F	Co. Dublin	Scholar

Clarke	Thomas	Castleknock	Dublin	56	M	Co. Dublin	Farmer
Finn	Bridget	Castleknock	Dublin	76	F	Co. Dublin	House Work
Finn	Margaret	Castleknock	Dublin	14	F	Co. Dublin	Scholar
Clarke	Edward	Castleknock	Dublin	6	M	Co. Dublin	Scholar
Clarke	Andrew	Castleknock	Dublin		M	City Dublin	Scholar
Clarke	Elizabeth	Castleknock	Dublin	35	F	Co. Dublin	Wife
Williams	Joseph	Castleknock	Dublin	22	M	Co Limerick	Groom Servant
Emmett	Christina	Castleknock	Dublin	16	F	Co. Dublin	-
Emmett	Thomas	Castleknock	Dublin	44	M	Co. Dublin	Farm Servant
Emmett	Alfred	Castleknock	Dublin	14	M	Co. Dublin	Scholars
Emmett	Patrick	Castleknock	Dublin	12	M	Co. Dublin	Scholars
Emmett	Thomas	Castleknock	Dublin	9	M	Co. Dublin	Scholars
Emmett	Leo	Castleknock	Dublin	6	M	Co. Dublin	Scholar
Emmett	Mary	Castleknock	Dublin	50	F	Westmeath	-
Poynton	Alice	Castleknock	Dublin	11	F	Co. Dublin	Scholars
Poynton	Annie	Castleknock	Dublin	4	F	Co. Dublin	Scholars
Poynton	James	Castleknock	Dublin	38	M	Co. Dublin	General Labourer
Poynton	Edward	Castleknock	Dublin	10	M	Co. Dublin	Scholars
Poynton	Thomas	Castleknock	Dublin	8	M	Co. Dublin	Scholars
Poynton	Godfrey	Castleknock	Dublin	2	M	Co. Dublin	Scholars
Poynton	Annie	Castleknock	Dublin	40	F	Co. Dublin	-
Jackson	Edward	Castleknock	Dublin	39	M	Co. Dublin	General Labourer
Jackson	Helena	Castleknock	Dublin	28	F	Co. Dublin	House Keeping
Tracey	John	Castleknock	Dublin	33	M	Co Kildare	Agr. Labourer
Tracey	Lizzie	Castleknock	Dublin	12	F	Co. Dublin	Scholars
Tracey	Mary	Castleknock	Dublin	18	F	Co. Dublin	Scholars
Tracey	Maggie	Castleknock	Dublin	14	F	Co. Dublin	Scholars
Tracey	Michael	Castleknock	Dublin	39	M	Co Kildare	Land Contractor
Tracey	John	Castleknock	Dublin	16	M	Co. Dublin	Scholars
Coady	James	Castleknock	Dublin	22	M	Co. Dublin	Land Contractor
Maguire	Bridget	Castleknock	Dublin	14	F	Co. Dublin	Scholars
Tracey	Margaret	Castleknock	Dublin	40	F	Co. Dublin	-
Gaffney	Esther	Castleknock	Dublin	5	F	Co Meath	-
Gaffney	Micheal	Castleknock	Dublin	29	M	Co Meath	Herdsman
Gaffney	Patrick	Castleknock	Dublin	3	M	Co Meath	-
Gaffney	Mary	Castleknock	Dublin	28	F	Co Meath	-
Roe	Mary	Castleknock	Dublin	35	F	England	Laundress Servant
Kavanagh	Elizabeth	Castleknock	Dublin	35	F	Co. Dublin	Dress Maker
Kavanagh	Margaret	Castleknock	Dublin	30	F	Co. Dublin	Dress Maker
Kavanagh	Teresa	Castleknock	Dublin	32	F	Co. Dublin	Machinist
Kavanagh	Anne	Castleknock	Dublin	69	F	Co. Dublin	-

Kavanagh	Joseph	Castleknock	Dublin	50	M	Co. Dublin	Shoe Maker
Kavanagh	Patrick	Castleknock	Dublin	29	M	Co. Dublin	Shoe Maker
Kavanagh	John	Castleknock	Dublin	44	M	Co. Dublin	Master Maker
Kelly	Honor	Castleknock	Dublin	4	F	Co. Dublin	Scholars
Kelly	Lizzie	Castleknock	Dublin	10	F	Co. Dublin	Scholars
Kelly	Joseph	Castleknock	Dublin	42	M	Co Kildare	Agr Labourer
Kelly	Michael	Castleknock	Dublin	13	M	Co. Dublin	Scholars
Kelly	Joseph	Castleknock	Dublin	8	M	Co. Dublin	Scholars
Kelly	John Wm	Castleknock	Dublin	17	M	Co. Dublin	Agr Labourer
Kelly	Eliza	Castleknock	Dublin	40	F	Co. Dublin	-
Peake	Mary K	Castleknock	Dublin	2	F	Co. Dublin	-
Peake	Joseph J	Castleknock	Dublin	30	M	Co. Dublin	Printer
Peake	Thomas J	Castleknock	Dublin	1	M	Dublin City	-
Peake	Adelaide	Castleknock	Dublin	30	F	City Dublin	No Occupation
Crean	Mary	Castleknock	Dublin	82	F	Co. Dublin	-
Whyte	Annie	Castleknock	Dublin	20	F	Westmeath	-
Whyte	Bridget	Castleknock	Dublin	18	F	Westmeath	-
Whyte	Mary	Castleknock	Dublin	16	F	Co. Dublin	-
Whyte	Rose	Castleknock	Dublin	14	F	Co. Dublin	-
Whyte	John	Castleknock	Dublin	52	M	Longford	Brick Layer
Whyte	William	Castleknock	Dublin	12	M	Co. Dublin	Scholar
Whyte	Michael	Castleknock	Dublin	22	M	Longford	Brick Layer
Whyte	Mary	Castleknock	Dublin	49	F	Longford	-
Cunningham	Patrick	Castleknock	Dublin	17	M	Westmeath	Ord Surveyor
Dardis	Nora	Castleknock	Dublin	7	F	Co. Dublin	Scholar
Dardis	M. Esther	Castleknock	Dublin	18	F	Co. Dublin	-
Dardis	Emily	Castleknock	Dublin	1	F	Co. Dublin	-
Dardis	Clare	Castleknock	Dublin	3	F	Co. Dublin	-
Dardis	Alice	Castleknock	Dublin	5	F	Co. Dublin	-
Dardis	Kate	Castleknock	Dublin	10	F	Co. Dublin	Scholar
Dardis	Teresa	Castleknock	Dublin	12	F	Co. Dublin	Scholar
Dardis	Rose	Castleknock	Dublin	16	F	Co. Dublin	-
Dardis	Thomas	Castleknock	Dublin	43	M	Westmeath	Royal Engineer
Dardis	Bertie	Castleknock	Dublin	13	M	Co. Dublin	Scholar
Dardis	Mary Jane	Castleknock	Dublin	39	F	Co. Dublin	-
Halpin	Angela	Castleknock	Dublin	7	F	Co. Dublin	Scholar
Halpin	Mary Anne	Castleknock	Dublin	57	F	Co. Dublin	House Keeper
Halpin	Joseph	Castleknock	Dublin	12	M	Co. Dublin	Scholar
Halpin	Francis	Castleknock	Dublin	8	M	Co. Dublin	Scholar
Slevin	Patrick	Castleknock	Dublin	40	M	Co. Dublin	Master Carpenter
Slevin	Anne	Castleknock	Dublin	30	F	Co. Dublin	Market Gardener

Slevin	Catherine	Castleknock	Dublin	28	F	Co. Dublin	Market Gardener
Drake	Mary	Castleknock	Dublin	12	F	Co. Dublin	Scholar
Drake	John	Castleknock	Dublin	40	M	Co. Dublin	Stable Man
Drake	James	Castleknock	Dublin	2	M	Co. Dublin	-
Drake	John	Castleknock	Dublin	8	M	Co. Dublin	-
Drake	Ellen	Castleknock	Dublin	40	F	Co Meath	-
Finn	Edward	Castleknock	Dublin	32	M	Co. Dublin	Dairy Farmer
Malborough	Mary	Castleknock	Dublin	16	F	Dublin City	Servant Domestic
Finn	Edward	Castleknock	Dublin	3	M	Co. Dublin	Scholar
Finn	William	Castleknock	Dublin	5	M	Co. Dublin	Scholar
Finn	Denis	Castleknock	Dublin	1	M	Co. Dublin	-
Finn	Elizabeth	Castleknock	Dublin	28	F	Co. Dublin	-
Halpin	Joseph	Castleknock	Dublin	64	M	Co. Dublin	Market Gardener
Halpin	Joseph	Castleknock	Dublin	22	M	Co. Dublin	-
Halpin	Francis	Castleknock	Dublin	17	M	Co. Dublin	-
Halpin	Angela	Castleknock	Dublin	16	F	Co. Dublin	
Emmett	Thomas	Castleknock	Dublin	50	M	Co. Dublin	General Laborer
Emmett	Mary	Castleknock	Dublin	52	F	Westmeath	-
Emmett	Bridget	Castleknock	Dublin	27	F	Co. Dublin	-
Emmett	Alfred	Castleknock	Dublin	23	M	Co. Dublin	General Laborer
Molloy	Mary	Castleknock	Dublin	22	F	Westmeath	Machinist
Molloy	Annie	Castleknock	Dublin	13	F	England	Scholar
Peake	Joseph	Castleknock	Dublin	41	M	Co. Dublin	Printer Ord Survey
Peake	Adelaide	Castleknock	Dublin	41	F	Dublin City	-
Peake	Catherine	Castleknock	Dublin	12	F	Co. Dublin	-
Peake	William H.	Castleknock	Dublin	7	M	Co. Dublin	-
Peake	Joseph P.	Castleknock	Dublin	4	M	Co. Dublin	-
Peake	Louisa M.	Castleknock	Dublin		F	Co. Dublin	-
Slevin	Catherine	Castleknock	Dublin	37	F	Co. Dublin	House Property
Slevin	Anne	Castleknock	Dublin	34	F	Co. Dublin	-
Fegan	John	Castleknock	Dublin	34	M	Co. Dublin	Merchant Tailor
Fegan	Mary	Castleknock	Dublin	32	F	Co. Dublin	-
Fegan	John	Castleknock	Dublin	11	M	Co. Dublin	Scholar
Fegan	Laurnce	Castleknock	Dublin	9	M	Co. Dublin	Scholar
Fegan	William	Castleknock	Dublin	7	M	Co. Dublin	Scholar
Fegan	Henry	Castleknock	Dublin	5	M	Co. Dublin	Scholar
Fegan	Bernard	Castleknock	Dublin	3	M	Co. Dublin	-
Fegan	Richard	Castleknock	Dublin		M	Co. Dublin	-
Scott	William	Castleknock	Dublin	35	M	Scotland	Tailor
Higgenbotham	William	Castleknock	Dublin	57	M	Wexford	Electrical Engineer
Higgenbotham	Elizabeth	Castleknock	Dublin	34	F	Wexford	-

Higgenbotham	Agatha	Castleknock	Dublin	30	F	Dublin	Typest Bookeeper
Higgenbotham	William	Castleknock	Dublin	27	M	Dublin	Electrical Engineer
Higgenbotham	Mary	Castleknock	Dublin	24	F	Co. Dublin	-
Higgenbotham	Alexander	Castleknock	Dublin	19	M	Co. Dublin	Electrical Engineer
Drake	Kate	Castleknock	Dublin	44	F	Co. Dublin	-
Drake	Kathleen	Castleknock	Dublin	16	F	Co. Dublin	-
Drake	John	Castleknock	Dublin	13	M	Co. Dublin	Scholars
Drake	Eva	Castleknock	Dublin	11	F	Co. Dublin	Scholars
Drake	Winifred	Castleknock	Dublin	7	F	Co. Dublin	Scholars
Bradley	Robert	Castleknock	Dublin	30	M	City Dublin	Postman
Bradley	Mary	Castleknock	Dublin	30	F	Co. Dublin	-
Keegan	Laurence	Castleknock	Dublin	42	M	Co. Dublin	Groom
Keegan	Catherine	Castleknock	Dublin	40	F	Co Meath	-
Keegan	Mary	Castleknock	Dublin	17	F	Co. Dublin	Scholar
Keegan	Kate	Castleknock	Dublin	15	F	Co. Dublin	Scholar
Keegan	John	Castleknock	Dublin	12	M	Co. Dublin	Scholar
Keegan	Laurence	Castleknock	Dublin	10	M	Co. Dublin	Scholar
Keegan	Charles	Castleknock	Dublin	8	M	Co. Dublin	Scholar
Keegan	Mark	Castleknock	Dublin	5	M	Co. Dublin	Scholar
Keegan	Nora	Castleknock	Dublin		F	Co. Dublin	-
Carty	Joseph	Castleknock	Dublin	56	M	Co. Dublin	Fitter
Carty	Teresa	Castleknock	Dublin	10	F	Co. Dublin	Scholar
Carty	Mary	Castleknock	Dublin	8	F	Co. Dublin	Scholar
Madden	Bridget	Castleknock	Dublin	47	F	Co Wicklow	Cook Servant
Madden	Marcella	Castleknock	Dublin	14	F	Co Kildare	Scholar
Hanlon	John	Castleknock	Dublin	55	M	Co. Dublin	Agr. Labourer
Hanlon	Mary	Castleknock	Dublin	50	F	Co. Dublin	-
Hanlon	Thomas	Castleknock	Dublin	28	M	Co. Dublin	Agr.Labourer
Hanlon	Patrick	Castleknock	Dublin	16	M	Co. Dublin	Agr. Labourer
Hanlon	Mary	Castleknock	Dublin	14	F	Co. Dublin	Scholar
Hanlon	Michael	Castleknock	Dublin	7	M	Co. Dublin	Scholar
Lynam	James	Castleknock	Dublin	54	M	Co. Dublin	Agr. Labourer
Lynam	Mary	Castleknock	Dublin	60	F	Co Meath	-
O'Neill	Annie	Castleknock	Dublin	12	F	City Dublin	Scholar
Dunne	Joseph	Castleknock	Dublin	13	M	City Dublin	Scholar
?eney	James	Castleknock	Dublin	10	M	City Dublin	Scholar
Jacob	Josephine	Castleknock	Dublin	21	F	City Dublin	-
Lennon	Thomas	Castleknock	Dublin	72	M	Rosco'mn	Gen Labourer
Lennon	Agnes	Castleknock	Dublin	65	F	Co. Dublin	-
Lennon	William	Castleknock	Dublin	28	M	Co. Dublin	Gen Labourer
Lennon	James	Castleknock	Dublin	22	M	Co. Dublin	Gen Labourer

Carty	Joseph	Castleknock	Dublin	56	M	Co. Dublin	Fitter
Carty	Teresa	Castleknock	Dublin	10	F	Co. Dublin	Scholar
Carty	Mary	Castleknock	Dublin	8	F	Co. Dublin	Scholar
Madden	Bridget	Castleknock	Dublin	47	F	Co Wicklow	Cook Servant
Madden	Marcella	Castleknock	Dublin	14	F	Co Kildare	Scholar
Jordan	Myles	Castleknock	Dublin	40	M	Wexford	Postman
Jordan	Bridget	Castleknock	Dublin	36	F	Queens Co	Laundry Maid
Jordan	Annie E	Castleknock	Dublin	5	F	Co. Dublin	Scholar
Jordan	Joseph	Castleknock	Dublin	2	M	Co. Dublin	Scholar
Kelly	Joseph	Castleknock	Dublin	36	M	Co. Dublin	Machine Moulder
Kelly	Bridget	Castleknock	Dublin	27	F	Co. Dublin	-
Kelly	J. Henery	Castleknock	Dublin	7	M	Co. Dublin	Scholar
Kelly	Patrick	Castleknock	Dublin	6	M	Co. Dublin	Scholar
Kelly	Maria	Castleknock	Dublin	3	F	Co. Dublin	Scholar
Kelly	Joseph	Castleknock	Dublin		M	Co. Dublin	-
Thomline	Walter	Castleknock	Dublin	38	M	City Dublin	Cycle Business
Thomline	Annie	Castleknock	Dublin	35	F	Co. Dublin	-
Thomline	Constance	Castleknock	Dublin	16	F	Co. Dublin	-
Thomline	Muriel	Castleknock	Dublin	12	F	Co. Dublin	Scholar
Thomline	Vivienne	Castleknock	Dublin	8	F	Co. Dublin	Scholar
Kelly	Joseph	Castleknock	Dublin	53	M	Co. Dublin	Gen Labourer
Kelly	Eliza	Castleknock	Dublin	48	F	Co. Dublin	-
Kelly	Mary	Castleknock	Dublin	26	F	Co. Dublin	-
Kelly	Honor	Castleknock	Dublin	13	F	Co. Dublin	Scholar
Brien	Richard	Castleknock	Dublin	44	M	Dublin Co	Gate Keeper
Brien	Ca?ter	Castleknock	Dublin	42	F	Dublin Co	-
Brien	Mary	Castleknock	Dublin	8	F	Dublin Co	Scholars
Brien	Ann	Castleknock	Dublin	6	F	Dublin Co	Scholars
Brien	Chris	Castleknock	Dublin	3	M	Dublin Co	-
Brien	Easter	Castleknock	Dublin	1	F	Dublin Co	-
Mahon	Thomas	Castleknock	Dublin	64	M	Co. Dublin	Gardener
Mahon	Catherine	Castleknock	Dublin	71	F	Co. Dublin	-
Mahon	John	Castleknock	Dublin	30	M	Co. Dublin	Clerk Ord Survey
Mahon	Rose	Castleknock	Dublin	31	F	Co. Dublin	-
Doyle	Michael J	Castleknock	Dublin	42	M	Co Wicklow	Vintner
Doyle	Margaret	Castleknock	Dublin	29	F	Co. Dublin	-
Doyle	James	Castleknock	Dublin	8	M	Co. Dublin	Scholars
Doyle	Michael J	Castleknock	Dublin	7	M	Co. Dublin	Scholars
Doyle	Peter V	Castleknock	Dublin	1	M	Co. Dublin	-
Murphy	James	Castleknock	Dublin	25	M	Wexford	Shop Assistant
Kennedy	Annie	Castleknock	Dublin	18	F	Tipperary	Cook Servant

White	John	Castleknock	Dublin	64	M	Longford	Bricklayer
White	Mary	Castleknock	Dublin	65	F	Longford	-
White	Annie	Castleknock	Dublin	30	F	Longford	Dress Maker
White	Rose	Castleknock	Dublin	25	F	Co. Dublin	-
White	William	Castleknock	Dublin	23	M	Co. Dublin	Bricklayer
Kavanagh	John	Castleknock	Dublin	50	M	Co. Dublin	Master Boot.
Kavanagh	Joseph	Castleknock	Dublin	56	M	Co. Dublin	Bootmaker
Kavanagh	Elizabeth	Castleknock	Dublin	48	F	Co. Dublin	-
Kavanagh	Teresa	Castleknock	Dublin	45	F	Co. Dublin	Machinist
Kavanagh	Margret	Castleknock	Dublin	43	F	Co. Dublin	Dressmaker
Kavanagh	Patrick	Castleknock	Dublin	41	M	Co. Dublin	Bootmaker
Pointon	James	Castleknock	Dublin	48	M	Co. Dublin	Farm Labourer
Pointon	Annie	Castleknock	Dublin	49	F	Co. Dublin	-
Pointon	Annie	Castleknock	Dublin	14	F	Co. Dublin	Scholar
Pointon	Godfrey	Castleknock	Dublin	12	M	Co. Dublin	Scholar
Pointon	Josephine	Castleknock	Dublin	9	F	Co. Dublin	Scholar
Pointon	Dora	Castleknock	Dublin	9	F	Co. Dublin	Scholar
Pointon	Florrie	Castleknock	Dublin	6	F	-	Scholar
Treacy	Michael	Castleknock	Dublin	46	M	Co Kildare	Sand Contractor
Treacy	Margaret	Castleknock	Dublin	50	F	Co. Dublin	-
Cody	James	Castleknock	Dublin	30	M	Co. Dublin	-
Treacy	John	Castleknock	Dublin	24	M	Co. Dublin	-
Treacy	Margaret	Castleknock	Dublin	23	F	Co. Dublin	-
Treacy	Elizabeth	Castleknock	Dublin	21	F	Co. Dublin	Tailoress
Herrieven	Charles	Castleknock	Dublin	26	M	England	Chauffeur Servant
Herrieven	Mary	Castleknock	Dublin	25	F	Co. Dublin	-
Herrieven	Bryan	Castleknock	Dublin	2	M	Co. Dublin	-
Herrieven	Mary	Castleknock	Dublin		F	Co. Dublin	-
Cashion	Kathleen	Castleknock	Dublin	11	F	Co. Dublin	Scholar
Stevens	William	Castleknock	Dublin	34	M	England	Gardener
Carmichael	George	Castleknock	Dublin	23	M	Scotland	Gardener
Addie	James	Castleknock	Dublin	20	M	Co. Dublin	Gardener
Smith	William	Castleknock	Dublin	21	M	England	Gardener
Kenna	Owen	Castleknock	Dublin	22	M	Queens Co	Gardener
Byrne	Thomas	Castleknock	Dublin	24	M	Co. Dublin	Gardener
Vincent	John	Castleknock	Dublin	49	M	London D.	Head Steward
Vincent	Mary	Castleknock	Dublin	42	F	London D.	-
Vincent	Edith	Castleknock	Dublin	20	F	Co. Dublin	-
Vincent	Thomas	Castleknock	Dublin	18	M	Co. Dublin	Apprentice
Vincent	Eileen	Castleknock	Dublin	13	F	Co. Dublin	Scholar
Vincent	Cecil	Castleknock	Dublin	7	M	Co. Dublin	Scholar

Surname	Forename	Townland	DED	Age	Sex	Birthplace	Occupation
Bale	Robert	Castleknock	Dublin	30	M	Roydon	Groom
Bale	Annie	Castleknock	Dublin	45	F	Chester	-
Bale	Robert	Castleknock	Dublin	10	M	London	Scholar
Buchanan	Jane	Castleknock	Dublin	39	F	Scotland	House Servant
May	Annie	Castleknock	Dublin	30	F	England	Maid Domestic
Ross	Maggie	Castleknock	Dublin	22	F	Scotland	Maid Domestic
Fraser	Blanche	Castleknock	Dublin	20	F	England	Maid Domestic
McKenzie	Annie	Castleknock	Dublin	18	F	England	Maid Domestic
Bore	Annie	Castleknock	Dublin	23	F	England	Kitchen Maid
Johnson	Sidney	Castleknock	Dublin	24	M	England	Footman Servant
Foster	Frederick	Castleknock	Dublin	17	M	England	Hall Boy Servant
Baker	O S	Castleknock	Dublin	-	-	-	-
Rogers	John	Castleknock	Dublin	38	M	Co. Dublin	Carpenter
Rogers	Kate	Castleknock	Dublin	27	F	Dublin	-
Rogers	Charles	Castleknock	Dublin	2	M	Co. Dublin	-
Rogers	John	Castleknock	Dublin	1	M	Co. Dublin	-
Drew	Eliza	Castleknock	Dublin	68	F	Co. Dublin	-
Byrne	Mary	Castleknock	Dublin	15	F	Dublin	Scholar
Ennis	William	Castleknock	Dublin	31	M	Co. Dublin	Groom Servant
Ennis	Mary	Castleknock	Dublin	26	F	Co. Dublin	-
Ennis	Margaret	Castleknock	Dublin	2	F	Co. Dublin	-
Jackson	Chris	Castleknock	Dublin	55	M	Co. Dublin	Agr. Labourer
Jackson	Catherine	Castleknock	Dublin	46	F	Co Leitrim	-

The townland of Castleknock covers part of the Strawberry Beds, It is that portion the runs from the Glen towards Knockmaroon hill. The census details of 1901 are included for this portion of the road as seen above, but are omitted for the census of 1911. The records are quite extensive and it is difficult to identify that specific section that is relevant to the Strawberry Beds. While I consider it unfortunate that this problem exists I believe the details of 1901 will give an accurate picture of those that were residing on the road at this time.

Diswellstown 1901

Surname	Forename	Townland	DED	Age	Sex	Birthplace	Occupation
Baker	William	Diswellstown	Castleknock	52	M	Limerick	Farmer
Baker	Anne	Diswellstown	Castleknock	60	F	Co. Dublin	-
Balfe	William	Diswellstown	Castleknock	5	M	Dublin	Scholars
Balfe	John	Diswellstown	Castleknock	3	M	Dublin	Scholars
Balfe	Patrick	Diswellstown	Castleknock	15	M	Dublin	Scholars
Balfe	Peter	Diswellstown	Castleknock	7	M	Dublin	Scholars
Balfe	Mary	Diswellstown	Castleknock	38	F	Dublin	Farmeress
Balfe	Mary	Diswellstown	Castleknock	6	F	Dublin	Scholars

Balfe	James	Diswellstown	Castleknock	14	M	Dublin	Scholars
Balfe	Catherine	Diswellstown	Castleknock	43	F	Co. Dublin	Farmer
Balfe	Mary	Diswellstown	Castleknock	20	F	Co. Dublin	Daughter
Balfe	Patrick	Diswellstown	Castleknock	23	M	Co. Dublin	Farmer's Son
Black	George	Diswellstown	Castleknock	38	M	Haddon	Gardener Servant
Black	Mary	Diswellstown	Castleknock	26	F	Co. Dublin	
Black	Mary	Diswellstown	Castleknock	0	F	Co. Dublin	
Bliss	Matilda	Diswellstown	Castleknock	42	F	England	Teacher
Bobbett	James	Diswellstown	Castleknock	21	M	England	Scholar
Bobbett	John	Diswellstown	Castleknock	24	M	England	Scholar
Bobbett	Louisa	Diswellstown	Castleknock	10	F	England	Scholar
Bobbett	Elizabeth	Diswellstown	Castleknock	19	F	England	Scholar
Bobbett	Richard	Diswellstown	Castleknock	52	M	Co Meath	Cattle Salesman
Bobbett	Rebecca	Diswellstown	Castleknock	42	F	England	
Brennan	Patrick	Diswellstown	Castleknock	57	M	Co Kildare	Coachman
Brooke	Baril G.	Diswellstown	Castleknock	7	M	Dublin	Scholar
Brooke	Emily	Diswellstown	Castleknock	10	F	Co Kildare	Scholar
Brooke	Rose D.	Diswellstown	Castleknock	5	F	Co. Dublin	
Brooke	Emily Alina	Diswellstown	Castleknock	46	F	Dublin	
Brooke	Geoffrey T	Diswellstown	Castleknock	4	M	Co. Dublin	
Brooke	George F	Diswellstown	Castleknock	51	M	Dublin	J P D L Merchant
Clarke	Mary Jane	Diswellstown	Castleknock	22	F	Meath	Nurse Servant
Cooney	Thomas	Diswellstown	Castleknock	21	M	W' Meath	Domestic
Coughlan	Harriet	Diswellstown	Castleknock	30	F	Belfast	Domestic
Cox	John	Diswellstown	Castleknock	20	M	Co Mayo	Gardener Servant
Dobbs	John	Diswellstown	Castleknock	45	M	Co. Dublin	Rural Post Man
Dobbs	Emily	Diswellstown	Castleknock	29	F	Co. Dublin	
Dobbs	George	Diswellstown	Castleknock	0	M	Co. Dublin	
Eccles	Margaret	Diswellstown	Castleknock	48	F	Co Tyrone	Housemaid
English	Norah	Diswellstown	Castleknock	40	F	Co Kerry	Laundress
Gallagher	Rebecca	Diswellstown	Castleknock	20	F	Co Carlow	Housemaid
Greenham	Richard	Diswellstown	Castleknock	24	M	Galway	Gardener Servant
Haddock	Annie	Diswellstown	Castleknock	30	F	Co Down	Nurse
Hicky	Thomas	Diswellstown	Castleknock	48	M	Kildare	Carter Labourer
Hughes	Andrew	Diswellstown	Castleknock	34	M	Co. Dublin	Agr. Labourer
Hughes	Ann	Diswellstown	Castleknock	36	F	Co Meath	
James	Margaret	Diswellstown	Castleknock	20	F	Co Kildare	Nursery Maid
Keegan	Bridget	Diswellstown	Castleknock	68	F	Co. Dublin	
Keegan	Thos	Diswellstown	Castleknock	31	M	Co. Dublin	Labourer Carter
Kynes	William	Diswellstown	Castleknock	66	M	Wexford	Butler
Ledwidge	Bridget	Diswellstown	Castleknock	38	F	Co. Dublin	House Keeper

Surname	Forename	Townland	DED	Age	Sex	Birthplace	Occupation
Ledwidge	Chris.	Diswellstown	Castleknock	23	M	Dublin	General Labourer
Ledwidge	Chris.	Diswellstown	Castleknock	40	F	Co. Dublin	Care Taker
Lofrin	Thomas S	Diswellstown	Castleknock	18	M	Co Carlow	Footman
Lovely	Catherine	Diswellstown	Castleknock	62	F	Co. Dublin	
Lovely	Simon	Diswellstown	Castleknock	28	M	Co. Dublin	General Assistant
Lovely	Esther	Diswellstown	Castleknock	30	F	Co. Dublin	
Lovely	John	Diswellstown	Castleknock	70	M	Co. Dublin	Market Gardener
Martin	R. Jasper	Diswellstown	Castleknock	54	M	Dublin	Literature
McDonald	Annie	Diswellstown	Castleknock	22	F	Queen Co	Kitchen Maid
McKeon	Annie	Diswellstown	Castleknock	50	F	Co. Dublin	
McKeon	Michael	Diswellstown	Castleknock	51	M	Ros'comn	Groom
McKeon	George	Diswellstown	Castleknock	24	M	Co Kildare	Gardener
McKeon	James	Diswellstown	Castleknock	7	M	Co Kildare	Scholar
McKeon	John	Diswellstown	Castleknock	9	M	Co Kildare	Scholar
Mitchell	Marcella	Diswellstown	Castleknock	50	F	Co Meath	Housekeeper
Mitchell	John	Diswellstown	Castleknock	46	M	Co Kildare	Coachman
Mitchell	Bernard	Diswellstown	Castleknock	20	M	Co Kildare	Draughtsman
Persse	Sarah H	Diswellstown	Castleknock	35	F	England	Interest on Money
Proudfoot	Patrick	Diswellstown	Castleknock	36	M	Co Meath	General Labourer
Proudfoot	Ann	Diswellstown	Castleknock	61	F	Co Meath	
Shields	Anne Jane	Diswellstown	Castleknock	16	F	Co Meath	Housemaid
Smyth	James	Diswellstown	Castleknock	26	M	Co Meath	Groom
Stratton	Ellen Mary	Diswellstown	Castleknock	35	F	England	Cook
Vaughan	Edward	Diswellstown	Castleknock	19	M	Co. Dublin	Farmer
Wardell	G. Alfred	Diswellstown	Castleknock	19	M	Wicklow	Pantry
Wilson	Maggie	Diswellstown	Castleknock	25	F	Dublin	House Keeper
Wilson	Thomas	Diswellstown	Castleknock	39	M	Dublin	Farmer
Wilson	Mary	Diswellstown	Castleknock	63	F	Dublin	Farmer
Wilson	John F	Diswellstown	Castleknock	25	M	Dublin	Farmer
Wilson	Richard	Diswellstown	Castleknock	8	M	Dublin	Scholar

Diswellstown 1911

Surname	Forename	Townland	DED	Age	Sex	Birthplace	Occupation
Aughan	Edward	Diswellstown	Castleknock	28	M	Co. Dublin	Farm Servt
Baker	William	Diswellstown	Castleknock	62	M	Limerick	Farmer
Baker	Anne	Diswellstown	Castleknock	80	F	Co. Dublin	
Balfe	Catherine	Diswellstown	Castleknock	58	F	Co. Dublin	Farmer
Balfe	Patrick	Diswellstown	Castleknock	33	M	Co. Dublin	Farmer Son
Brennan	Elizabeth	Diswellstown	Castleknock	35	F	Co. Dublin	
Brophy	Bridget	Diswellstown	Castleknock	46	F	Tipperary	House Maid

Chamberlain	Neville K B	Diswellstown	Castleknock 55	M	England	R.I.C. Retired. Colonel Indian Staff Corps	
Chamberlain	Nora	Diswellstown	Castleknock 23	F	India		
Chamberlain	Mary	Diswellstown	Castleknock 45	F	Scotland		
Davis	Fred	Diswellstown	Castleknock 30	M	England	Groom	
Davis	Margaret	Diswellstown	Castleknock 31	F	Co Mayo		
Doolan	Ellen	Diswellstown	Castleknock 17	F	Co. Dublin		
Doolan	Margaret	Diswellstown	Castleknock 13	F	Co. Dublin	Scholar	
Doolan	Bridget	Diswellstown	Castleknock 44	F	Co. Dublin		
Doolan	Bridget	Diswellstown	Castleknock 20	F	Co. Dublin		
Doolan	Joseph	Diswellstown	Castleknock 9	M	Co. Dublin	Scholar	
Doolan	Winifred	Diswellstown	Castleknock 10	F	Co. Dublin	Scholar	
Farrell	Denis	Diswellstown	Castleknock 28	M	Longford	General Lab	
Finlay	Fannie	Diswellstown	Castleknock 22	F	Co Carlow	Parlour Maid	
Flannery	Elizabeth	Diswellstown	Castleknock 32	F	Co Meath	Cook	
Flannery	William	Diswellstown	Castleknock 43	M	Galway	Butcher and Valet	
Flannery	Eileen	Diswellstown	Castleknock 1	F	Co. Dublin	Infant	
Fullerton	John Alex	Diswellstown	Castleknock 61	M	Armagh	Gardener	
Fullerton	Eileen Lucy	Diswellstown	Castleknock 16	F	Co. Dublin		
Fullerton	Annie E	Diswellstown	Castleknock 26	F	Co. Dublin	Dress Maker	
Fullerton	Herbert G	Diswellstown	Castleknock 12	M	Co. Dublin	Scholar	
Gay	Julia	Diswellstown	Castleknock 29	F	King's Co		
Gay	Patrick	Diswellstown	Castleknock 33	M	W'meath	Groom	
Gill	Ellen	Diswellstown	Castleknock 10	F	Co. Dublin	Scholar	
Gill	James	Diswellstown	Castleknock 14	M	Co. Dublin	Scholar	
Gill	John	Diswellstown	Castleknock 20	M	Co Leitrim	General Labourer	
Gill	Thomas	Diswellstown	Castleknock 52	M	Longford	General Labourer	
Gill	Mary	Diswellstown	Castleknock 50	F	Westmeath		
Glenney	James	Diswellstown	Castleknock 34	M	Limerick	Coachman	
Glenney	Catherine	Diswellstown	Castleknock 34	F	Monaghan		
Graham	Mary	Diswellstown	Castleknock 45	F	Tyrone		
Graham	John Wm	Diswellstown	Castleknock 40	M	Cavan	Gardener	
Graham	T. Wm	Diswellstown	Castleknock 8	M	Co. Dublin		
Green	William	Diswellstown	Castleknock 3	M	Co. Dublin		
Green	Kathleen	Diswellstown	Castleknock 5	F	Co. Dublin		
Green	Henry	Diswellstown	Castleknock 38	M	Co. Dublin	General Labourer	
Green	Ellen	Diswellstown	Castleknock 30	F	Co Kildare		
Hartigan	Mary	Diswellstown	Castleknock 40	F	Co Louth	Parlour Maid	
Hughes	Kate	Diswellstown	Castleknock 19	F	Co. Dublin		
Hughes	James	Diswellstown	Castleknock 17	M	Co. Dublin	General Labourer	

The Strawberry Beds

Hughes	James	Diswellstown	Castleknock	52	M	Co. Dublin	General Labourer
Hughes	Mary	Diswellstown	Castleknock	54	F	Co Kilkenny	
Hynes	Michael	Diswellstown	Castleknock	40	M		Groom
Kavanagh	Peter	Diswellstown	Castleknock	33	M	Queens Co	Groom
Kavanagh	Kathleen	Diswellstown	Castleknock	5	F	Co. Dublin	Scholar
Kavanagh	Patrick	Diswellstown	Castleknock	1	M	Co. Dublin	
Kavanagh	Annie	Diswellstown	Castleknock	3	F	Co. Dublin	
Kavanagh	Annie	Diswellstown	Castleknock	28	F	Queens Co	
Kennan	Thomas	Diswellstown	Castleknock	51	M	Co. Dublin	Colonel Capt 6th Royal Irish Rifles
Lockington	Elizabeth	Diswellstown	Castleknock	27	F	Co Tyrone	Lady's Maid
Lovely	Simon	Diswellstown	Castleknock	38	M	Co. Dublin	Market Gardener
Lynch	William	Diswellstown	Castleknock	29	M	Co Kildare	Groom
Mc?agh	Mary	Diswellstown	Castleknock	12	F	Dublin	Scholar
McDermott	John	Diswellstown	Castleknock	13	M	City Dublin	Scholar
McGuirk	Thomas	Diswellstown	Castleknock	24	M	Co. Dublin	General Labourer
McGuirk	Susan	Diswellstown	Castleknock	23	F	Co. Dublin	
McGuirk	Mary	Diswellstown	Castleknock	0	F	Co. Dublin	
McGuirk	Annie	Diswellstown	Castleknock	1	F	Co. Dublin	
Murphy	Mary	Diswellstown	Castleknock	3	F	City Dublin	
Nolan	Lizzy	Diswellstown	Castleknock	34	F	Queens Co	
Nolan	Mary	Diswellstown	Castleknock	7	F	Co. Dublin	Scholar
Nolan	Margaret	Diswellstown	Castleknock	4	F	Co. Dublin	Scholar
Nolan	John	Diswellstown	Castleknock	38	M	Co. Dublin	Groom
Nolan	Lizzy	Diswellstown	Castleknock	12	F	Co. Dublin	Scholar
Nolan	Thomas	Diswellstown	Castleknock	0	M	Co. Dublin	
Victory	Annie	Diswellstown	Castleknock	23	F	Co Meath	Kitchen Maid
Ward	Catherine	Diswellstown	Castleknock	44	F	Co. Dublin	
Ward	Patrick	Diswellstown	Castleknock	11	M	Co. Dublin	Scholar
Ward	Charles	Diswellstown	Castleknock	5	M	Co. Dublin	Scholar
Ward	Patrick	Diswellstown	Castleknock	45	M	Co. Dublin	General Labourer
Ward	John	Diswellstown	Castleknock	21	M	Co. Dublin	Groom
Ward	Esther	Diswellstown	Castleknock	13	F	Co. Dublin	Scholar
Wildbore	Annie	Diswellstown	Castleknock	35	F	England	Cook House
Wilson	Thomas	Diswellstown	Castleknock	40	M	Co. Dublin	Farmer
Winters	Patrick	Diswellston	Castleknock	55	M	Co. Dublin	Farm Servant

Porterstown 1901

Surname	Forename	Townland	DED	Age	Sex	Birthplace	Occupation
Bentley	Edward	Porterstown	Castleknock	23	M	Co Galway	Railway Checker
Bentley	Nathaniel	Porterstown	Castleknock	61	M	Westmeath	Railway Police

Bentley	Bridget	Porterstown	Castleknock	60	F	Westmeath	
Bonass	Richard	Porterstown	Castleknock	29	M	Co Meath	Groom
Bonass	Katie	Porterstown	Castleknock	26	F	Co. Dublin	
Brennan	Patrick	Porterstown	Castleknock	24	M	Co. Dublin	Railway Signalman
Callaghan	Patrick	Porterstown	Castleknock	2	M	Co. Dublin	
Callaghan	Maggie	Porterstown	Castleknock	13	F	Co Meath	Scholar
Callaghan	Henry	Porterstown	Castleknock	9	M	Co. Dublin	Scholar
Callaghan	Thomas	Porterstown	Castleknock	6	M	Co. Dublin	Scholar
Callaghan	Mary	Porterstown	Castleknock	14	F	Co Meath	Scholar
Callaghan	Annie	Porterstown	Castleknock	8	F	Co. Dublin	Scholar
Callaghan	Sarah	Porterstown	Castleknock	11	F	Co. Dublin	Scholar
Callaghan	Kate	Porterstown	Castleknock	4	F	Co. Dublin	Scholar
Callaghan	Sarah	Porterstown	Castleknock	38	F	Co Meath	
Callaghan	Henry	Porterstown	Castleknock	44	M	Co Meath	Cattle Dealer
Coffey	John	Porterstown	Castleknock	36	M	Co Kildare	Groom
Coffey	Mary	Porterstown	Castleknock	7	F	Co. Dublin	Scholar
Coffey	Julia	Porterstown	Castleknock	0	F	Co. Dublin	
Coffey	Kate	Porterstown	Castleknock	34	F	Co. Dublin	Nil
Coffey	Bernard	Porterstown	Castleknock	2	M	Co. Dublin	
Cullen	Peter	Porterstown	Castleknock	40	M	Co. Dublin	Agr. Labourer
Cullen	Catherine	Porterstown	Castleknock	4	F	Co. Dublin	Scholar
Cullen	Rose	Porterstown	Castleknock	30	F	Co. Dublin	
Donnelly	Cathrine	Porterstown	Castleknock	30	F	Co. Dublin	General Servant
Donnelly	Kathleen	Porterstown	Castleknock	4	F	Co. Dublin	
Farrell	Thomas	Porterstown	Castleknock	60	M	Co Kildare	Agr. Labourer
Farrell	John	Porterstown	Castleknock	20	M	City Dublin	Agr. Labourer
Farrell	Mary	Porterstown	Castleknock	53	F	Wexford	
Fox	Bridget	Porterstown	Castleknock	44	F	Co. Dublin	
Fox	John	Porterstown	Castleknock	24	M	Co. Dublin	Agr. Labourer
Fox	Maryan	Porterstown	Castleknock	22	F	Co. Dublin	Cook Servant
Gannon	Margret	Porterstown	Castleknock	30	F	Co. Dublin	
Gannon	Joseph	Porterstown	Castleknock	34	M	Co. Dublin	General Labourer
Gannon	Patrick	Porterstown	Castleknock	40	M	Co. Dublin	Farmer
Gannon	Anne	Porterstown	Castleknock	6	F	Co. Dublin	Scholar
Gannon	Patrick	Porterstown	Castleknock	1	M	Co. Dublin	
Gannon	Bridget	Porterstown	Castleknock	30	F	Co Kildare	
Gannon	Bridget	Porterstown	Castleknock	8	F	Co. Dublin	Scholar
Gilbert	Bobert	Porterstown	Castleknock	4	M	Co. Dublin	
Gilbert	Mary	Porterstown	Castleknock	6	F	Co. Dublin	
Gilbert	Jane	Porterstown	Castleknock	3	F	Co. Dublin	
Gilbert	Jane	Porterstown	Castleknock	28	F	Co Meath	

Gilbert	Chris	Porterstown	Castleknock	1	M	Co. Dublin	
Glynn	Patrick	Porterstown	Castleknock	22	M	Co Galway	Blacksmith
Gurney	Mary Jane	Porterstown	Castleknock	0	F	Dublin	
Gurney	Jane	Porterstown	Castleknock	30	F	Co Kildare	
Howe	Mary	Porterstown	Castleknock	15	F	Co. Dublin	Scholar
Howe	Elizabeth	Porterstown	Castleknock	9	F	Co. Dublin	Scholar
Howe	Ellen	Porterstown	Castleknock	4	F	Co. Dublin	Scholar
Howe	Joseph	Porterstown	Castleknock	38	M	Co. Dublin	Labourer
Howe	Theresa	Porterstown	Castleknock	7	F	Co. Dublin	Scholar
Howe	Chrisdina	Porterstown	Castleknock	0	F	Co. Dublin	
Howe	Frances	Porterstown	Castleknock	2	F	Co. Dublin	
Howe	Elizabeth	Porterstown	Castleknock	36	F	Co. Dublin	House Keeper
Hughes	Mary	Porterstown	Castleknock	45	F	Co. Dublin	
Hughes	James	Porterstown	Castleknock	42	M	Co. Dublin	Farm Labourer
Hughes	Kathleen	Porterstown	Castleknock	9	F	Co. Dublin	Scholar
Hughes	James	Porterstown	Castleknock	7	M	Co. Dublin	Scholar
Hynes	Patrick	Porterstown	Castleknock	38	M	Co. Dublin	Agr. Labourer
Hynes	Esther	Porterstown	Castleknock	30	F	City Dublin	
Hynes	Margaret	Porterstown	Castleknock	9	F	Co. Dublin	Scholar
Hynes	Patrick	Porterstown	Castleknock	2	M	Co. Dublin	
Hynes	Esther	Porterstown	Castleknock	5	F	Co. Dublin	Scholar
Kane	Mary Ellen	Porterstown	Castleknock	18	F	Co. Dublin	
Kane	Jane	Porterstown	Castleknock	7	F	Co. Dublin	Scholar
Kane	Mary	Porterstown	Castleknock	70	F	Co Kildare	
Kane	Kathleen	Porterstown	Castleknock	9	F	Co. Dublin	Scholar
Kane	Patrick	Porterstown	Castleknock	17	M	Co. Dublin	Market Gardener
Kane	Laurence	Porterstown	Castleknock	11	M	Co. Dublin	Scholar
Kane	Michael	Porterstown	Castleknock	50	M	Co. Dublin	Market Gardener
Kane	Annie	Porterstown	Castleknock	5	F	Co. Dublin	Scholar
Kane	Michael	Porterstown	Castleknock	13	M	Co. Dublin	Scholar
Leonard	Matthew	Porterstown	Castleknock	42	M	Co. Dublin	Farmer
Lynam	Laurence	Porterstown	Castleknock	23	M	Co. Dublin	Farmers Son
Lynam	Mary	Porterstown	Castleknock	45	F	Co. Dublin	Farmers Wife
Lynam	Patrick	Porterstown	Castleknock	50	M	Co. Dublin	Farmer
Lynam	William	Porterstown	Castleknock	25	M	Co. Dublin	Farmer Son
Lynam	Patrick	Porterstown	Castleknock	30	M	Co. Dublin	Farmer Son
Lynam	James	Porterstown	Castleknock	28	M	Co. Dublin	Farmer Son
Macken	Michael	Porterstown	Castleknock	4	M	Co. Dublin	
Macken	Margaret	Porterstown	Castleknock	6	F	Co. Dublin	Scholar
Macken	Patrick	Porterstown	Castleknock	1	M	Co. Dublin	
Macken	Patrick	Porterstown	Castleknock	32	M	Co Meath	Coachman

Macken	Margaret	Porterstown	Castleknock	30	F	Co Meath	
Mc Loughlin	Patrick	Porterstown	Castleknock	25	M	Co. Dublin	Blacksmith
McGrane	Mary	Porterstown	Castleknock	8	F	Co. Dublin	Scholar
McGrane	Margaret	Porterstown	Castleknock	7	F	Co. Dublin	Scholar
McGrane	Alice	Porterstown	Castleknock	9	F	Co. Dublin	Scholar
McGrane	Christophr	Porterstown	Castleknock	45	M	Dublin City	Horse Dealevete
McGrane	Christophr	Porterstown	Castleknock	5	M	Co. Dublin	
McGrane	Frederick	Porterstown	Castleknock	4	M	Co. Dublin	
McGrane	Mary	Porterstown	Castleknock	41	F	Canada	Teacher N School
McGrane	Robert	Porterstown	Castleknock	2	M	Co. Dublin	
McIntosh	Mary	Porterstown	Castleknock	38	F	Co Meath	General Servant
Moran	Eliza	Porterstown	Castleknock	60	F	Co Kildare	
Murphy	Thomas	Porterstown	Castleknock	46	M	Co. Dublin	Blacksmith
Murphy	John	Porterstown	Castleknock	21	M	Co. Dublin	Blacksmith
Murphy	Elizabeth	Porterstown	Castleknock	16	F	Co. Dublin	Scholar
Murphy	Charles	Porterstown	Castleknock	13	M	Co. Dublin	Scholar
Murphy	Margaret	Porterstown	Castleknock	42	F	Co. Dublin	
Murphy	Thomas	Porterstown	Castleknock	19	M	Co. Dublin	Clerk
O Neill	John	Porterstown	Castleknock	53	M	Wicklow	Farmer
O Neill	Sarah	Porterstown	Castleknock	7	F	Dublin City	
O Neill	Christophr	Porterstown	Castleknock	11	M	Dublin City	
O Neill	Mary	Porterstown	Castleknock	20	F	Dublin City	Daughter
O Neill	James	Porterstown	Castleknock	21	M	Dublin City	Farmer's Son
O Neill	Patrick	Porterstown	Castleknock	9	M	Dublin City	
O Neill	Elizabeth	Porterstown	Castleknock	46	F	Co. Dublin	
Proudfoot	Thomas	Porterstown	Castleknock	40	M	Co Meath	Labourer
Proudfoot	Mary	Porterstown	Castleknock	34	F	Co. Dublin	Domestic Servant
Proudfoot	Michael	Porterstown	Castleknock	6	M	Co. Dublin	Scholar
Proudfoot	Maggie	Porterstown	Castleknock	10	F	Co. Dublin	Scholar
Proudfoot	Richard	Porterstown	Castleknock	8	M	Co. Dublin	Scholar
Proudfoot	John	Porterstown	Castleknock	2	M	Co. Dublin	Scholar
Proudfoot	Josph	Porterstown	Castleknock	0	M	Co. Dublin	Scholar
Reilly	John	Porterstown	Castleknock	82	M	Co. Dublin	
Reilly	Sarah A	Porterstown	Castleknock	12	F	City Belfast	Scholar
Reilly	Mary A	Porterstown	Castleknock	65	F	Co Wicklow	
Seery	Ellen	Porterstown	Castleknock	76	F	Co. Dublin	
Seery	Anne	Porterstown	Castleknock	36	F	Co. Dublin	
Seery	Henry	Porterstown	Castleknock	38	M	Co. Dublin	Agr Labour
Seery	Peter	Porterstown	Castleknock	33	M	Co. Dublin	Agr Labour
Walker	Anna	Porterstown	Castleknock	38	F	Longford	Seamstress

| Walker | Henry | Porterstown | Castleknock | 12 | M | Dublin | Scholar |
| Walker | William | Porterstown | Castleknock | 74 | M | Kings Co. | Pensione Sexton |

Porterstown 1911

Surname	Forename	Townland	DED	Age	Sex	Birthplace	Occupation
Bentley	Bridget	Porterstown	Castleknock	68	F	Westmeath	
Bentley	Edward	Porterstown	Castleknock	33	M	Co Galway	General labourer
Bentley	Nathaniel	Porterstown	Castleknock	72	M	Westmeath	Railway Gateman
Callaghan	Henry	Porterstown	Castleknock	56	M	Co. Dublin	Cattle Dealer
Callaghan	Mary	Porterstown	Castleknock	24	F	Co. Dublin	
Callaghan	Kattleen	Porterstown	Castleknock	14	F	Co. Dublin	Scholar
Callaghan	Mabel	Porterstown	Castleknock	8	F	Co. Dublin	Scholar
Callaghan	Patrick K	Porterstown	Castleknock	12	M	Co. Dublin	Scholar
Callaghan	Sarah	Porterstown	Castleknock	53	F	Co. Dublin	
Callaghan	Henry	Porterstown	Castleknock	19	M	Co. Dublin	Agr Labourer
Cullen	Kathleen	Porterstown	Castleknock	14	F	Co. Dublin	Scholar
Cullen	Rose	Porterstown	Castleknock	44	F	Co. Dublin	
Cullen	Peter	Porterstown	Castleknock	55	M	Co. Dublin	General Labourer
Dalton	Patrick	Porterstown	Castleknock	26	M	Co Kildare	Groom
Dalton	Lena	Porterstown	Castleknock	24	F	Co. Dublin	
Dobbs	Emily	Porterstown	Castleknock	40	F	Wexford	
Dobbs	John	Porterstown	Castleknock	6	M	Co. Dublin	Scholar
Dobbs	William	Porterstown	Castleknock	2	M	Clonsilla	
Dobbs	John	Porterstown	Castleknock	59	M	Co. Dublin	Rural Post Man
Dobbs	George	Porterstown	Castleknock	10	M	Co. Dublin	Scholar
Gannon	Joseph	Porterstown	Castleknock	42	M	Co. Dublin	Labourer
Gannon	Patrick	Porterstown	Castleknock	50	M	Co. Dublin	Agricultural
Gannon	Annie	Porterstown	Castleknock	17	F	Co. Dublin	
Gannon	Patrick	Porterstown	Castleknock	12	M	Co. Dublin	Scholar
Gannon	Bridget	Porterstown	Castleknock	19	F	Co. Dublin	
Gannon	Bridget	Porterstown	Castleknock	43	F	Co Kildare	
Gannon	Maggie	Porterstown	Castleknock	10	F	Co. Dublin	Scholar
Gilbert	Mary	Porterstown	Castleknock	16	F	Co. Dublin	
Gilbert	Jane	Porterstown	Castleknock	13	F	Dublin	Scholar
Gilbert	Christophr	Porterstown	Castleknock	11	M	Co. Dublin	Scholar
Gilbert	Patrick	Porterstown	Castleknock	6	M	Co. Dublin	Scholar
Gilbert	Robert	Porterstown	Castleknock	14	M	Co. Dublin	Telegraph Mess.
Gilbert	Jane	Porterstown	Castleknock	38	F	Co Meath	
Gurney	Jane	Porterstown	Castleknock	40	F	Co Kildare	
Gurney	John	Porterstown	Castleknock	38	M	England	Butter Valet
Gurney	Mary Jane	Porterstown	Castleknock	11	F	City Dublin	Scholar

Hennessy	Ellen	Porterstown	Castleknock	40	F	Co Clare	Servant Domestic
Howe	Teresa	Porterstown	Castleknock	17	F	Co. Dublin	
Howe	Elizabeth	Porterstown	Castleknock	19	F	Co. Dublin	
Howe	Mary	Porterstown	Castleknock	25	F	Co. Dublin	General Servant
Howe	Ellen	Porterstown	Castleknock	14	F	Co. Dublin	
Howe	Eliza	Porterstown	Castleknock	46	F	Co. Dublin	
Howe	Joseph	Porterstown	Castleknock	48	M	Co. Dublin	Labourer
Howe	Frances	Porterstown	Castleknock	12	F	Co. Dublin	Scholar
Howe	Gilbert	Porterstown	Castleknock	5	M	Co. Dublin	Scholar
Howe	Helena	Porterstown	Castleknock	8	F	Co. Dublin	Scholar
Kane	Mary	Porterstown	Castleknock	82	F	Co Kildare	
Keane	Mary	Porterstown	Castleknock	28	F	Co. Dublin	
Keane	Michael	Porterstown	Castleknock	23	M	Co. Dublin	Agr Labourer
Keane	Catherine	Porterstown	Castleknock	48	F	Co. Dublin	
Keane	Patrick	Porterstown	Castleknock	50	M	Co. Dublin	Labourer
Keane	Maurice	Porterstown	Castleknock	50	M	Co. Dublin	Agricultural
Keane	Laurence	Porterstown	Castleknock	21	M	Co. Dublin	Agricultural
Keane	Annie	Porterstown	Castleknock	15	F	Co. Dublin	Scholar
Leonard	Mathew	Porterstown	Castleknock	53	M	Co. Dublin	Farmer
Lynam	Mollie	Porterstown	Castleknock	4	F	Co. Dublin	Scholar
Lynam	Mary	Porterstown	Castleknock	36	F	Co. Dublin	
Lynam	Larry	Porterstown	Castleknock	6	M	Co. Dublin	Scholar
Lynam	James	Porterstown	Castleknock	9	M	Co. Dublin	Scholar
Lynam	George	Porterstown	Castleknock	8	M	Co. Dublin	Scholar
Lynam	Patrick	Porterstown	Castleknock	1	M	Co. Dublin	
Lynam	Laurence	Porterstown	Castleknock	36	M	Co. Dublin	Farmer
Lynham	Patrick	Porterstown	Castleknock	74	M	Co. Dublin	Farmer
Lynham	William	Porterstown	Castleknock	28	M	Co. Dublin	Farmers Son
Lynham	Catherine	Porterstown	Castleknock	70	F	Co. Dublin	Old Age Pensioner
Lynham	Laurence	Porterstown	Castleknock				
Lynham	James	Porterstown	Castleknock	30	M	Co. Dublin	Farmers Son
Murphy	Elizabeth	Porterstown	Castleknock	24	F	Co. Dublin	
Murphy	Thomas	Porterstown	Castleknock	61	M	Co Kildare	Black Smith
Murphy	John	Porterstown	Castleknock	28	M	Co. Dublin	Blacksmith
Murphy	Charles	Porterstown	Castleknock	22	M	Co. Dublin	Blacksmith
Murphy	Margaret	Porterstown	Castleknock	59	F	Co. Dublin	
Murphy	Thomas	Porterstown	Castleknock	26	M	Co. Dublin	Blacksmith
OKeefe	John	Porterstown	Castleknock	40	M	Co Wicklow	Farmer
OKeefe	Bridget	Porterstown	Castleknock	50	F	Co. Dublin	
OKeefe	John	Porterstown	Castleknock	14	M	Co Wicklow	
ONeill	John	Porterstown	Castleknock	61	M	Co Wicklow	Farmer

Surname	Forename	Townland	DED	Age	Sex	Birthplace	Occupation
ONeill	Christophr	Porterstown	Castleknock	22	M	City Dublin	Agr Labour
ONeill	Patrick	Porterstown	Castleknock	20	M	City Dublin	Agr Labour
ONeill	James	Porterstown	Castleknock	32	M	City Dublin	Agr Labourer
ONeill	Lizzie	Porterstown	Castleknock	56	F	Co. Dublin	
ONeill	Mary	Porterstown	Castleknock	30	F	City Dublin	
ONeill	Sarah	Porterstown	Castleknock	18	F	Co. Dublin	
Proudfoot	Thomas	Porterstown	Castleknock	50	M	Co Meath	Agr Labourer
Proudfoot	Michael	Porterstown	Castleknock	16	M	Co. Dublin	Agr Labourer
Proudfoot	John	Porterstown	Castleknock	13	M	Co. Dublin	Scholar
Proudfoot	Laurence	Porterstown	Castleknock	7	M	Co. Dublin	Scholar
Proudfoot	Peter	Porterstown	Castleknock	0	M	Co. Dublin	
Proudfoot	Margaret	Porterstown	Castleknock	20	F	Co. Dublin	
Proudfoot	Francis	Porterstown	Castleknock	5	M	Co. Dublin	Scholar
Proudfoot	Mary	Porterstown	Castleknock	43	F	Co. Dublin	
Proudfoot	Joseph	Porterstown	Castleknock	10	M	Co. Dublin	Scholar
Seery	Anne	Porterstown	Castleknock	45	F	Co. Dublin	Farmers Daughter
Seery	Peter	Porterstown	Castleknock	43	M	Co. Dublin	Agr Labourer
Seery	Ellen	Porterstown	Castleknock	80	F	Co. Dublin	Farmer
Seery	Henry	Porterstown	Castleknock	47	M	Co. Dublin	Farmers Son
Seery	Patrick	Porterstown	Castleknock	17	M	City Dublin	
Thornton	Kathleen	Porterstown	Castleknock	14	F	Co. Dublin	Scholar
Thornton	Bridget	Porterstown	Castleknock	3	F	Co. Dublin	

Woodlands 1901

Surname	Forename	Townland	DED	Age	Sex	Birthplace	Occupation
Barton	Anna	Woodlands	Clonsilla	71	F	England	Householder
Bennett	Albert Ed	Woodlands	Clonsilla	40	M	England	Coachman
Bingham	Edward	Woodlands	Clonsilla	20	M	Co Dublin	Groom
Burton	Jane	Woodlands	Clonsilla	28	F	Scotland	Domestic Servant
Byrne	Lydia	Woodlands	Clonsilla	19	F	Co Wicklow	Domestic Servant
Cruickshank	Jane	Woodlands	Clonsilla	31	F	Scotland	Domestic Servant
Delany	Roady	Woodlands	Clonsilla	14	M	Co Dublin	Plummer
Delany	Timothy	Woodlands	Clonsilla	18	M	Co Dublin	Plummer
Delany	Timothy	Woodlands	Clonsilla	59	M	Kings Co	Pensioner (Army)
Delany	Anastatia	Woodlands	Clonsilla	44	F	Queens Co	House Keeper
Dent	Jessie Mary	Woodlands	Clonsilla	2	F	England	
Dent	James	Woodlands	Clonsilla	33	M	England	Gardener
Dent	Euphemia	Woodlands	Clonsilla	32	F	Scotland	
Doyle	Michael	Woodlands	Clonsilla	30	M	Co Dublin	Gardener
Doyle	Michael	Woodlands	Clonsilla	2	M	Co Dublin	Scholars
Doyle	M Anne	Woodlands	Clonsilla	0	F	Co Dublin	

Surname	Forename	Townland	Parish	Age	Sex	Origin	Occupation
Doyle	William	Woodlands	Clonsilla	4	M	Co Dublin	Scholars
Doyle	M Anne	Woodlands	Clonsilla	24	F	Co Dublin	
Flora	Annie	Woodlands	Clonsilla	26	F	Co Cavan	Domestic Servant
Johnson	Robert	Woodlands	Clonsilla	22	M	Co Tipperary	Gardener
Kerr	William	Woodlands	Clonsilla	64	M	Scotland	Game Keeper
Kerr	Anne	Woodlands	Clonsilla	27	F	Galway	House Keeper
Lovewell	George	Woodlands	Clonsilla	29	M	England	Domestic Servant
Lucas	Robert	Woodlands	Clonsilla	19	M	Belfast	Gardener
Lynch	John	Woodlands	Clonsilla	20	M	Dublin	Agricultural
Melcalf	Norman	Woodlands	Clonsilla	24	M	England	Domestic Servant
Moore	Catherine	Woodlands	Clonsilla	40	F	Dublin	
Moore	Catherine	Woodlands	Clonsilla	5	F	Dublin	Scholar
Moore	James	Woodlands	Clonsilla	13	M	Dublin	Scholar
Moore	Mary	Woodlands	Clonsilla	12	F	Dublin	Scholar
Moore	William	Woodlands	Clonsilla	7	M	Dublin	Scholar
Murray	Ellen	Woodlands	Clonsilla	31	F	Wexford	
Murray	Michael	Woodlands	Clonsilla	1	M	Co Dublin	
Murray	Nellie	Woodlands	Clonsilla	2	F	Co Dublin	
Murray	Edward	Woodlands	Clonsilla	31	M	Co Dublin	Painter
Murray	Philomena	Woodlands	Clonsilla	6	F	Co Dublin	Scholar
Murray	May	Woodlands	Clonsilla	4	F	Co Dublin	Scholar
Norton	William	Woodlands	Clonsilla	60	M	Dublin	Ploughman
O'Brine	Bridget	Woodlands	Clonsilla	53	F	Longford	
O'Brine	John	Woodlands	Clonsilla	62	M	Clare	Pensioner (Army)
Platt	Sophia	Woodlands	Clonsilla	21	F	Co Cavan	Domestic Servant
Plunkett	James	Woodlands	Clonsilla	56	M	Meath	General Labourer
Plunkett	Rosanna	Woodlands	Clonsilla	10	F	Meath	Scholar
Plunkett	Bridget	Woodlands	Clonsilla	12	F	Meath	Scholar
Plunkett	George	Woodlands	Clonsilla	20	M	Meath	Gardener
Plunkett	Jane	Woodlands	Clonsilla	17	F	Meath	Labourer's Daughter
Plunkett	Catherine	Woodlands	Clonsilla	56	F	Meath	
Plunkett	Batholomew	Woodlands	Clonsilla	14	M	Meath	Scholar
Plunkett	Catherine	Woodlands	Clonsilla	18	F	Meath	Labourer's Daughter
Reid	Lizzie	Woodlands	Clonsilla	27	F	Meath	
Reid	Christopher	Woodlands	Clonsilla	3	M	Dublin	
Reid	John	Woodlands	Clonsilla	35	M	Dublin	Labourer
Reid	Thomas	Woodlands	Clonsilla	6	M	Dublin	Scholar
Roper	Agnes	Woodlands	Clonsilla	26	F	Scotland	Domestic Servant
Smyth	Julia F	Woodlands	Clonsilla	5	F	Co Meath	Scholar
Smyth	John J	Woodlands	Clonsilla	13	M	Co Meath	Scholar
Smyth	Catherine	Woodlands	Clonsilla	11	F	Co Meath	Scholar

Smyth	Thomas	Woodlands	Clonsilla	43	M	Co Meath	Shepherd
Smyth	Catherine	Woodlands	Clonsilla	42	F	Co Meath	
Smyth	Annie	Woodlands	Clonsilla	15	F	Co Meath	Seamstress
Sterne	Ellen	Woodlands	Clonsilla	34	F	Co Wexford	
Sterne	William	Woodlands	Clonsilla	38	M	Co Wexford	Gardener
Thomson	Josephine	Woodlands	Clonsilla	43	F	Scotland	Domestic Servant
Townshed	Fanny	Woodlands	Clonsilla	20	F	Scotland	Domestic Servant
Usher	James	Woodlands	Clonsilla	24	M	Co Cavan	Gardener

Woodlands 1911

Surname	Forename	Townland	DED	Age	Sex	Birthplace	Occupation
Baldie	Elizabeth	Woodlands	Clonsilla	41	F	Scotland	Housemaid
Barrowman	Margaret	Woodlands	Clonsilla	47	F	Scotland	None
Brooke	Francis	Woodlands	Clonsilla	28	M	Dublin	Wine Merchant
Brooke	Raymond	Woodlands	Clonsilla	25	M	Dublin	Wine Merchant
Buchan	Alexander	Woodlands	Clonsilla	22	M	Scotland	Herdsman
Burne	William	Woodlands	Clonsilla	21	M	England	Gardner
Clinton	Mary	Woodlands	Clonsilla	34	F	Co. Dublin	Kitchenmaid
Coghlan	Mary	Woodlands	Clonsilla	31	F	Co. Dublin	Housemaid
Corey	Leonard	Woodlands	Clonsilla	21	M	England	Foreman
Dagge	Teresa	Woodlands	Clonsilla	30	F	Kildare	
Dagge	Isabella	Woodlands	Clonsilla	3	F	Dublin	
Dagge	Reginald	Woodlands	Clonsilla	34	M	Dublin	Groom
Dagge	May	Woodlands	Clonsilla	5	F	Dublin	Scholar
Dagge	John	Woodlands	Clonsilla	7	M	Dublin	Scholar
Dagge	Teresa	Woodlands	Clonsilla	0	F	Dublin	
Dallas	Elisa	Woodlands	Clonsilla	23	F	Scotland	Housemaid
Delaney	Anestasia	Woodlands	Clonsilla	56	F	Queens Co.	Lodge Keeper
Dent	James	Woodlands	Clonsilla	43	M	England	Gardner
Dent	Euphemia	Woodlands	Clonsilla	43	F		
Doyle	William	Woodlands	Clonsilla	13	M	Co. Dublin	Scholar
Doyle	Julia	Woodlands	Clonsilla	8	F	Co. Dublin	Scholar
Doyle	Michael	Woodlands	Clonsilla	12	M	Co. Dublin	Scholar
Doyle	Michael	Woodlands	Clonsilla	46	M	Co. Dublin	Yardman
Doyle	Mary Anne	Woodlands	Clonsilla	33	F	Co. Dublin	House Keeper
Doyle	Mary	Woodlands	Clonsilla	10	F	Co. Dublin	Scholar
Doyle	Elizabeth	Woodlands	Clonsilla	26	F	Co. Dublin	Cook Servant
Dupuis	Marie	Woodlands	Clonsilla	44	F	Switzerland	Teacher
Fegan	William	Woodlands	Clonsilla	8	M	Kildare	Scholar
Fegan	Patrick	Woodlands	Clonsilla	40	M	Co Meath	Shepherd
Fegan	Anna	Woodlands	Clonsilla	39	F	Co Meath	

Fegan	Patrick	Woodlands	Clonsilla	10	M	Kildare	Scholar
Fegan	Thomas	Woodlands	Clonsilla	6	M	Kildare	Scholar
Flynn	Mary	Woodlands	Clonsilla	37	F	Dublin City	
Flynn	Nicholas	Woodlands	Clonsilla	5	M	Dublin City	Scholar
Flynn	Julia	Woodlands	Clonsilla	19	F	Dublin City	
Flynn	Luke	Woodlands	Clonsilla	37	M	Dublin City	Motor Driver
Fox	Alicia	Woodlands	Clonsilla	56	F	Co. Dublin	
Guidon	Alice	Woodlands	Clonsilla	27	F	Co. Dublin	
Guidon	Thomas	Woodlands	Clonsilla	62	M	Co. Dublin	Labourer
Head	William	Woodlands	Clonsilla	18	M	England	Footman,
Laidlaw	Elizabeth	Woodlands	Clonsilla	40	F	United States	
Laidlaw	Thomas K	Woodlands	Clonsilla	46	M	Scotland	Rtd. Engineer
Laidlaw	Margaret	Woodlands	Clonsilla	9	F	Scotland	Scholar
Laidlaw	Elizabeth	Woodlands	Clonsilla	2	F	Co. Dublin	
McCormáic	Padraig	Woodlands	Clonsilla	21	M		Chauffeur
MacDiarmd	Marjory	Woodlands	Clonsilla	23	F	Scotland	Kitchenmaid
MacKenzie	Annie	Woodlands	Clonsilla	52	F	Scotland	Cook Servant
McCluskey	Nannie	Woodlands	Clonsilla	42	F	Wicklow	
McCluskey	Charles	Woodlands	Clonsilla	45	M	Co. Dublin	Herdsman
Murray	Ellen	Woodlands	Clonsilla	12	F	Co. Dublin	Scholars
Murray	Michael	Woodlands	Clonsilla	11	M	Co. Dublin	Scholars
Murray	Edward	Woodlands	Clonsilla	41	M	Co. Dublin	Painter
Murray	James	Woodlands	Clonsilla	4	M	City Dublin	Scholars
Murray	Mary Ann	Woodlands	Clonsilla	14	F	Co. Dublin	Scholars
Murray	Ellen	Woodlands	Clonsilla	41	F	Wexford	
Murray	Catherine	Woodlands	Clonsilla	2	F	Co. Dublin	
Murray	Philomena	Woodlands	Clonsilla	16	F	Co. Dublin	
Murray	Bridgid	Woodlands	Clonsilla	9	F	Co. Dublin	Scholars
O'Neill	Christopher	Woodlands	Clonsilla	22	M	Dublin	Servant
O'Brien	Brigget	Woodlands	Clonsilla	69	F	Longford	
O'Brien	John	Woodlands	Clonsilla	72	M	Co Clare	Lodge Keeper
Plunkett	James	Woodlands	Clonsilla	66	M	Co Meath	Farm Labourer
Plunkett	James	Woodlands	Clonsilla	33	M	Co Meath	Farm Labourer
Plunkett	Bridget	Woodlands	Clonsilla	23	F	Co Meath	
Plunkett	George	Woodlands	Clonsilla	31	M	Co Meath	Farm Labourer
Plunkett	Catherine	Woodlands	Clonsilla	63	F	Co Meath	
Reid	Philip	Woodlands	Clonsilla	18	M	Co. Dublin	Garden Boy
Reid	Thomas	Woodlands	Clonsilla	15	M	Co. Dublin	Ag Labourer
Reid	Eliza	Woodlands	Clonsilla	41	F	Co. Dublin	
Reid	John	Woodlands	Clonsilla	44	M	Co. Dublin	Ag Labourer
Reid	Peter	Woodlands	Clonsilla	9	M	Co. Dublin	Scholar

Reid	John	Woodlands Clonsilla	2	M	Co. Dublin	
Reid	William	Woodlands Clonsilla	5	M	Co. Dublin	Scholar
Reid	Christy	Woodlands Clonsilla	13	M	Co. Dublin	Scholar
Shackleton	Jane Christi	Woodlands Clonsilla	32	F	C. Dublin	
Shackleton	George	Woodlands Clonsilla	38	M	Co. Dublin	Flour Miller
Shackleton	Reb. Harvey	Woodlands Clonsilla	37	F	Co. Dublin	
Shackleton	John. Wigham	Woodlands Clonsilla	35	M	Co. Dublin	Flour Miller
Sheil	James	Woodlands Clonsilla	33	M	Carlow	Gardner
Sheil	Mary	Woodlands Clonsilla	25	F	Dublin	
Sheil	Patrick	Woodlands Clonsilla	6	M	Dublin	Scholar
Sheil	Thomas	Woodlands Clonsilla	2	M	Dublin	
Sheil	Bridget	Woodlands Clonsilla	4	F	Dublin	
Smyth	John J	Woodlands Clonsilla	21	M	Co Meath	J' Gardener
Sterne	Ellen	Woodlands Clonsilla	45	F	Wexford	
Sterne	William	Woodlands Clonsilla	50	M	Wexford	Gardener
Usher	Sam John	Woodlands Clonsilla	28	M	Co Cavan	Foreman
Wright	Annabella	Woodlands Clonsilla	24	F	Scotland	Housemaid

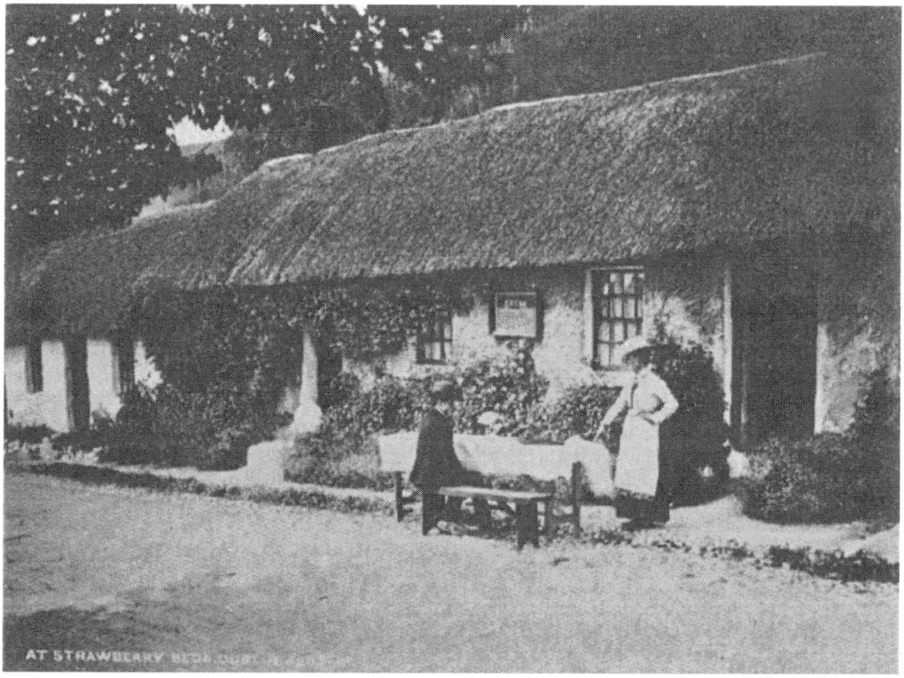
AT STRAWBERRY

ROINN OIDEACHAIS.

OIDEACHAS NAISIÚNTA.
NATIONAL EDUCATION.

REVISION OF RULES AND REGULATIONS.
Amendment of Rule 187.

Rule 187 has been amended as set forth below in order to provide for the amalgamation of boys' and girls' schools adjoining or in close proximity at one or both of which the average daily attendance for the preceding calendar year was under 40.

The rule as amended takes effect from the 1st April, 1929, inclusive :—

187 (1.) Separate ordinary boys' and girls' schools adjoining or in close proximity and under the same management at one or both of which there has been for any calendar year an average daily attendance of less than 40 shall be deemed to be amalgamated as from the 1st January of the succeeding year ; provided that where the average daily attendance at one or both of such schools for the calendar year 1928 has been less than 40, the schools shall be deemed to be amalgamated as from the 1st April, 1929.

(2.) On the amalgamation of the schools, the principal teacher of one of the former separate schools may be retained as privileged assistant in the amalgamated school, irrespective of the average attendance.

(3.) An assistant teacher or a junior assistant mistress recognised prior to the amalgamation in any of the schools amalgamated under this rule will be declared redundant, but may continue to be recognised as an ordinary assistant or as junior assistant mistress, as the case may be, on the same conditions in regard to average daily attendance as applied in the former boys' or girls' school, pending

(i) in the case of a junior assistant mistress, the occurrence of an available vacancy in a school in the same parish or neighbourhood, or

(ii) in the case of an assistant master or assistant mistress, the occurrence of an available vacancy which the Department may consider it reasonable for such assistant master or assistant mistress to accept.

(4.) In the case of a school amalgamated under this rule in which either one or two junior assistant mistresses are included in the staff, one junior assistant mistress may be excluded from the redundant list and may be retained on the teaching staff so long as the average daily attendance for the preceding calendar year is not less than 60.

(5.) If there is more than one junior assistant mistress in the amalgamated school, the choice of the junior assistant mistress to be so retained shall be determined by the Manager, subject to the approval of the Department, or, by the Department in the event of the failure of the manager to indicate to the Department the junior assistant mistress he desires should be retained.

Amalgamation of Schools Act 1929.

(6.) As from the 1st January next following the calendar year in which the combined average daily attendance at the amalgamated school falls below 60, the junior assistant mistress excluded from the redundant list will cease to be so excluded and may be retained in the school only on the conditions specified in Section (3) of this rule.

(7.) In any school amalgamated under this rule the staff of which consists of a principal, a privileged assistant and one or two ordinary assistants, one of the assistants may be excluded from the redundant list and may be retained on the teaching staff so long as the average daily attendance for the preceding calendar year was not less than 70.

(8.) In any school amalgamated under this rule the staff of which consists of a principal teacher, a privileged assistant, an assistant teacher and a junior assistant mistress, both the assistant teacher and the junior assistant mistress may be excluded from the redundant list and may be retained on the teaching staff so long as the average daily attendance for the preceding calendar year was not less than 80.

(9.) In any case of an amalgamation under this rule where the question arises as to which of two ordinary assistant teachers is to be retained, the choice of the assistant teacher to be so retained shall be determined by the manager, subject to the approval of the Department, or, by the Department in the event of the failure of the manager to indicate to the Department the assistant teacher he desires should be retained.

(10.) An assistant teacher excluded from the redundant list under Section (7) or Section (8) of this rule will cease to be so excluded and will be retained in the school only on the conditions specified in Section (3) of this Rule as from the 1st January next following a calendar year in which the average attendance has fallen below 70 or 80, as the case may be.

(11.) No new appointment of a junior assistant mistress to any school may be made without the prior approval of the Department.

(12.) Should a junior assistant mistress who has been declared redundant refuse to accept a vacancy offered to her in a school in the same parish or in the same neighbourhood, the Department may withdraw recognition from her unless satisfied that she has a reasonable cause for declining to accept the position.

(13.) Should an assistant teacher who has been declared redundant refuse to accept a vacancy which the Department considers that such assistant should accept, the Department may withdraw recognition from such assistant teacher.

SEÓSAMH Ó NÉILL,
Rúnaí.

AN ROINN OIDEACHAIS,
   BAILE ÁTHA CLIATH,
    Marta, 1929.

REFERENCES:

Amalgamation of Schools Act	1929
National Library Of Ireland Photographs	1890
Ordinance Survey Of Ireland Maps	1836, 1870
Ordinance Survey Of Ireland Maps	1907, 1936
Taylor And Skinner Map	1778
Down Survey (Ref) Map	1657
Rocques. Map Of Dublin (Ref) Map	1750
Burkes Guide To Country Houses Mark Bruce - Jones	1978
Griffiths Valuation	1843
Mineral Waters Of Ireland Dr. Butty	1750
History Of County Dublin Dr. Ball	1920
The Neighbour Hood Of Dublin W. St. J. Joyce	1939
Lewis Topographical Dictionary Of Ireland	1837
The History Of County Dublin John D'alton	1838
The Brimming River Raymond Brook	1954
Cnucha James O Driscoll	1977
A Candle In The Window Jim Lacey	2007
St Mochta's Church Charles And Mary Hulgraine	1990
Millers And Mills Of Ireland	1850

National Archives Of Ireland Census   1901

National Archives Of Ireland Census   1911

National School Registers (Lower Road)   1904 -1971

Royal Society Of Antiquities In Ireland Photographs   1898

****